THE UNIVERSITY OF LIVERPOOL
SYDNEY JONES LIBRARY

Please return or renew, on or before the last date below. A fine is payable on late returned items. Items may be recalled after one week for the use of another reader. Items may be renewed by telephone:- 0151 794 - 2678.

For conditions of borrowing, see Library Regulations

For conditions of borrowing, see Library Regulations

ELEMENTS OF ARCHITECTURE

From form to place

Pierre von Meiss
Professor of Architecture
l' Ecole Polytechnique Fédérale de Lausanne

Forewords by Kenneth Frampton and Franz Oswald

VNR
International

Van Nostrand Reinhold (International)

First published in 1986 by
Presses polytechniques romandes
CH-1015 Lausanne, Switzerland
© 1986, 1990 Presses polytechniques romandes

This edition published in 1990 by
Van Nostrand Reinhold (International) Co. Ltd
11 New Fetter Lane, London EC4P 4EE
Published in the USA by
Van Nostrand Reinhold
115 Fifth Avenue, New York NY 10003

Translated by Katherine Henault

Typeset in Clarendon 9/11pt by
Witwell Ltd, Southport
Printed in Hong Kong by
Thomas Nelson (Hong Kong) Ltd

ISBN 0 7476 0014 7
      0 442 31151 6(USA)

Library of Congress Cataloging in Publication Data

Meiss, Pierre von, 1938–
   [De la forme au lieu. English]
   The elements of architecture: from form to place/Pierre von
Meiss: forewords by Kenneth Frampton and Franz Oswald.
   p. cm.
   Translation of: De la forme au lieu.
   "First published in 1986 by Presses polytechniques romandes . . .
Lausanne, Switzerland"—T.p. verso.
   Includes bibliographical references.
   ISBN 0 442 31151 6 (U.S.)
   1. Architecture—Composition, proportion, etc.   2. Space
(Architecture)   I. Title.
NA2760.M4413   1989
720—dc20   89–2495
                                             CIP

British Library Cataloguing
in Publication Data

Von Meiss, Pierre
   Elements of architecture: from
form to place.
   1. Architecture
   I. Title
   720
ISBN 0 7476 0014 7

Contents

Acknowledgements

Thanks to all those who contributed to the formation of certain passages in this book by their criticism, and to those who patiently corrected the manuscript: Marie-Christine Aubry, Michel Bassand, Mario Bevilacqua, Marc Collomb, Michel Dufourd, Pierre Foretay, Franz Fueg, Jacques Gubler, Margrit Lambert, Michel Malet, Vincent Mangeat, Larry Mitnick, Franz Oswald and Angela Pèzanou.

Foreword

Kenneth Frampton

Among those who are familiar with the professional and academic architectural scene, it may well be thought that the last thing we need is another book on architectural theory. And indeed the author of this work would probably be the first to admit that the architectural libraries of the world are bursting at their seams with books on theory, many of which contain contradictory or repetitive hypotheses and most of which remain largely unread by the vast majority of students and practising architects. This book, however, has a good chance of breaking through this barrier of deadening indifference, often displayed today by many members of the profession and even by a large number of students, for this is a refreshingly direct and unpretentious compendium of the elements of architecture as these can be reasonably derived from architectural practice.

The subtitle *From form to place* at once reveals the critical stance of the author, his conviction that as a society we must start to redress the debilitating and environmentally destructive practice of proliferating free-standing buildings. He is convinced that, save for the rare institutional commission, every building ought to be construed as an occasion for making a place or for adding to the continuous articulation of the human habitat, rather than as another moment in which to display the ego of the client and the competitive prowess of the designer. This is the unusual *parti pris* that runs through this work, to such an extent that it may well be the first theoretical exposition of architectural practice that is at the same time a book on the principles of urban design.

Recognizing, as other recent theoretists have done, that all attempts to find an absolutely scientific basis for architectural theory and practice have each successively ended in tautological contradictions, von Meiss has opted to take a pragmatic, but nonetheless critical, phenomenological approach to architectural theory; one that puts logic, science and techno-science in their respective places, when it comes to the production of architecture. At the same time he is prompt to acknowledge that it is the direct impact of techno-science on the craft of building that has made it increasingly difficult to evolve and maintain a common standard of quality for the built environment. This may be exemplified, as von Meiss points out, by the ubiquitous wrap-around curtain wall that has effectively stripped the traditional window of its integrated constructional logic. Similarly light-weight framing and dry walling techniques have also served to deprive us tectonically of such expressive elements as load-bearing brickwork and the timber truss. Thus our current confusion and incapacity arises out of an excess of means rather than the lack of it. As von Meiss puts it, with full awareness of the paradox involved, techno-science is strangely incapable of assuring the quality of reality or more precisely of meeting our innermost desires in terms of everyday experience.

This last no doubt explains why Gestalt psychology and phenomenology play such prominent roles in von Meiss's theoretical approach. However it is important to note that they do so in such a way as to remain linked to specific forms of architectural practice. This accounts for von Meiss's *musée imaginaire* that he uses as a didactic device in order to exemplify, through illustration, the different salient aspects of his overview. Thus he passes from the legibility of the figure ground to the formal precepts of repetition, symmetry, grouping, gradation, hierarchy and transparency and from various dialogical phenomena such as goal versus route, entrance v. exit and centre v. periphery to a more ontological consideration of the ambient tactile qualities of space and material, that is to say, to an awareness of the way in which the five senses rather than sight alone are affected by architecture. In this regard von Meiss rightly stresses the fundamental qualities that separate architecture from the other plastic arts, that is to say he emphasizes the roles played by hollow space and gravity in its constitution; the first engendering spatial and typological criteria and the second assuring the essential structural and constructional nature of the entire undertaking. As he puts it, 'Stage sets are a kind of architecture, but architecture is not a stage set.' Elsewhere he remarks on the ambiguous influence that modern sculpture and painting has had on twentieth-century architecture, particularly with regard to the spatial articulation of that which had hitherto always been conceived as a confined volume. He has in mind the so-called liberation of the free plan (le Corbusier) and the destruction of the box (Frank Lloyd Wright).

For the degree to which they express hierarchy and institutional difference, within the continuity of their respective environments, the author's personal haunts of Morgés, Lausanne and Hydra are compared for their capacity to provide identity and to admit appropriate forms of inflection. Needless to say it is the abstract, gridded, internal street systems of the twentieth century that are found wanting in this regard, for the new EPFL campus outside Lausanne is a gridded mega-building; one that is so far removed from the natural legibility of Morgés that without the provision of graphic indicators, at each intersection, the occupants would remain perennially lost.

von Meiss is to apply this same phenomenological critique to other mechanistic devices and methods deployed in the late twentieth century: the soul-destroying, filing-cabinet, high-rise slab that lacks any adequate threshold or form of hierarchy; the ubiquitous air conditioner, adopted and applied on purely ideological grounds in temperate climates; the open office landscape that provides for neither identity nor appropriation; the bulldozer that is ruthlessly applied to contoured sites in order to achieve small economies in the maximization of constructional efficiency. This last is unfortunately all too common and von Meiss appeals, like Vittorio Gregrotti, for a new territorial ethic with which to limit the ecological transformation of any given site.

Given his overall position the author treats the tectonic dimension of architecture in a somewhat cursory way although he attests (after Tessenow) to the fact that no structure or construction can simply express the totality of its material production. Structure leads him via Louis Kahn to a brilliant and revealing disquisition on the role of light in architecture and von Meiss is at his most prescient when he argues that it is not the light source that is critical in the environment, but rather luminosity and shape of the objects illuminated. Unfortunately diurnal and seasonal variations in natural light are among the most invisible and frequently neglected aspects of the architectural phenomenon; a fact that is all the more regrettable in that these variations possess a dynamic and subtle capacity, for evoking the ineffable.

Sceptical with regard to behaviourism and casting an informed but knowing eye on physiological data and ergonomics, von Meiss seems to have been influenced by two separate lines of German thought: the first coming through England and America and the second passing through France. The first of these lines, stressing the psychological, symbolic and semiotic aspects of the arts, stems from Ernst Cassirer and passes through the Warburg Institute and its prime *émigré* pupils Ernst Gombrich and Rudolf Wittkower. These last were to have an impact on the theoretical writings of Colin Rowe, Robert Slutzky and Bernard Hoesli, all of whom were, at various times, colleagues of the author. A sub-set stemming from this line and emphasizing Gestalt psychology is also in evidence here, above all in the writings of Rudolf Arnheim. In the end, however, it is the Franco-German tradition that is decisive, for this imparts to von Meiss's thesis its critical edge and power. This line of thought, stemming from Husserl and passing through Heidegger, culminates in the critical-phenomenological position of such writers as Gaston Bachelard and Michel Serres; authors that von Meiss cites to great effect.

One of the most common problems in teaching and practising architecture today is the general difficulty encountered in deciding on our formal preferences and we often find ourselves hard-pressed to say why our design has come to assume this particular form rather than another. The discredited hypothesis of functional efficiency as the sole mover of form has now given way to an unstable combination of ruthless instrumentality and architectural dyslexia. Impelled by the clamour of the media and by ever-escalating oscillations in the pendulum of taste, students, architects and clients alike find themselves frequently caught between a desperate search for novelty and sporadic waves of reactionary nostalgia. In recapitulating and reconstituting the elements of architecture, this book could hardly have come at a more opportune time and we shall no doubt find ourselves beholden to the tenets of von Meiss's thesis, as we come imperceptibly to adopt them, largely because (as Albert Einstein said of Le Corbusier's *Modulor*) 'the bad, difficult and the good, easy'.

Kenneth Frampton
January 1989

Foreword

Franz Oswald

'*From form to place*'– the subtitle incorporates a sense of direction. It marks a position and indicates the intention of this book to describe an approach to architecture. Could there be anything more natural than to start with the visible form and then gradually to penetrate into the realm of the invisible? The architect must be able to manipulate the invisible so as to render reality visible; he has to be able to envisage reality to transform it. The study of architecture is always oriented towards two poles: towards seeing objects for the purpose of creation; towards creating objects for the purpose of seeing.

Elements of Architecture is a welcome guideline to the science of design. It provides those eager to study the discipline of architecture with the requisite terms of reference and concepts for that study. It serves as an introduction to the territory of architecture. 'Architecture is spatial art.' Form is less the ultimate end to that purpose, but rather a means of conferring upon places and pathways a distinctive identity, of arranging places and pathways to be utilized and to create an impression on the mind. Form is the architect's tool which he uses to fashion reality. At the same time it is a tool for recognizing reality. The recognition of form is the prerequisite for the creation of new form and essential if the architect is to avoid ossifying into blind formalism. Even when form is reproduced, especially in its more seductive variation of form forgery, the recognition of form is a prerequisite.

Based on the experience that a project is produced through the interconnection of arguments, from the ordering of ideas, from the evaluation of criteria – in short: from linking different elements, *From form to place* puts a series of useful tools at the designer's disposal. It demonstrates to him that the project is a product of mental processes involving analysis and condensation. Designing is like spiralling around an amorphous core which gradually crystallizes into a project. The amorphous core consists of abstract materials and models of an architecture as yet temporally and geographically undefined. The outlines of this are described in this book. In addition, it demonstrates that a project is created less through the schematic application of rules, but rather through the patient interpretation of purpose, location and by creative means. This is a great achievement.

It also requires courage to write a book on design in a culture such as ours, with its belief in the freedom of design and pluralistic values. The teacher of architecture and the architect are here confronted with difficult questions. How can teaching and design carry conviction if – derived from that very conviction – the momentary mood of taste is already sufficient to establish the form of a house, if examples from architectural history are used only as a model for the application of decorative patterns on buildings, if they are hardly recognized as authorities pointing the way and are consequently interchanged at will; if symbols of architectural language, products of a long and continued evolution, serve merely as signals of ephemeral attitudes? Designing is not an act of caprice or chance. The form of a project is rooted in time and place. The free will to design manifests itself by limiting and evaluating approaches to form. If such designs – approaches to form – are to be included or excluded, then this requires that we take a critical look at the content which the architect wants to convert into the language of architecture. Like other human languages, this one too has its constraints and functions. We must recognize these if we wish to make statements that are rich in content. Pierre von Meiss provides the basis and arguments for the critical discourse associated with a project during the period of its creation. Well aware that a locked educational edifice would represent a contradiction of our cultural situation and an evasion of our questions concerning design, he describes instead a system of co-ordinates. Although open to different interpretations of architecture, this system of co-ordinates is nevertheless a reliable one. It demonstrates which ideas first have to be evaluated so that an architectural project can be realized at all – and then to create a building which is valuable enough as to be memorable.

In this country too, as far as I can see, the teaching of architecture is undergoing a period of radical change. Many contemporaries seem unable to maintain their belief in the hopes which were placed in them and their architecture at the beginning of our present civilization. Doubts and uncertainty lead, here and there, to the deliberate surrender of the fundamental principles, the starting points and models of action for architecture in our time. They are dismissed as meaningless and some are therefore neither willing to subject them to critical investigation nor prepared to create anything new for the future that is based on the present. 'Let us forget the future and progress towards the past' is the motto of today's revolutionaries, who are thereby establishing fashionable schools with every superficial refinement. 'Space', that elusive concept of modern architecture, has disappeared from our mental field of vision. Instead, our minds are flooded with 'images'. Of course, the glut of images with which our historians and the media present us makes it difficult for contemporaries to recognize a central problem of design. We carry too many images of architectural solutions before even having understood the ideas behind them. '*From form to place*' prompts us to reflect on the guidelines for architectural education by affirming its belief in the basic principles of modern architecture and trying to convey them through subtle deliberations.

Books have a destiny. May this book help a few in their discovery and invention of architecture.

Franz Oswald
September 1986

1

OPENINGS

1.1 The window in crisis

The window – sign of human life, wink to the passerby, eye of the building allowing one to gaze at the outside world without being seen, welcomer of the daylight and the sun's ray highlighting surfaces and objects, source of fresh air and sometimes place of exchange of words and smells ... but also a break in the wall's structural continuity, and thus place of vulnerability, fragility, thermal sensitivity, leakage. A basic element in architecture, the window happily takes its place in the introduction to this book. Eye, mouth, nose and ear concurrently it is not only a determining feature in the building's appearance, but also the intermediary which allows the occupants of a building to see, hear and feel the place of which they are part.

The forms and dimensions of windows have their history. In the primitive hut, one minimal opening served as entrance, view, towards the outside world, source of light and of ventilation. One or two more modest openings were sometimes added. Much later came the glazed window which offers the user the choice between opening and closing it without having to be plunged into darkness. Hitherto the form of windows has been to a certain extent dependent on building techniques for controlling interior lighting and temperature. The lighting efficiency of a window is several times greater when it is near the ceiling than when it is near the ground. Thus the most economical window would be positioned near the ceiling, if it did not also have to take into account view and spatial articulation.

The window therefore encompasses three design functions: that of light, that of view and that of articulation between interior and exterior. Religious and introverted buildings are mainly designed for light. Since the Renaissance several architects have exploited the potential of isolating the design for light from that for view by providing openings or oculi for lighting above the windows which provide the view. The most common traditional window inserted into the masonry wall is still the 'vertical window', which combines the three design functions in a single architectural element with a minimal lintel. This was the archetypal window up until the twentieth century (Figure 1).

Figure 1 The vertical window: design for light, design for view and design for articulation between interior and exterior.

3

Figure 2 One of the first 'fenêtres en longueur' or strip windows supplying light to the embroideresses of Appenzell, Switzerland, in the eighteenth century.

Figures 3 and 4 Steel and reinforced concrete introduce the frame principle, which transforms the bearing wall into a non-bearing membrane; Fagus factory by Walter Gropius 1911–13, and the Convent of La Tourette by Le Corbusier 1957–60.

Exceptions exist. The *'fenêtre en longueur'* or strip window, in the houses of eighteenth-century Appenzell, in Switzerland, are no more than a clever response to the need to provide light for the dozens of embroideresses sitting behind this early 'curtain-wall' (Figure 2). This is, above all, an example of design for light, and only incidentally for view.

Thousands of years of traditional practice have now been challenged by new building methods: steel and reinforced concrete have introduced frame construction, which has transformed the bearing wall into a non-bearing membrane (Figures 3 and 4). Artificial lighting has done away with the limitations of natural lighting. The vertical window has lost its relationship with the economy of construction and thus been reduced to just one among a number of possibilities. Architecture is no longer guided by the imperatives of limited techniques of construction. Indeed free façades, glazed bays, vertical slots, picture windows, corner windows, glazed verandas, curtain walls and other devices offer many new solutions for modelling space and light.

This liberation from material constraints is not unique to the window; it involves the whole organization of the building. These new conditions made it possible for the architectural *avant-garde* to ally itself with such abstract art movements as Cubism and Purism.[1] Built form having acquired relative autonomy with respect to the constraints traditionally imposed by the logic of construction, henceforth the three functions – light, view and spatial articulation – could be made by different openings, precisely and uncompromisingly adapted to each function. An opening framing a selected view no longer had to provide light, which could just as well be provided overhead (compare, for example, works by Louis Kahn and Mario Botta, among others). Glass, steel and sealants have opened new ways to *reduce* the separation between interior and exterior (see, for example, works by Gerritt Rietveld, Ludwig Mies van der Rohe, Phillip Johnson and others).

This freedom is not won without tears; it has led to a great formal diversity of not only windows, but of the built work as a whole. When each window or each building follows its own logic, without respecting its neighbour or its predecessors, the result narrows the gap between the picturesque, on the one hand, and chaos on the other. Whilst in classical architecture the window could be considered a *beautiful object in itself* (which also justified separate analysis of this single element), the beautiful modern window can only be understood in relation to the whole spatial layout. It has ceased to be an object in itself.

To be a student or a teacher of architecture within this context is more demanding; where are the certainties of the vertical window when its lintel no longer needs to carry the weight of the wall? And where are the certainties when, searching the horizon of contemporary building output, we find simultaneously the picturesque, haphazard arrangement of the windows of Lucien Kroll, the powerful wall openings of Mario Botta, which draw together different types of fenestration in one major element, the obsessional square of Aldo Rossi, the partial dissolution of the wall creating a play of spatial interpenetration in the case of John Hejduk and Richard Meier, the transparent façade of Ludwig Mies van der Rohe and the reflective one of Norman Foster, the implicit reference to conventional motifs in the work of Robert Venturi and the deliberate distortion of imagery of the past in that of Leon Krier and Ricardo Bofill (Figure 5)?

This diversity is not, however, only the result of new techniques. It is firstly linked to our material wealth which no longer requires extreme simplicity, and secondly to the democratic nature of our society in which neither the intelligentsia, nor the state, nor avaricious banks can claim the right to determine what is appropriate and what is not.

The multitude of windows is only one example of the conceptual plurality inherent in contemporary architecture in general. Today's architect in search of paradigms encounters great difficulties in the face of the overwhelming choice between opposing but co-existing directions. The 'truths' are multiple, contradictory and ephemeral. Construction can be objectivized; architecture and urban design can only be so within relatively stable systems of human values linked to activities and to places. Consider that in the history of mankind, accumulated knowledge has never been so abundant nor so accessible to individuals. Archives have been established and gigantic libraries computerize their holdings. Architectural journals instantaneously provide the broadest possible range of the latest thinking, research and design work. The common feature of this élitist plurality lies in the attempt to snatch architecture from purely economic, technological and frivolous preoccupations. Our hope is to reinvest it with more meaningful objects for human life.

What objectives? The ambiguities of the plurality of approaches and the instability of social and aesthetic values caused by the great technological and sociological changes of the twentieth century underlie the premises of this book. They also highlight and form a critique of diversity of form in our daily environment when it starts to appear chaotic and becomes the cause of our difficulty in organizing house and city into 'a bunch of places'.[2]

In order to teach ourselves how to think about how to build a mere window in the most appropriate way, this book takes two approaches:

it presents fundamental principles of form and order in building, in particular those which are relatively independent of style and period; and
it considers contemporary architectural intervention relative to the existing state of affairs, as an insertion of a meaningful new fragment rather than a personal artistic invention.

These approaches are perhaps the only ones that can compensate for the disorientating effect caused by the speed of change within our society and its images.

If this book offers neither 'religion' nor recipe, it seeks neverthe-

Kahn

Botta

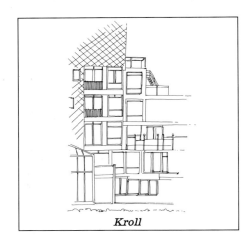

Kroll

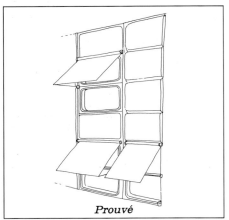

Prouvé

Figure 5 Where are the certainties of the vertical window when its lintel no longer needs to carry the weight of the wall? The skin of the building with its enclosure and openings contradicting, sometimes in a daring manner, material and constructional realities, in an exploration of the potential of plastic or symbolic expression.

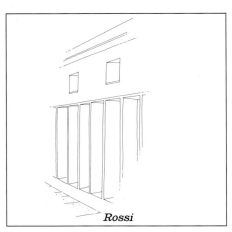

Rossi

Reichlin et Reinhart

Mies van der Rohe

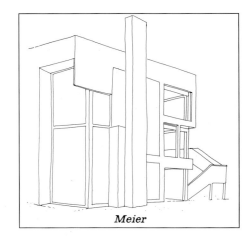

Meier

less to understand the world of forms and spaces which constitute the very substance of architecture.

1.2 In search of universal principles

That which constitutes perfectly the principles upon which an art is founded, is when there is no means by which you can move away from these principles.

E. L. Boullée[3]

The existence of relatively stable principles in architecture is contested today by a certain number of architectural historians. In fact historical diversity (the Greek temple, the Gothic cathedral, the chapel of Ronchamp ...) and contemporary plurality (the houses of Mario Botta, of Siza or of Moore ...) sustain the argument. There is no possible consensus and these different architectural approaches express more about the point of view of the interpreter than about the object interpreted.[4]

I am not a historian and I therefore have neither the same obligations nor the same objectives. Teaching in the field of architecture, I do not first of all look for the obvious or subtle differences, but the underlying or structural consistencies: yes, even the consistency linking a Greek temple, a Gothic cathedral, a Renaissance palace, a house by Loos, Hoffman or Botta and any vernacular village designed by history. I look at them, I compare them, and in order to teach I learn from them what they have in common and what is relatively stable.

The history of theories of architecture since Vitruvius (80 BC) is characterized by the search for universal principles likely to remain valid without reference to their position in history. It is a tricky undertaking. Alberto Perez-Gomez says, on the subject of notes by Memmo on the teaching of Lodoli in the eighteenth century, who was seeking precisely an aesthetic norm independent of history.

Memmo discussed in the same enlightened mood Greek and Roman architecture, the theories of Vitruvius, and Renaissance and modern authors. Memmo then ventured a conclusion supported by his historical research: Although Vitruvius had defined architecture as a science, this art still lacked fixed and immutable principles. It was not even necessary to discuss this point. It was sufficient to recognize the great diversity of existing ideas about the essence of architecture to be convinced that 'we are still in darkness'. And since the most famous authors did not share one single clear idea, 'we should at least have the courage to doubt'.[5]

The situation is not very different today, despite the increase in scientific knowledge. The difficulty lies in the fact that, in architecture, Cartesian rationality is not sufficient. Architectural problems are, in fact, to a great extent underdefined and their assumptions often conflicting. We are obliged to make critical choices. In this sense the theory of architecture belongs first to a branch of philosophy before it constitutes the foundation of practice. But, in fact, architectural theorists have also almost all been practitioners. There is, thus, a great temptation to extend the search for principles to systems such as the *classical orders, the elements* of the Beaux-Arts or the *'five points'* of modern architecture by Le Corbusier, or others. In his book, *Einführung in die Geschichte der Architekturtheorie*, Georg Germann describes the development of thinking about what these principles might be. Those which are of particular interest to us are those which say that one form is 'right' and another 'wrong'.[6]

Before the Middle Ages and again from the Renaissance to the nineteenth century, theories of architectural aesthetics used Greek Antiquity as a standard with which any new design was to be compared. These treatises have three obsessions:[7]

the taxis or geometrical order of grid and tripartition to organize the position of architectural elements and their spacing;
the genera or code for sets of elements such as Doric, Ionic, Corinthian ...;
the symmetry or rhythm and proportions which regulate the relationship of parts to the whole.

There is a substantial difference between the three preoccupations. The genera provide models or, in the best instances, a typology of elements, whilst the search for systems of logical order and pleasing proportions offers more abstract and more general possibilities for application, less linked to any specific form or technique. In this sense such a concern is more modern, or closer to the objectives of this book. We shall examine these systems in the light of present knowledge in Chapter 4.

Where can we find the sources of truth, whether it be a form or systems of proportion? Vitruvius justifies the form of Greek columns and their capitals in terms relative to human stature (Chapter 4). We are more inclined to share our faith in man with Zanotti who was already saying, in 1750, that if architecture was really to imitate something, it should preferably imitate God, rather than his works.[8] That is to say that in the matter of architecture, humanity holds sway for better or worse. It is responsible.

Architectural theorists have always tried to make their statements and the results of their research and thinking last beyond the period in which they have been formulated. To a certain extent they have succeeded, because the study of ancient treatises on architecture still provides one of the founts of wisdom which sustains our own thinking and actions, either because their propositions shape and confirm our own vague impressions, or because they force us to refute them with sound reasoning.

Our purpose is not to carry out an analysis of these treatises; we shall be content to recall one or two particular aspects relating to the premises of this book, notably the balance between art and science.

Vitruvius[9] strove to place architecture on the level of a 'science' which integrates the art of building, functionality and aesthetics. The value of the models of Antiquity is postulated. He gives a 'Darwinian' explanation of the form of the Greek temple which would have had a wooden structure as its origin. The objective of his theoretical proposition is the establishment of architecture among arts and sciences.

For Vitruvius, and later the Renaissance theorists (Alberti, Filarete, Martini, Serlio ... Palladio), the works of Antiquity are the primary reference, not so much as fragments of history but rather as models to be reinterpreted. The ten volumes of Alberti, however, outstrip Vitruvius in terms of clarity and range of subject matter. He devotes considerable space to the layout of sites of towns. If the term 'science' is used in this treatise, its nature remains more that of a great master who offers advice and who shares his concerns and experiences: the scientific rigour of Galileo, Descartes and Newton will come later. For Alberti, theory is the objectivizing explanation of a practice based on common sense and experience, 'the science of know-how'. It is the same in the four books of Palladio[10] who illustrates his treatise with his own schemes refined for the purpose. The studies of proportions in music and architecture constitute perhaps the most objective aspect of these treatises.

The birth of Cartesian rationalism and exact sciences in the seventeenth and eighteenth centuries could not be ignored by architectural theorists. François Blondel said '... genius alone will not make an architect. He must through study, application, long practice and experience acquire a perfect knowledge of the rules of his art and of proportions and the skill to choose between them ...'.[11]

This quotation sums up well the dilemma of architectural theory in the Age of Enlightenment. 'The genius', the artist, is not in question; 'the rules' are an allusion to stable principles, especially proportions, which one would obtain from the study of the most beautiful buildings. 'Science' refers to the understanding and the orderly organization of rules and their judicious application. The ambiguity comes from the fact that the different rules and 'eternal' laws expounded by Blondel and others do not have the same scientific value. The relation between the integers for a certain musical harmony are not to be questioned; the same does not apply in their transposition to architectural proportions. It is in fact difficult to distinguish between conventions of beauty established empirically, and laws which subsist when these conventions are discarded, as is the case in the twentieth century.

In this difficulty in describing the world of architecture in terms of eternal laws such as those in physics or biology, we discover an area where there are indications of a shift towards sensory or artistic discretion, which characterizes certain tendencies in the nineteenth and twentieth centuries. 'Discretion' is not used here with a negative connotation, but to denote a difference between judgement and scientific analysis. The idea of *progress* is again challenged by the separation of the arts and science. Charles Perrault suggests that the arts develop and perish, that there is no continuous progress, whereas the sciences progress.[12]

Attempts to bring science and art closer together assumed a particular form in the nineteenth century. The architectural treatises from Durand (1802) to Guadet (1903) reflect the academic rationalism of Beaux-Arts, an authority during this period in the Western world. For Durand, beauty is reached by uniting economy and simplicity. To this end, he drew up a catalogue of models which corresponded to his interpretation of this assumption.[13] One of the aims was to make architecture 'teachable'. Durand said that architecture is both a science and an art, but by art he meant the faculty of *applying knowledge*.

Guadet said, one hundred years later: '*Science has its axioms, art has its principles. Of all the arts, architecure has the most rigorous principles ... But the principles do not manifest themselves in the same way as the axioms ...*'.[14] By principles he no longer means just the order or genera, but knowledge of the elements of architecture (walls, doors, windows, staircases, roofs...) and elements of composition which are acquired by analogy with the most beautiful models of history. The weakness of such teaching by analogy lies in the tendency to perpetuate the same models instead of a more profound understanding of the essence which they embody.

The authority of the Beaux-Arts was already shaken in the nineteenth century by theorists such as Gottfried Semper[15] and Viollet-le-Duc. They presaged the decline of the 'principles' and the arrival, in force, of the exact sciences through the intermediary of the art of the engineer, which would compromise the conventional codes of architecture and open the way for change in techniques and forms 'stripped of artistic choice'. Viollet-le-Duc sees architecture from two different aspects:

(1) Theory, which deals with that which is permanent and always valid, notably the rules of art and the laws of statics; and

(2) Practice, which seeks to adapt these eternal laws to the variable conditions of time and space.[16]

This return to reason paves the way for the reversal of the supremacy of the codified academic architecture of the Beaux-Arts and the birth of those formal inventions which, at the beginning of the twentieth century, were to make a decisive break with historical references in order to find their own revolutionary and authentic path forward.

The programmes and manifestoes of the beginning of this century are particularly eloquent. '*The aesthetics of the engineer, architecture, two interdependent consecutive things, one in full bloom, the other in painful decline*'[17] said Le Corbusier in 1920. Even if the Bauchaus then gave first place to arts and crafts, the principles of this art have nevertheless fundamentally changed and the sciences have made their honourable entry into the teaching of architecture.

The last quarter of our century has led to a threshold of considerable change in scientific thought. First of all we have witnessed an important development, not only in exact sciences, but also in social sciences, notably in psychology, sociology and history. These form a precarious bridge between the certainties of exact sciences and the approximations of art. Precarious, because for about twenty years the most informed scientists have been questioning the relationship between science and reality as experienced. Phenomenological approaches are multiplying and metaphysics is gradually regaining ground.

Malraux said: '*The twenty-first century will either be religious or it will not be*'.

Alberto Perez-Gormez points out: in *Architecture and the crisis of modern science*:

Truth–demonstrable through the laws of science – constitutes the fundamental basis upon which human decisions are made over and above 'reality', which is always ambiguous and accessible only through the realm of 'poetics'. Today, theory in any discipline is generally identified with methodology; it has become a specialized set of prescriptive rules concerned with technological values, that is, with process rather than ultimate objectives, a process that seeks maximum efficiency with minimum effort. Once life itself began to be regarded as process, whether biological or teleological, theory was able to disregard ethical considerations in favor of applicability. Modern theory, leaning on the early nineteenth century model of the physico-mathematical sciences with their utopian ideals, has designated the most crucial human problems illegitimate, beyond the transformation and control of the material world.[18]

This quotation suggests some of the motivations for May 1968, a reflection of our ambiguous relationship with technological progress stemming from science. It contains a justified criticism which must nevertheless be accepted cautiously. If it is true that great human decisions are no longer taken by consulting a clairvoyant or the oracle at Delphi, it is also true that these decisions are not taken 'scientifically'. We use science to obtain a better appreciation of that part of reality that *we want* to grasp; for the actual decisions we refer to our value systems. Our ethics override objective facts more often than we like to admit. Ethics and myth aid and abet each other. Myth, while bringing us closer to life, spreads confusion over what were certainties, but when myth does not leave space for doubt and itself becomes certainty, it might become terrifying.

Despite appearances, the architecture of the pioneers of this century has never been 'scientific', even in the case of the almost unwavering believers in a rational and scientific approach, such as Hanes Meyer (see his competition plan for the SDN in 1929). Some of them, after starting to tackle the laws of form in a purely logical or mathematical manner, slid progressively towards a reinstatement of the irrational. The young architectural theorist Christopher Alexander, who was not deprived of mathematical genius, said in 1964 that his ultimate dream was to succeed in capturing mathematically the beauty and complexity of a rose. His book *Notes on the Synthesis of Form*'[19] reflects this search for the absolute, but *Pattern Language*'[20], published about twenty years later, grasped techniques, myths and realities in a mixture of positivism and phenomenology. In the same way, there remains little of the fascination that Le Corbusier had in the years following 1910 for the art of the engineer in his mature work of 1957, the convent of La Tourette.

1.3 In search of an introduction to the study of architecture

With *Space, Time and Architecture* Siegfried Giedion offered the students of forty years ago a new and coherent vision of what constitutes the roots and essence of modern architecture. At about the same time, Bruno Zevi was succeeding with his book, *Learning how to see architecture* in initiating the novice into reading architecture as space rather than objects. What happened since?

The upheaval caused by the revolution of the Modern Movement at the beginning of the century gave the *coup de grace* to the architectural treatises and the idea of 'unchangeable and unquestionable principles'. Contemporary culture reacts; writings on art and architecture such as renditions, collections of key texts, manifestos and aphorisms, historical depth studies, practice surveys and monographs, proliferate, purposely avoiding the positivism of a treatise. A gigantic bank of knowledge from diverse sources is accumulating and, with this in mind, the attempt to embrace the whole of architecture in just one introductory book necessitates a limited selection and a certain modesty of scientific ambition in favour of a didactic aim.

Every day the teacher is faced with the need to lead students to discover the range and principal aspects of a discipline which organizes the place for human life for today and tomorrow. The many-sided aspect of this discipline must therefore be presented with simplicity. This task is carried out in one way or another in all schools of architecture, *but it is no longer written about*. Consequently the argument varies from one teacher to another. The student starting out runs up against a diversity of concepts and language concerning the same basic principles of architecture.

In reality it is often more a difference of presentation than content. Some base their introductory talk on a critical and in-depth analysis of a few case studies. Others think it preferable to tackle the subject by a comparative study of typical elements (the column, wall, base, corner, parapet, window, door, staircase, square, street, etc.), and others choose more generic themes of composition, which is what we have opted for in this work. Whatever the methods of presentation chosen, what is important for the student is to be able to obtain a clear idea of the discipline, to discover a few basic facts, and to begin to build up references which will enable him to continue to learn.

This is the cultural context of this book. With the risk of inevitable omissions, the first part is built around the themes of geometry and environmental perception in order to give some *grammatical references*. These references organize the acquired knowledge of built form as such and as a design tool. Form is considered here sometimes with a certain degree of autonomy in relation to meaning. It is first of all 'empty of sense'[21] before taking on various meanings which are changing through time.

Our 'textbook' will seek, for example, to explain the phenomena of form which result in certain urban settings (Hydra, San Giminiano, Berne, etc.) being regarded as having a great formal coherence or, on the contrary, for what reasons the contemporary town is often perceived as chaotic. The same exercise can be undertaken for the disposition of openings in a façade. We shall also try to show why certain plans and spatial dispositions appear more balanced than others; due to which causes one building plays a role as an object and another as a stitch in the urban fabric; how architectural space can be defined with an economy of means, and what are the essential principles for establishing links between spaces; what are the spatial characteristics of certain geometries and how they can be manipulated, etc.

The dissection and classification of attributes of architectural form are not entirely safe procedures. They reflect neither the perception of the physical world, which is always seen in a subjective totality, nor the process of architectural design. In order to teach and learn we must, nevertheless, proceed by way of an analysis of the *structures* of the world of forms. The reader will quickly realize that this is not a treatise, a dictionary, or a book of architectural recipes, but rather an introduction to our discipline.

In the second part the author states his own position regarding the contemporary architectural scene from the angle of three selected themes: *place*, relationship between *form and matter*, and design as an *instrument for acquiring knowledge.*

The vision adopted places architecture between the world of physical realities and that of desire and the imaginary. Architecture cannot therefore be a science, but it uses sciences: the exact sciences for its stability and durability, its thermal and acoustic capabilities; social sciences for a better understanding of man's relationship with place and time. The responsible architect checks the artistic and cultural intuitions expressed in his design by rational means. He acts, knowing enough about established scientific facts and experience. The attractive vision of an entirely rational, scientific architecture based on facts and stripped of all speculation, is, on the other hand, a trap; or in the words of Colin Rowe:

> If the laws of statics can be safely assumed to be established beyond dispute, the 'laws' of use and pleasure, of convenience and delight, have certainly not as yet been subjected to any Newtonian revolution; and, while it is not inconceivable that in the future they may be, until that time, any ideas as to the useful and the beautiful will rest as untestifiable hypotheses.[22]

In architecture, as in life itself, science and art occupy positions of equal importance. Since we are dealing more particularly with *form*, what we call 'principles' is finally made up of observations and hypotheses on the most permanent components of architecture. Where scientific research has helped to reinforce certainties we shall make special mention of it. Elsewhere our approach will remain phenomenological and pragmatic. We shall try to establish our rules with a maximum of relevance. History, the body of 'experience', will therefore be of precious assistance.

If some of the principles might prove more ephemeral than expected, that will reduce their value but will not, however, negate it. As the Abbé Laugier said, in a similar context, in 1753:

> It seems to me that in the arts which are not purely applied arts, practice alone is not sufficient. It is above all important to learn to think. An artist must be able to justify what he does. To this end he needs principles which determine his judgements and justify his choices to the extent that he cannot merely say instinctively what is good or bad, but express his judgement as a man who knows the paths of Beauty and who can justify them.[23]

In an age when the trends and 'schools' that we mentioned at the beginning are so numerous and rather ephemeral, it seems useful that a discussion on architecture should try to integrate, reveal and clarify what these trends have in common. This book is a collection of observations, research, experiences and ordered thoughts which seek to be of use to the architects' *reasoned critique* of their own work and of the projects and designs of others.

The form of presentation which has been chosen for this work is that of an invitation to a guided tour of a small 'imaginary museum' compiled by the author, who will comment on his thematic collection. The pictures and text form an integral whole. The references will perhaps encourage readers to further their studies by consulting more specialized works as curiosity or needs urge them to do so. The collection reveals preferences of the author: modern architectural movements of the first third of this century, Greek antiquity, Byzantium, the Renaissance and sometimes the Baroque.

Overleaf
Le Corbusier, Convent of La Tourette,
Evreux-sur-l'Arbresle

2.1 The pleasure of looking at, listening to, feeling, touching and moving through architecture

Be warned: for a person who has the use of all his senses, the experience of architecture is primarily visual and kinaesthetic (using the sense of movement of the parts of the body). The main part of the book is devoted to this. *That does not mean that you are allowed to be deaf and insensitive to smell and touch.* That would be to deny oneself the fullness of sensations. Isn't it sometimes a failure on a single one of these points which are deemed to be of secondary importance which destroys all visual qualities? Aesthetic experiencing of the environment is a matter of all our senses and there are even some situations where hearing, smell and tactility are more important than vision; they are experienced with extraordinary intensity. As designers we must never forget that! Let us try to imagine the echo in the spaces that we are designing, the smells that will be given off by the materials or the activities that will take place there, the tactile experience that they will arouse. Let the five 'images' which follow serve as a reminder (Figures 6–10).

Hearing is not only involved in areas of entertainment where its demands are well known; it also has a role to play in the paving of streets, in the materials for staircases, in the ceilings and floors for a work place, etc. A school classroom, however large, well laid-out, well lit, or of splendid spatial composition, becomes a place of suffering if echoing exceeds certain limits, whether caused by the materials or by excessive height. An acoustically 'dead' church loses its religious character. A gravel path leading to a house announces the visitor's steps, whereas if it is asphalted (for the purpose of tidiness) it no longer delivers its message. If sometimes we close our eyes to remove the dominance of the visual world in order to listen more intently, that is real proof of the sheer pleasure of auditory experience. Think of the sound of a footstep!

Smell – perfumes of gardens, the smells of wood, of concrete, smells of cooking, the smell of soot, steam from laundries, incense in church, the dryness of granaries, dust, damp smells of cellars (which we experience even in the engravings of Piranesi) – small identifies places and moments for a lifetime. Perhaps it is the relative rarity of these experiences which makes them all the stronger. We can pick out their preciseness and detail and we can recall them throughout the whole of our lives; the smell of grandmother's house can be so firmly rooted in our memory that the simple fact of encountering it again in a completely different context twenty years later is sufficient to conjure up images of the old house with amazing precision.

Tactility occupies a special place in architecture for two reasons: on one hand it is inevitable because of gravity, and on the other it is anticipated by our ability to see forms and textures. A person's standing or walking are in permanent tactile contact with the ground – smooth or rough, hard or soft, flat or sloping. When we are permitted to choose, it is often that which is most convenient which triumphs. And our hands? It is well known that it is not enough just to look at beautiful objects on display: we want to touch them, examine the weight and the textural quality of the surface and its form. *Smooth* vertical elements, sculptures, tiles, columns etc., invite us to caress them.

And the buttocks? They too feel drawn by certain formal layouts of steps, plinths, benches and seats, the eye and sometimes the hand making a prior examination, judging their sensuality. And the skin? Cold, hot, unpleasant or refreshing draughts, stuffiness or freshness of the air offer just as many concerns for architectural design. Study Frank Lloyd Wright!

The movement of the body, if it is not itself one of our five senses, provides us, nevertheless, with a measure for things and space. Passing through, visiting, dancing, gesture – all allow us to appreciate the splendour and exploration of that which is hidden: (to move closer, move away, go round, go up, go down, go into, escape,) are all actions which invite us to organize for ourselves what we want to see, hear, feel, smell and touch in a given environment. Architecture is image only in a drawing or photograph. As soon as it is built it becomes the scene and sometimes the scenario of comings and goings, of gestures, even of a succession of sensations.

The sense of hearing (*listening*), smell (*perfume*) and the tactile sensation (*caress*), like vision and the kinaesthetic sense, are not only simple physiological functions, but also skills that can be learnt. The ear, the nose and the skin *are no more 'innocent'* than our eyes. Our intellectual faculties, our capacity to learn and to memorize turn them into sensing devices linked to our own experience, our culture and our time. The smells, noises and tunes of the nineteenth century are not experienced in the same way in the twentieth.

Let us conclude this brief evocation of the senses by repeating that they almost never act in isolation; they help each other, mix with each other and sometimes contradict each other, or, to conclude with the particularly relevant words of Michel Serres:

> ... nobody has ever smelt and only smelt the unique perfume of one rose. Hearing perhaps, the tongue without doubt, practises this isolation or selectiveness. The body smells a rose and a thousand smells around it at the same time as it touches wool, looks at a varied landscape, trembles at sound waves, at the same time as it rejects this flood of sensations in order to take time to imagine, muse abstractedly or go into ecstasy, work actively or interpret in ten different ways its state without ceasing to experience it.[162]

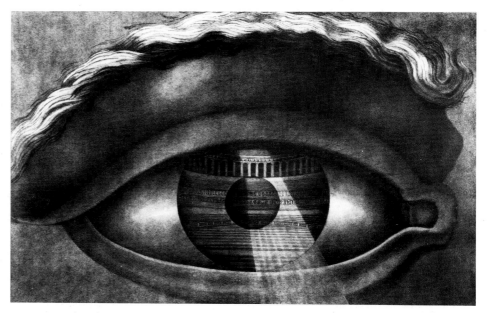

Figure 6 The gaze

'Your gaze scans the streets as if they were written pages: the city says everything you must think, makes you repeat her discourse ...

Rarely does the eye light on a thing, and then only when it has recognized that thing as the sign of another thing: a print in the sand indicates the tiger's passage ...

It is the mood of the beholder which gives the city of Zemrude its form. If you go by whistling, your nose a-tilt behind the whistle, you will know it from below: window sills flapping curtains, fountains. If you walk along hanging your head, your nails dug into the palms of your hands, your gaze will be held on the ground, in the gutters, the manhole covers, the fish scales, waste-paper. You cannot say that one aspect of the city is truer than the other ...

Your footsteps follow not what is outside the eyes, but what is within, buried, erased. If, of two arcades, one continues to seem more joyous, it is because thirty years ago a girl went by there, with broad, embroidered sleeves, or else it is only because that arcade catches the light at a certain hour like that other arcade, you cannot recall where.'

(Italo Calvino, The Invisible Cities)[161]

Illustration: Claude Nicolas Ledoux, Besancon Theatre

Figure 7 Listening

'It is not the voice that commands the story: it is the ear.' (Italo Calvino, The Invisible Cities*)*[161]

'... I listen. My ear grown to the size of an amphitheatre, an auricle of marble. Hearing laid on the ground, vertically, which tries to hear the harmony of the world ...'
(Michel Serres, Les cinq sens*)*[162]

Illustration: Epidaurus, aerial view.

Figure 8 Perfume

'Smell appears to be the sense of the singular. Shapes return to the same position, constant or modified, harmonies are transformed, stable despite variations, perfume indicates the specific. Eyes closed, ears blocked, feet and fists bound, lips tight, we choose between a thousand things, years later, such and such a forest at that season at sunset, before the rain ... a rare sense of the singular smell slips from knowledge to memory and from space to time ...' (*Michel Serres*, The Five Senses).[162]

Illustration: Russian Baptism.

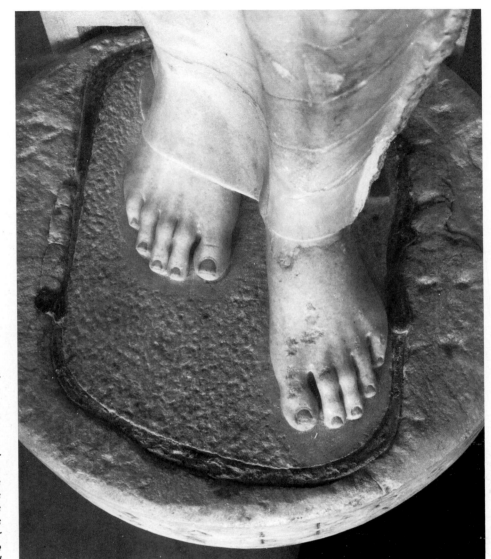

Figure 9 Caress

The skin can explore surrounding areas, limits, adhesions, lumps and bumps ...

Many philosophies refer to the visual; few to the auditory; still fewer put their trust in tactility ...

Some look, contemplate, see; others caress the world or let themselves be caressed by it, throw themselves into it, roll in it, bathe in it, dive into it and, sometimes, are beaten by it. The former do not know the weight of things, smooth and flat skin in which large eyes are set, the others surrender themselves under that weight. Their epidermis takes the pressure, over different parts of the body, like a bombardment, their skin is tattooed, striped like a zebra, like a tiger, matched, pearled, studded and sown chaotically with tones and shades, sores or swellings.

The skin sees ... It shivers, speaks, breathes, listens, sees, loves and is loved, receives, refuses, retreats, bristles in horror, is covered in cracks, blotches, wounds of the soul ... (Michel Serres, The Five Senses).[162]

Illustration: detail of a caryatid on the Acropolis, Athens.

Figure 10 The movement of the body

The spirit sees, language sees ... the body visits. It always transcends its location by virtue of its movement. Movements made in order to see make use of roads, crossroads, interchanges, so that the examination will either become more detailed or will become a general synopsis: change of dimension, of sense and direction. The visit explores and enumerates all the senses of feeling ...

The body does not act as a simple, passive receiver ... it exercises, trains, almost of its own accord, loves movement, becomes willingly involved in it, is happy to spring into action, jumps, runs or dances, is only aware of itself, instantly and without speech, in and through its involvement, discovers its existence in the burning of its muscles, out of breath, at the limits of fatique ... (*Michel Serres*, The Five Senses).[162]

Illustration: Oskar Schlemmer, Bauhaustreppe, 1932.

2.2 Seeing and noticing

Visual laws

Before carrying out the extension to the Kunstmuseum in Berne, Atelier 5 erected, in 1984, near its office, an experimental room to try to perfect a natural lighting system, overhead and extremely refined, which would avoid glare, uneven lighting between the top and bottom of the wall, direct sunlight, undesirable contrasts etc., in order to conserve and present paintings in the best possible conditions. The visitor to this experimental room went away perplexed, this setting for pictures seeming too 'antiseptic'. Perhaps he remembered pictures in a beaufiul house, lit in varying ways by the morning or evening light, with, from time to time, a ray of sunshine to give them a special vividness.

Once the museum was completed the visitor obviously scrutinized its contents with the greatest curiosity. When an architect makes his first visit to a new museum built by eminent colleagues, he does not usually go there in order to see the pictures on display. And yet, in this exceptional case he discovered that he had in the end forgotten to look at the museum and had *only seen the paintings!*

It is perhaps one of the greatest compliments that can be paid to a work of architecture. That does not mean that it must always be so and that well-designed architecture should be condemned to 'disappear' behind its content. There are many cases in which architecture is called upon to play a more active and forceful role, but for the exhibition of works of art it does well to put itself in second place. The fashionable anti-functionalist tendency needs to ask itself some questions.

The Castlevecchio museum of Carlo Scarpa in Verona (1957–64) is, in many respects, in direct contrast to that of Atelier 5. The architecture is so powerful that it is difficult to remember the objects on display. But the problem was, in this case, very different. For Scarpa it was a question of 'exhibiting', at the same time as the objects and pictures, the palace itself as a product of history.

Within the objective that he had set himself, Scarpa knew how to modulate the different means at his disposal. Outside and on the ground floor where the longest and most dissimilar objects are displayed, the play between the old and new architecture is accentuated in a dialectic manner, exhibiting both these objects and the palace itself. Upstairs, where the most valuable canvases are displayed, the architecture fades into a quiet background for the paintings.

What happened in Berne and in Verona? These architects knew and respected the most relevant visual laws. They subordinated the architectural form to the *raison d' être* of the space. That is real progress in comparison with the enormous warehouses of the Louvre and other ancient museums.

What are the visual laws which will help the architect in the design process?

Some of the laws are of a *physiological* nature, such as ocular stereometry, sensitivity of the retina, adaptation of the iris to the level of lighting, angle and precision of view, etc. They are important, but we will not tackle them here, because numerous works on physiology and architecture,[24] lighting engineering[25] or technical design[26] are already easily accessible.

Other laws originated from the *psychology of perception* and more especially from 'Gestalt' theorie (the theory of form). This particular branch, under the impulse of researchers like Koffka,[27] Wertheimer,[28] Katz,[29] Guillaume[30] and Metzger,[31] followed by researchers who, while subscribing to these theories, also stand apart, such as Gregory[32] and Gibson,[33] managed to establish some visual rules which have not subsequently been refuted. They are of interest to us because they frequently impinge on the notion of *preferences*, which can provide useful elements for an aesthetic theory. The first part of this book refers to this. It will be easily recognizable in the chapters 'Order and Disorder', 'Fabric and Object' and 'Space'.

The third group of theories concentrates on the mental activity which draws on perception. We are thinking of epistemology, information theory, genetics, anthropology, etc., which will appear in a more generalized manner, particularly in the chapter on 'place'.

What interests us for the moment is that some principles of the psychology of perception can be applied to architecture and to the graphic arts, since they originated from empirical experiments on vision, instead of being speculative. The results bring to our attention phenomena which are relatively more permanent than taste or style. The qualifying word – *'relatively'* – refers to a partial lingering doubt. One wonders to what extent it is our tradition or our immersion in Judaeo-Christian civilization which produces this way of seeing things.

Rudolf Arnheim[34,35] and Ernst Gombrich[36] have helped to extend Gestalt psychology to art. Bruno Zevi has used some of its principles in a relevant and didactic way in his 'classic' on teaching, *Learning how to see architecture.*[37] Christian Norberg-Schulz, more than twenty years ago, made a first attempt at proposing a theory of architectural form which would be based, at least partially, on the principles of perception.[38]

Norberg-Schulz subsequently disassociated himself from an explanation of the nature of the architectural phenomenon from the point of view of visual perception. However, it cannot be denied that, without eyes, one's experience of the physical environment is quite different. Numerous works on the perception of the blind exist as evidence of this.

The *readability of forms as figures* is one of the obvious objectives in the compositions of architects, painters, sculptors, graphic artists, typographers and many others. Conversely, the 'user' of forms cannot choose freely what he wants to see in a given context. Certain forms register more easily than others even before one considers their content or meaning. They become autonomous *figures* in front of a *ground*. The figure/ground phenomenon can therefore be considered fundamental for visual perception. It is a physiological phenomenon.

A *figure* finds its autonomy to a large extent by its edges, its contours, therefore by the contact it has with its exterior, the rest of the world. It is not accidental if in classical architecture the base, corners and cornice are accentuated. It is as if there were a greater concentration of information and excitation at the edge than at other points. The background can also consist of figures itself, but they play a secondary role (Figure 11).

The edges of figures are the precarious results of opposing forces. Each neighbouring surface claims the edge and when these forces are of equal value it causes an ambiguity between figure and ground (Figure 12). But the *ambiguity* between figure and ground is more prevalent in two-dimensional phenomena causing hesitation or illusions, rather than a three-dimensional working notion for the architect. The psychologist and the painter have the freedom to extract an element from reality; the architect is *in* reality.

There are rules which govern the good fit of figures; it is a question of the formal characteristics which tend to make them dominant in relation to other forms in the visual field. When the shape is relatively *convex, small and closed* (for example the moon, a window, etc. Figure 13) and when it *contrasts* with a ground which, on the other hand, seems to extend indefinitely, it tends to become a figure. The presence of elementary geometric form rein-

Figure 11 Inversion of figure and ground: one figure becomes a ground to another. Morandi, Still Life, 1946.

Figure 12 Progression from the ground towards the figure and vice-versa. M. C. Escher, The Sky and the Sea II.

Figure 13 The figure character is reinforced by a closed and convex form.

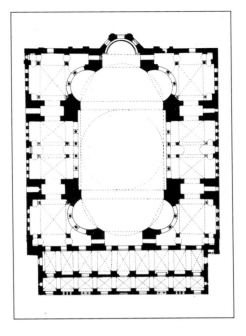

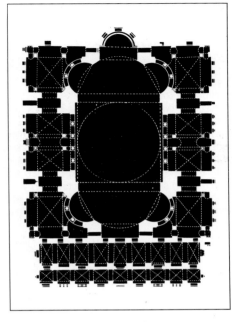

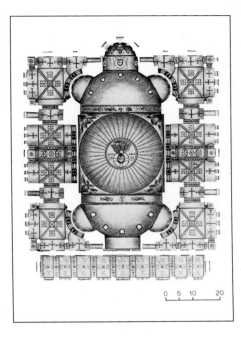

Figure 14 Drawing a plan attributes to the outline of the walls the character of a figure. Saint Sophia in Constantinople, 532–537 AD.

Figure 15 To invert the drawing of the plan on a white background is the equivalent of attributing the figure character to the space contained by the walls which now blend in with the ground.

Figure 16 Spatial subtleties of the section and the openings can be made visible by a plan in which the space assumes the role of a figure with shades of grey according to its degree of definition. Here we have slightly manipulated a drawing of the ceiling of Saint Sophia, by E. M. Antoniades in 1909, in order to obtain a similar effect.

forces this tendency towards an autonomous figure (for example circle, spiral, prism, etc). A weakly defined figure can, however, become a good fit when we are familiar with it.

Autonomy and formal identity must not be confused. *Identity* can come from its outline, but just as much from associated information that can be discerned on its surface or in its volume (for example the human face with nose, mouth, eyes; the rose with its petals; the cathedral with its doorway, buttresses and

turrets). We shall come back later on to this not-so-innocent eye.

For more detailed study of the figure/ground phenomenon and the perception of depth, it is useful to refer to the fifth chapter of *Art and Visual Perception* by Rudolf Arnheim.[39] A special adaptation of this concept to the built environment will be made in Chapter 5, when we shall talk about the *object* which becomes a figure.

It is an area where the complementary nature of the relationship

between figure and ground can be used as a graphic *tool* by architects in order to get a clearer idea of *the form of spaces*. When we draw a plan, we give concrete expression to the walls and objects; we draw *what surrounds* the space rather than the space itself (Figure 14).

If we wanted to perceive better the form of the spaces themselves, we would have to transform the volume (or its projection on a plan) into a figure. That can be done by drawing the surfaces rather than the walls

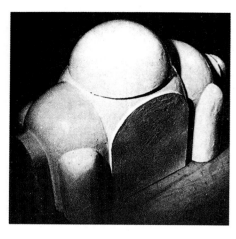

Figure 17 Space transformed to solid prohibits any mental penetration.

Figure 18 The sectional axonometric which combines the information of the plan with that of the section and the view of the interior volume is an effective means of giving an objective representation of the space.

Figure 19 Perspective, although limited and static, remains an informative representation of interior space. Our experience allows us to 'travel mentally' – even if only a little. Moreover it conveys part of 'the atmosphere', which other means achieve only with difficulty.

which define them. It would then be a question of a sort of working with the negative. But it is not sufficient simply to present a negative plan, because one would again read the white lines which were black before. That is due to the law which requires a ground to have an 'infinite' field relative to the figure (Figure 15).

This same technique can be applied with more subtlety by using shades of black and grey according to the degree of enclosures of a space (explicit or implicit), or by reflecting the relief of the ceiling for example (Figure 16).

One could also have made a model representing space as a moulded solid (Figure 17). By this means, we obtain a rather strange form, even if it comes from a marvellous space. It remains alien to what that space is and to the way in which it can be understood. Being a solid object, it prohibits any mental penetration. This academic exercise is costly and not of anywhere near the same interest as the figure/ground inversion as a way of accentuating the formal characteristics of the void (Figure 15). The axonometric and the perspective are other meaningful means of representation of space (Figures 18 and 19).

Arnheim suggests that architects should replace the notion of figure/ground by that of objects producing a field of energies. The space would then be described by vectors or 'magnetic fields' modified by distances, expansions and contractions (Figure 20). He thus is interested in the work of Paolo Portoghesi whose 'grids' bear a greater resemblance to ripples produced by the walls than to a system of abstract organization (Figure 21). The notion of figure and its relationship with ground will be very useful elsewhere when we talk about fabric and object.

In the next chapter, 'Order and Disorder' we will, on the other hand, use Gestaltist laws which demonstrate the tendency of the eye to gather certain elements in the visual field into 'families' or 'groups': minimal heterogeneity, proximity, resemblance, enclosure, common orientation, repetition, symmetry etc., are those factors, well presented by Metzger,[40] which influence our sense of unity or incoherence for a given environment (Figure 22).

Although these laws often act very forcefully on our images, we must not lose sight of the fact that our perceptions are not only the result of a 'mechanical process' of vision, but that they are filtered through our memory and intelligence.

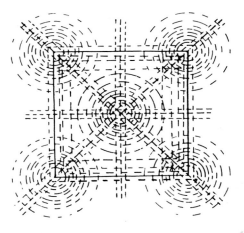

Figure 20 *The structural skeleton of the square by Rudolf Arnheim.*

Figure 21 *Walls which generate space or space which generates walls? Paolo Portoghesi and V. Gigliotti, Papanice house, the maxtrix of composition.*

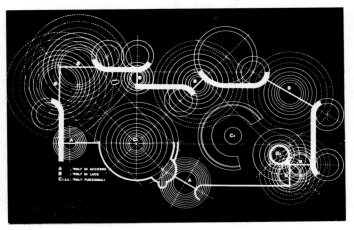

The law of proximity. There are not six spots, but two × three spots; the spots which are close together join into a group.

The law of similarity in competition with the law of proximity. Proximity requires three spots on the left and three on the right: similarity requires three spots (hatched, outlined or small) at the top and three (large and solid) at the bottom.

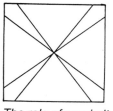 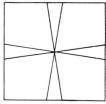

The role of proximity and distance: on the left one sees primarily a diagonal cross, while on the right one sees instead a vertical/horizontal cross.

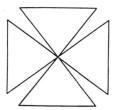 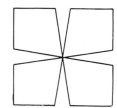

Enclosure wins over proximity. The narrow sectors can no longer be read as the arms of a cross because they are missing a small part of the edge.

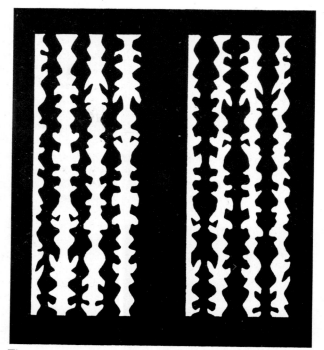

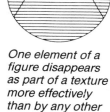

One element of a figure disappears as part of a texture more effectively than by any other means of integration; we see an angle and not a triangle.

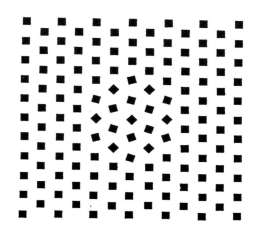

The strength of symmetry: one tends to see white figures on the left and black figures on the right.

Groups are formed according to regular or irregular orientation.

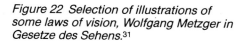

Figure 22 Selection of illustrations of some laws of vision, Wolfgang Metzger in Gesetze des Sehens.[31]

The eye is not innocent

There is a difference between seeing and perceiving. Le Corbusier, travelling in Belgium, was amazed by the enormous pyramids he saw through the country. When he noticed that, in fact, they were slag-heaps of mining spoil, his enthusiasm waned '... suddenly I measure the abyss that can open up between the appearance of a thing and the quality of thought that it evokes ....'[41]

The gaze holds hidden experiences, knowledge and expectations. Perception is not neutral; we continually compare what we see with situations that we have previously met and assimilated. This is what makes the scientific observations of perception precarious and 'Gestalt' laws incomplete. The figure-character is reinforced by the *familiarity* that we have with an image and by its underlying *meaning*. We 'prefer' a meaningful image to other information coming from the field of vision, even when the latter is a better fit in terms of shape.

That holds true as well when we only perceive a fragment or when this figure charged with meaning is blurred (Figure 23). We do not see what we see but what we expect to find. We need these expectations because '... a world in which nothing is predictable, in which everything changes continually, is a world in which intelligence has no hold on reality, where one is continually expecting the unexpected'.[42] Our memory acts on our perceptions and influences our judgements beyond 'objective' truths.

A doctor recognizes anomalies on an X-ray where we see only a general image composed of dark and light areas. He has learnt to know the norm, which enables him to detect divergences. A Bedouin is able to detect the presence of a herd of camels in the distance where for us there is only a desert of stones as far as the eye can see. For him it is a question of survival; he has learnt to see. A student of architecture learns to perceive consciously the appearance of landscapes, towns and buildings. He develops an aptitude for seeing and recognizing signs in the environment which enable him to *distinguish* more sharply, to *judge*

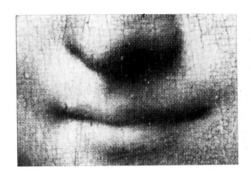

Figure 23 *Whose smile? Past experience helps us to recognize a whole image when looking at only a fragment of it.*

between order and disorder, proportion and disproportion, balance and imbalance, homogeneity and hierarchy, solidity and fragility, significant forms and forms that are accidental or devoid of meaning. The student of architecture wandering through the alleyways of Vicenza, even without knowing Palladio, will pick out more easily than a layman which are the particular qualities which distinguish this master's buildings from others in the same street. Visiting Le Corbusier's Villa Savoie or Frank Lloyd Wright's Kaufmann house (Falling Water), he will assess the methods and details which have contributed to the exceptional richness of these works which take on more easily for him than for the layman, a figure-character.

Moreover, the architect cannot limit himself to seeing buildings by means of their visible enveloping planes. *He sees the invisible*, his vision anticipates the hypotheses that he will be able to make on the interior organization, thickness, structure, space and all that follows.

Landscapes, towns and buildings are part of each person's daily visual experience; they are not reserved for specialists. Of course the impressions of the public remain most often intuitive and hazy. Its views are, however, governed by a combination of visual laws, acquired cultural values that have been imposed or accepted, by the memory of one's own experiences and by particular objectives that one is pursuing at the moment of confrontation with the environment in question – buying a newspaper, visiting a town or going to a show. The motives which determine an action condition the perception of the world in which it takes place.

Being capable of seeing what few others perceive straight away, the architect bears a great responsibility. We can build what others are hardly capable of seeing, we can erect something that shocks or something that pleases. We can speculate on the fact that one day the public will discover at least part of our intentions by incorporating them it its memory. Whatever happens, through his schemes the architect plays a public role. His 'didactic' role can help others to perceive and enjoy the built environment with greater subtlety.

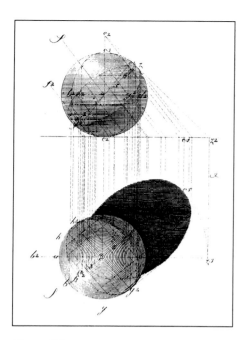

Figure 24

Figure 25

The sphere and the rose

Great masters of architecture throughout time have declared themselves in favour of aesthetics linked to the simplicity of volume. '*Less is more*' is not the sole prerogative of Mies van der Rohe.

Boullée, who aspired to an 'articulate' architecture, said that the figure of irregular bodies escapes our understanding[43] (Figure 24). Gombrich affirms that simplicity is a prerequisite for being able to learn – to learn to see and to perceive. He establishes the hypothesis that ease of perception is linked to simplicity of construction. He also thinks that preference for simple forms could well be due to the fact that they are recognizable outside the acute angle (between 1 and 2 degrees) of the eye's sharp focus.[44] The simplicity and regularity of a daisy delights and reassures.

Researches in psychology have, however, shown that the complexity of the stimulus arouses *interest*. 'Subjects whose age is under ten seem most sensitive to an optical complexity situated somewhere between simplicity and maximal complexity.'[45] Let us take the example of a rose at the moment of flowering. It hardly ever disappoints aesthetic sensibility. In spite of all its complexity, indescribable or at least unpredictable by mathematics or language, it is taken in at just one glance. It is capable of arousing our emotions there and then. It can perhaps elude our reason, but not our sensibility (Figure 25). Would it be a challenge to all logical discussion on the formal structure of a beautiful object?

It is a question of regularity without repetition. What offsets the enormous complexity of the figure or the image of the rose, is *its internal coherence and its dependence on an origin, on a stem and on a centre:* tensions and releases, curves and counter-curves, centrality and the *common effort of the petals* are a substitute for geometric simplicity. In short, it is a question of a highly organized and hierarchical totality which is fundamentally different from a random assemblage.

Moreover, the rose is, unlike buildings, sufficiently small to be perceived by the narrow angle of focus. If we were obliged to find our way *inside* the labyrinth of a giant rose, our sensual pleasure would perhaps be transformed into a nightmare. Geometric simplicity and complexity do not, therefore, have the same significance when it is a matter of perception of the whole or from a distance, rather than a close and fragmentary perception. We shall return in the next chapter to the themes of simplicity and complexity, or regularity and irregularity. We are as moved by the convergent complexity of Hans Scharoun's Philharmonic Hall as by the clarity of Mies van der Rohe's Art Gallery, both built in the same period in Berlin. But there is one thread between the sphere and the potato or between the rose and chaos.

3

ORDER AND DISORDER

Overleaf
Random order. Monemvassia.

3.1 Inevitable order

We are not talking here about classical 'order' in the sense of a code for architectural composition in antiquity or from the sixteenth to the nineteenth centuries. The Doric, Corinthian, Ionic, Tuscan orders, if we sometimes refer to them, do not interest us for their value as a cultural code, but for the geometrical structure. Fundamental and permanent rules seem to govern the interdependence of the elements of architectural form. Buildings and urban groupings are always more or less structured. What is this order?

Order only has meaning in relation to disorder and chaos. It has no value in itself except at its limits. Perfect order and total chaos are equally difficult situations to bear for a long period. The works we construct are situated somewhere between the two.[46]

Order in building

Nature: order or disorder? And then again, what nature? Wild untouched nature, because it is too vast, does not give an impression of chaos. Cycles, tides and waves give visible order. Rocks, rivers, plants or insects allow their structure to be observed. But, taken together, they represent an order which, at the visual level with which we are concerned, becomes unmeasurable. We accept the variety. We also admire it and yet man has traditionally imposed the measurable, the city, upon nature.

We have to live 'against nature' and therefore we build by ordering. 'In order that nature can be considered as landscape, it must cease to be too wild; because to be a specta-tor, one must not feel threatened. The world is more beautiful since it has been explored' (Hellpach). Man imposes the mark of his control on the earth, water and the vegetable kingdom to the furthest corners of the world. He must assume the enormous responsibility that such a desire involves.

To build we must use fairly simple geometry. It is first of all *a necessity for design and above all for building.* Thus, to design and lay out roads, construct houses, prepare the site, cut the stones, mould or press the bricks and concrete panels, make the structural frame, and finally fit it all together, we have always sought to economize our efforts by using *the repetition of elements that can be assembled.* Regularity is thus the very essence of building. Heinrich Tessenow said: 'Order is always more or less miserable ... but you have to take the world as it is, and for that a certain inelegance is required. The construction of our streets, bridges, houses and furniture is always somewhat makeshift and it is for that reason that we particularly need order.'[47]

Repetition, alignment and juxtaposition of identical elements and similar methods of construction impose order on our buildings and our towns. A colonial town on a grid layout, such as Turin or Manhattan, a Gothic cathedral, a building by Louis Kahn or a bridge by Robert Maillart celebrate order from structure or from technical necessities. The order which arises from construction finally educates the eye and influences our sense of the beautiful. This taste for regularity, once it has been established, acts on architectural design by transcending, on this occasion, purely constructional requirements. Order acquires its own autonomy. That does not mean that one ignores the demands of construction, but that one superimposes other criteria. Each period and, to a certain extent, each architect, establishes its or his own ethics relative to the degree of autonomy permitted (Chapter 8).

Our search for order is not simply that of knowing in what way things have been made, what purpose they serve or what they represent. Objects also act on our senses as forms having their own intrinsic and geometric logic.

The sense of order

The discussion of perceptive phenomena in the previous chapter gave a glimpse of the fact that regularity is *necessary* to man. The more complex the environment, the more we need to simplify and summarize to understand and get our bearings. Since we operate by making analogies to perfect our knowledge of the environment, we do not want order to change completely from one day to the next. We need to accustom ourselves. Gombrich reverses this idea by saying: 'The power of habit comes from our sense of order. It comes from our resistance to change and from our search for continuity.'[48] Just as the sense of balance is innate, developing from the inner ear, it seems possible that our sense of order runs very deep. Even if it is not entirely innate, this sense of order has already developed by early childhood.

Without wishing to make an analogy with what happens in the animal kingdom, the example of the cuckoo is disconcerting. Born in a strange nest, raised by a sparrow and having never seen its parents, it is a confident migrant. It spends the winter in tropical forests. It travels alone and at night without following the example set by other birds. It seems that man, too, has an innate sense of order. Genetic pychology, which deals with these problems, will perhaps give us an explanation one day.

On this innate sense of order is superimposed a learning process varying according to the environment and culture, which helps us to orientate ourselves. There will, therefore, never be just one order, one measure or one ideal balance. However we can, by taking discoveries of psychology and the history of architecture, clarify the principal means at our disposal. We work with them implicitly every day. We still need to make them more explicit in order to be able to teach and develop criticism.

3.2 Factors of coherence

We have seen that the eye selects and combines elements, that it seeks the simplest and most synoptic form and that it tries to integrate the various parts. Architecture, once again, is at the crossroads between the arts and the sciences: the coherence of a work of art can have its internal logic, that is recognized neither by the natural sciences nor by construction. A figure, even if it is abstract, has other characteristics than its edges. We can compose it from parts which, together, give the effect of a grouping. This principle of grouping is reinforced by repetition, similarity, proximity, common enclosure, symmetry and orientation of the parts. It is not our aim to discuss the relationship between form and content, but it is important to point out that semantic unity can reinforce and sometimes even replace formal coherence. The construction of a church begun in the Romanesque period, continued in the Gothic and completed in the Renaissance can appear unified in spite of stylistic disparities. It is the 'idea' of 'church' which predominates and unites the whole.

Factors of formal coherence are omnipresent and fundamental to architecture and urban design. Their principles are illustrated here by a series of pictures from one small town. Part of the pleasures and difficulties we experience with the built environment can be explained by our ease or difficulty in mentally grouping different elements from the visual field into synoptic units. When one studies integration in an existing grouping, these phenomena require the closest attention. Architecture is an art which acts on the dependence between elements to establish coherence.

Figure 26 Group of triangles, group of circles and groups of triangles and circles.

Repetition and similarity

The eye tends to group together things of the same type (Figure 26). Even when the elements taken in pairs are somewhat different, we find that the structural resemblance dominates these differences (Figure 27). Repetition in the form of rhythm, as much in music as in architecture, is an extremely simple principle of composition which tends to give a sense of coherence. All forms of repetition can, moreover, be the result of addition, or of division of a whole, or simply constitute a series without a clearly identifiable overall form. On the scale of architecture and urban design, the absence of a limit, of a beginning or an obvious end, easily becomes disruptive; there is coherence of detail 'without aim' or without the coherence of the whole.

When the elements are heterogeneous, a grouping effect can in any case be obtained because of the partially common characteristics, as for example the proportions of the windows, their position in the wall and their relationship with the solid areas. Unity of materials and texture is another example of partial characteristics which reinforce the tendency towards coherence in spite of the individuality of each building (Figures 28 and 29).

Figures 26 to 40 The illustration of each phenomenon is accompanied by a series of photographs of the little town of Hydra, 12 km east of the Péloponèse. Its sea front, developed in the eighteenth century, provides an exemplary case demonstrating the interaction of forces that establish great coherence, in spite of the absence of identical repetition.

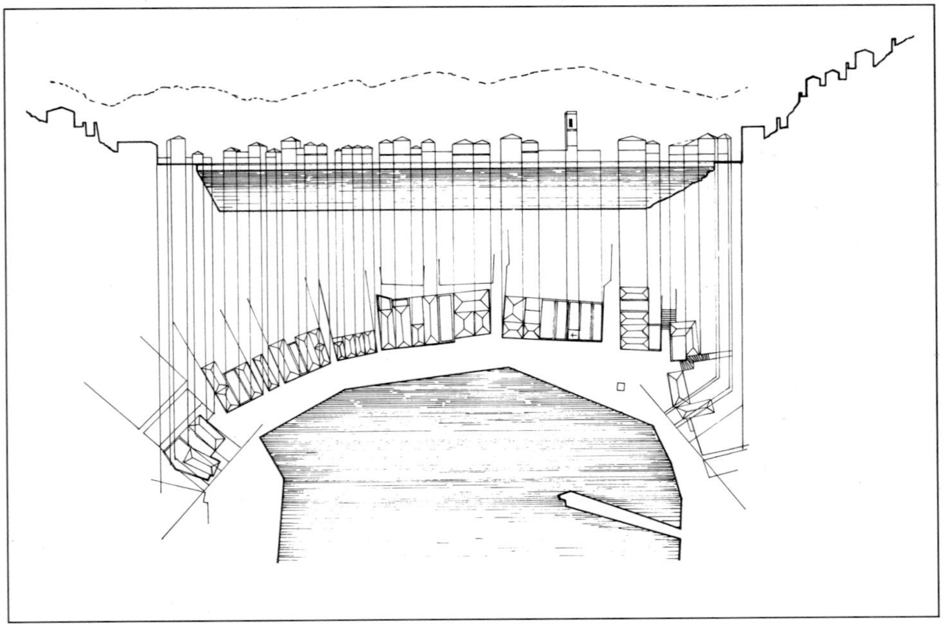

Figure 27 The plan suggests a relative equivalence of the facade module. All the same, it varies from single to triple, but this irregularity is offset by other factors which we shall talk about later. The four-sided roof is the norm, but exceptions do exist without causing disruption. Similarity is therefore not simply a question of the form of the roof. There is approximate repetition, but never identical.

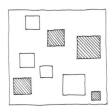

Figure 28 Group of hatched squares; group of plain squares.

Figure 29 Similarity of details – the construction and dimension of the walls, corners, cornices, windows and doors – vigorously counterbalances individual differences of size and proportion of the houses.

Common scale, indeed even the comparative size of elements, is an effective factor in grouping by similarity (Figures 30 and 31). It must be emphasized that this would not be sufficient if it were the *only* common characteristic. When the objects differ in other ways, such as materials, texture, openings or roofs, the unity is destroyed in spite of the similarity of scale.

Figure 30 Group of large elements and group of small elements.

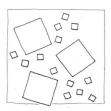

Figure 31 The waterfront of the harbour at Hydra, owing to the topography, is not formed only by the houses in the first row. The stone-faced 'giants', houses of ships' masters, captains and privateers, should disrupt the urban coherence. In fact, by their scale, they form a sub-group apart, without breaking up the urban fabric.

Proximity

The eye tends to group elements which are close together and to distinguish them from those which are further apart (Figure 32).

Figure 32 Dissimilarity is counteracted by proximity.

This grouping principle is very powerful. It makes it possible to join together that which is different by using small gaps to create an articulation between elements (Figure 33). There is no established size for these gaps, because the cohesion depends on the relative size of the elements and on the context. When the distance is greater than the size of the smallest element, one often resorts to other means (similarity, orientation, etc), to reinforce coherence.

Figure 33 Two groups of three windows, not just large and small windows. Similarity has become less powerful than proximity, common white background and symmetry.

Common enclosure and common ground

Figure 34 Group of figures on a 'carpet' and a group of exterior figures.

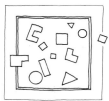

Figure 35 Group of figures inside an enclosure figure overlapping enclosure and figure outside.

An enclosure, a ground, even a carpet, define a field. What is included within the field is distinguished from what is outside it, even if the elements within are heterogeneous (Figures 34 and 35).

This is a very effective method of unification which we frequently use. Moreover, the elements which define the enclosure form a separate sub-group (Figure 36).

Conversely, the absence of clear limits to most of the recent extensions to our towns and villages prevents us from forming an image of the city (see also section 7.2).

Orientation of elements: parallelism or convergence towards a void or a solid

The eye also tends to group elements which have the same position: vertical, horizontal, parallel elements ... (Figures 37 and 38).

Heterogeneous figures form a group by the position that the elements take in relation to a street, square or building (Figures 39 and 40). The same phenomenon is sometimes used to organize a façade by grouping, for example, the windows in relation to the front door. The door acquires an importance which is hierarchically superior to the other elements.

Symmetry is a particular example of this principle. It can even contribute to the unification of such fundamentally different elements as building and nature. These acquire a common belonging by their relation to an axis which may be either real

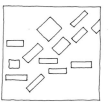

Figure 37 Group of horizontal figures and a group of oblique figures.

Figure 38 Group of figures which belong to the 'street' and a group of other figures.

or virtual. Trees set along a common axis with a building detach themselves from the surrounding nature and become part of the building complex. We shall come back to symmetry in the following chapter.

Figure 36 Homogeneity of the whole town in front of the mountain backdrop. The string of houses on the waterfront constitutes the sub-group of the enclosure.

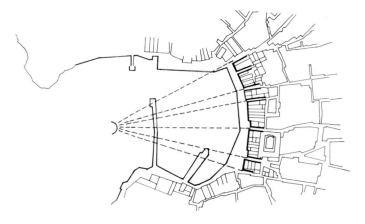

Figure 39 Convergence of alleyways and façades towards a theoretical focus in the natural harbour.

Figure 40 Parallelism and orientation: the space of the quay is one entity owing to the alignment of the façades in a broken curving line. No projecting building breaks this regularity. The line of the quay widens at the point where the activities or importance of the buildings so demand (businesses, main church, etc.).

Interaction of factors

In most organizations several factors come into play simultaneously. Reality is complex and pure situations are rare. Sometimes one factor dominates the others.

The example of the harbour at Hydra shows the power of a strong *redundancy* of factors of coherence. Owing to the simultaneous action of four factors (similarity, proximity, enclosure, orientation) which act on different scales, this 'ensemble', though still heterogeneous and not even symmetrical, is welded into one indissoluble whole. Once these principles of coherence are well established, one discovers that there is room for enormous variation. Of course, Rietveld's Schroeder house would be difficult to insert into it, rejecting the principle of frontality and the wall with openings. But the coherence of the whole would not be jeopardized by the insertion of Loos's Moller house, or Le Corbusier's Cook house. On the contrary, it would be enriched and we could have had fun doing a photo-montage as a demonstration.

These observations demonstrate the extreme theoretic fragility of planning rules which claim to preserve the town and its historic centre from the 'arbitrariness' of some contemporary architecture. The attempt, perhaps praiseworthy in itself, uses means that are too crude. It addresses only the symptoms. Strict alignments, colour and facing materials, storey height and cornice line, preservation of existing façades, type and colour of the roof, type of tiles, etc. – none of that is respected in Hydra ... and yet, what formal coherence!

3.3 From order to chaos

The study of the town of Hydra shows an example of interaction between repetition, similarity, proximity, enclosure and orientation. We use these methods to organize our environment. According to the choices which we make, we end up with groupings which can be grasped at a glance, or, on the contrary, which are complex, more difficult to understand and which require investigation. *The elements* and above all the *relationships* between the elements can be more or less organized starting from the use of a uniform texture, through hierarchy and complexity to a collection of elements without identifiable relationships – chaos (Figure 41).

The fewer links there are in the visual information the observer receives, the greater the effort he has to make. The architect, then, introduces structures which make it possible to group the elements by strengthening their relationships.

Most towns and architectural works are characterized by several superimposed levels of organization in a hierarchy specific to the composition. The level of interest of a work does not lie so much in the use of one or other of these methods or organization, but the knowledge of these methods increases our consciousness of the design resources available and our skill in handling them.

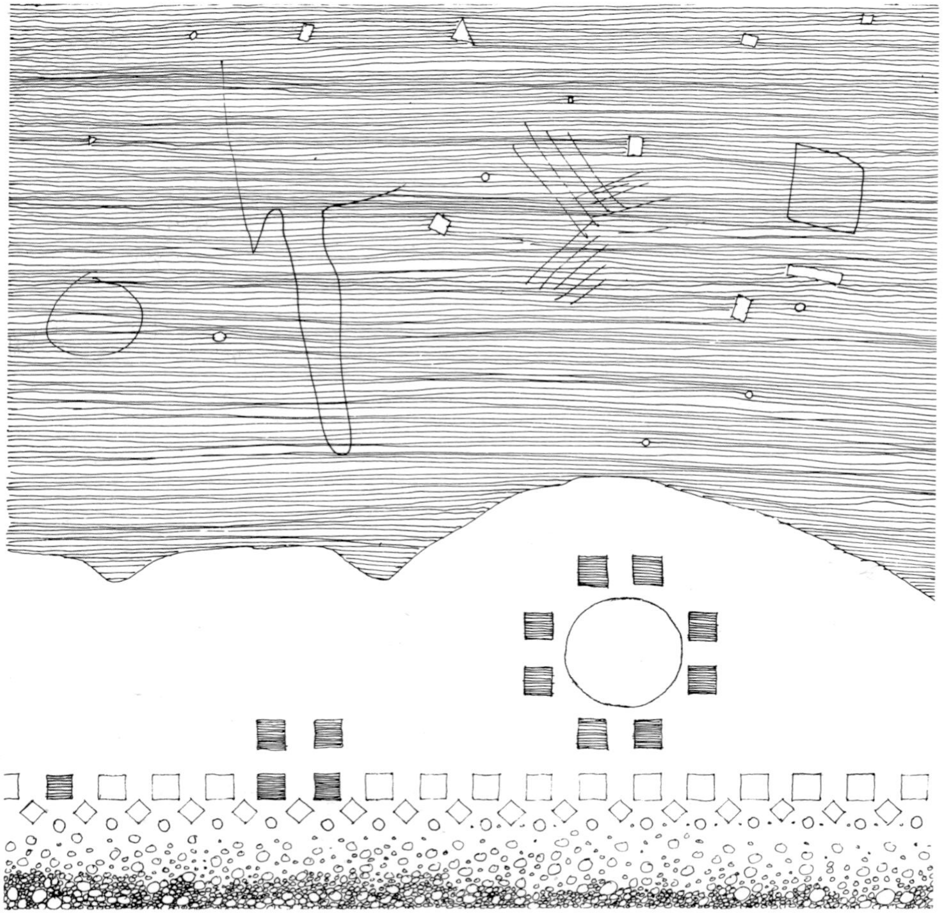

Figure 41 Texture – series – hierarchy – contrast – complexity (drawing by Larry Mitnick).

Homogeneity and texture

The eye perceives texture when the parts of a surface are sufficiently close, similar and numerous that they are no longer seen individually as figures. By analogy we can talk about a homogeneous structure when the same principle is applied to objects or buildings in space (for example a forest, a medina in North Africa, etc.).

The most elementary structure is thus created simply by *proximity, repetition, similarity and, sometimes, by the orientation* of the elements.

Textures are of two types. The forest, the gravel on a path or certain clusters of buildings in southern Europe form an order which we could call random (Figures 42 and 43). Other groupings reflect an explicit or underlying system of coordinates, 'a web' (Figure 44). The threads of this web are often nonphysical. They are suggested by the positions of the solids, organizing the space between elements, as, for example, the streets between houses. The mixture of random orders and webs characterizes the aerial view of Hydra (Figure 45). The urban structure often appears to be more random in places where topography asserts itself, whereas it is 'weblike' where flat land is available to accommodate the will of man. On a smaller scale, in the streets of Hydra we again find a homogeneity of nearby elements (forms and sizes of houses, doors, staircases, facings, colours, scales). The bird's eye view presents a generalization of reality and extent of the variations within an urban system, which must be qualified as experiences by walking through them. Texture is the significant order of collectivity, an easy and reassuring order by its similari-

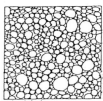

Figure 42

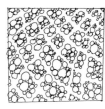

Figure 44

Figure 43 Skyros, Greece.

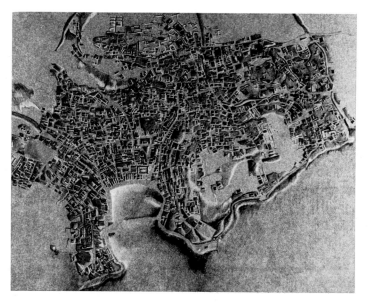

Figure 45 Co-ordinated texture; Hydra.

Figure 46 Fragmentary texture; Pully (on the same scale as Figure 45!).

ties in structure and scale, whilst at the same time allowing individual differences. Certain textures are in danger of disintegrating because they contain too many breaks and irregularities (Figure 46). The introduction of roads and buildings on the random alignment of previous agricultural subdivisions is often the root cause of the confusion of our modern suburbs. No sooner is a rule established than it is broken. The fabric does not get its chance to be woven.

We have based our argument on aerial views because they are comparable documents. We could just as well have observed the texture of façades or of fragments of façades.

Alignments and series

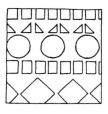

Figure 47

There is a particular configuration of texture in which order is obtained by repetition of aligned elements. All the parts are of similar or equivalent importance but, contrary to the homogeneous structure, there is a preferred direction through alignment (Figure 47).

Think of the example of a necklace or arcade. When the necklace is in double or triple strands, transverse relationships are established. When these become too important, we return to the web texture.

All the factors of coherence can come into play in the series, but similarity and proximity of the elements are the pre-condition for it.

The basis of this type of structure is *linearity and rhythm*. All series are rhythmical with beats and intervals. What at first sight appears to be nothing more than a simple, pleasant repetition when looking at the ensemble of the square at Telč (Figures 48 and 49) is, in fact, a complex combination which ensures that the ensemble is more than one house simply tacked onto another: the rhythm of arcades ... A - A - A ... and windows ... B - B - B - C - B - B - B - C ... is only slightly disrupted towards the base by the house units, while the rhythm of the gables ... D - D - D

... and d – d – d ... re-establishes the unity of each house. Could these horizontal strands therefore be split into two or three: the uniform rhythm of the arcades, the ambiguous one of the windows and that of the gables? A second examination shows that the rhythm of the gables is subtly extended down to ground level. The series are vertically co-ordinated: the individuality of the houses continues to exist, although diminished, as far down as the arcades, owing to a slight difference in proportion and colour. *Three* archways and *three* windows are slightly different from neighbouring ones. The figure three has a '*centre*', therefore a symmetry. The symmetry is explicit at the gable and implicit at ground level.

The over-all view, which is no doubt fascinating for most of us, is not simply the result of skilful control of form. Order is linked here to urban realities; it integrates facts of life. The aligned façades and the homogeneous arcade at ground level accentuate the collective role of the square. Towards the top, each floor progressively affirms the relative individuality of the builders/financiers/inhabitants.

What we can learn from this example is that a series need not all be based on an identical rhythm, but that one can join together several beats into larger units on condition that these groupings are not arbitrary. When these beats correspond to a reality of life, they are even more satisfying.

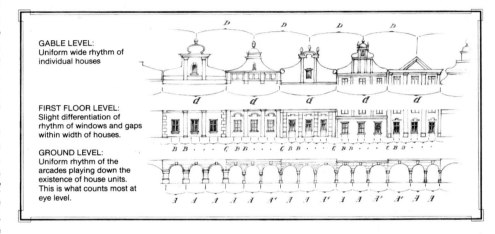

GABLE LEVEL:
Uniform wide rhythm of individual houses

FIRST FLOOR LEVEL:
Slight differentiation of rhythm of windows and gaps within width of houses.

GROUND LEVEL:
Uniform rhythm of the arcades playing down the existence of house units. This is what counts most at eye level.

Figure 48 Co-ordination of series, Telč, Czechoslovakia.

Figure 49 Telč, Czechoslovakia.

Gradation

In a repetitive structure like texture or series, the intervals or elements may gradually change their form, size or orientation. Gradation thus combines two contradictory characteristics: relationship and difference without a pronounced hierarchy (Figures 50 and 51). Gradation is found everywhere in our environment. Many of the elements of nature are structured in this way (Chapter 5). Without attaching too much importance to an analogy between the human body and the façade of the Convent of La Tourette (Figure 52), one must admit that the analogy incorporates the idea of crescendo and de-crescendo in time and distance, apparently without repetition. Frequently found in nature, gradation is, however, little used in architecture. More regular rhythms are generally preferred, for obvious reasons of economy of building methods. Other constructions, more demanding as regards function and structure/weight relationship do, however, resort to it, as for example the wings of a glider, whose very sensuality is breathtaking.

There exists one particular form of gradation which is used more often in plan and section than in façades: *progression* (Figure 53). In a progression there is a beginning and an end or an aim, which, for this

Figure 53

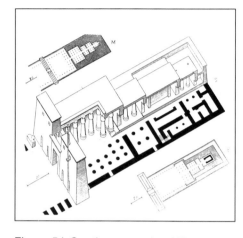

Figure 54 Southern temple of Thebes (according to Choisy).

reason, assumes a dominant position. It is a continuous gradation of crescendo without cyclical variation. Thus a hierarchy is established as can clearly be seen in the drawings of the southern temple at Thebes by Auguste Choisy (Figure 54) where the progression towards the heart of the sanctury can be read not only in the plan but also in section. It is not the highest and the largest which is the most important, but the opposite. Hierarchy is not a question of size but of the relative position of an element in its context.

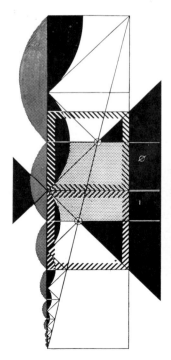

Figure 51 Le Corbusier, The Modulor, definitive diagram. 1950.

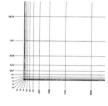

Figure 50

Figure 52 Gradation of glazing; Le Corbusier, Convent of La Tourette.

Hierarchy

Hierarchy is a more complex order because of the combination of elements in relation to a scale of importance. There is not necessarily an affinity between the elements. To create a hierarchy we can resort not only to the means of variation of relative *sizes*, but also to that of *disposition* and *singularity of form* in relation to a context (for example: centrality, axiality, orientation, geometric opposition, etc.) (Figure 55).

It is important for the architect to know the implicit hierarchy of certain geometric configurations. Thus the different loci of a space with a square, rectangular or circular plan are not of identical value since the centre, corners or circumference adopt a particular value in each case (Figure 20).

A hierarchy implies primary and secondary elements. There is a dependent relationship between these elements; one or several of them dominate the others. Within these elements the same phenomenon can take place: by concentrating attention on one element, this one can become primary and we then discover secondary elements. In diversity, hierarchy is a powerful unifying factor. It makes it possible to combine elements in bigger, simpler and more recognizable entities.

The discovery of dominant and subordinate elements in a group of buildings is applicable not only to solids (for example to a mass or a façade) but equally so to architectural space (Figure 56).

Whoever talks about 'hierarchy' in the built environment thinks only too readily of 'axis', 'symmetry', 'centrality', etc. It would be pointless to enumerate all the means which can contribute to *the dominance* of an element in its context. In any case, symmetry is not the only means of achieving it. Even the simple changing of the orientation of a building in relation to others is sufficient, by being an exception, to establish an unambiguous hierarchy (Figure 57).

Hierarchy thus implies a dominance of spaces or objects. We use hierarchies every day in the organization of our thoughts. We need these references to facilitate our orientation in complex space. When there are too many hierarchies of equal value, the clarity of the hierarchy breaks down.

Figure 55 Hierarchy of the centre.

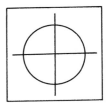

Figure 57 The mere rotation of a building in relation to others at once introduces a hierarchy. Le Corbusier, Carpenter Centre, Cambridge, Massachussetts, 1961–64.

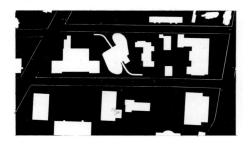

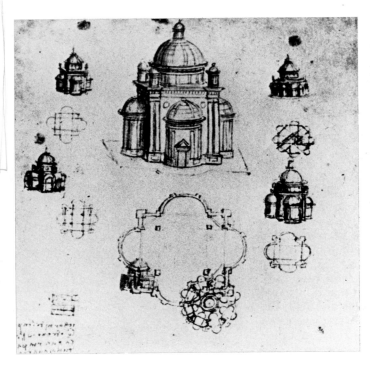

Figure 56 Study of buildings with centralized plans. Leonardo da Vinci.

Contrast

Contrast serves to give an immediate and unambiguous identity to two formal systems. It leads to mutual reinforcement without necessarily resorting to explicit hierarchy. The interdependence of the elements is achieved by tension resulting from their opposing characteristics (Figure 58). There can be many expressions of opposition, but in order that there be a dialogue, a certain proximity, even superimposition, must be respected:

- *positive and negative*
  solid/void (Figure 59), convex/concave (Figure 59), curved/straight (Figure 60).
- *light and dark*
  light/shade, reflective/absorbent
- *large and small*
  wide/narrow, high/low
- *horizontal and vertical*
- *natural and artificial*
  rough/smooth, vegetable/mineral
- *etc.*

Contrast enables us to establish differences: we have seen it with the figure/ground phenomenon. Moreover, two opposites placed in a contrasting situation establish a 'dialogue' between them. With three, four or more, that becomes difficult, or even impossible. Contrast is a principle for ordering our environment. The meaning of a form is accentuated by its opposite. When Slutzky says that, with Le Corbusier, '... the negative spaces (voids) are invested with a formal value equivalent to that of the objects which generate them'[49] he is referring to the primary requirement of composition by contrast: to inflect a form by the action of another, the space itself being able to serve as an expression of opposition. In order that the opposites enter into a 'dialogue', the differences must, however, be sufficiently pronounced. There are virtually no known rules for achieving this, the nature of oppositions taking so many different forms. The eye remains the principal judge.

Figure 58

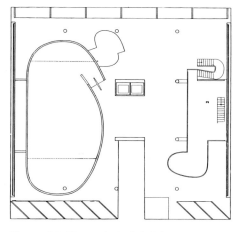

Figure 60 'Curved-straight': Le Corbusier, headquarters of the Association of Spinners, plan of level 4, Ahmedabad, 1954.

Figure 59 'Concave-convex': Francesco Borromini, Sant' Ivo della Sapienza, Rome 1642–60.

44

The concept of complexity in architecture can be defined by its opposition to simplicity, indeed to what is clear and elementary (Figure 61). Looking at the Parthenon from an oblique angle, we can guess at the sides hidden from view. All its elements, base, columns, capitals, architraves, etc., blend to create a unity, preventing all ambiguity of interpretation. Whilst being infinitely refined, this temple remains, at the same time, of utmost simplicity. *The eye is invited to accept it more than to explore it.* It is quite a different matter with Michelangelo's façade of San Lorenzo. In spite of the symmetry, which is a powerful unifying factor, we find ourselves in the presence of several co-ordinated and superimposed similar formal structures. The elements are grouped in such a way as to present more than

Figure 62 Michelangelo, facade for the funerary chapel of San Lorenzo in Florence, 1516–34; one of the first sketches still shows symmetry without much complexity (see Figure 102). That is the case for the majority of symmetrical buildings. Michelangelo was not satisfied with it; the final design plays down the preponderance of the axis. Numerous interpretatons are possible and almost equivalent, as can be seen from this selection from a series of analyses carried out by Colin Rowe and Robert Slutzky, published in Perspecta *No. 13/14, Yale, 1971.*

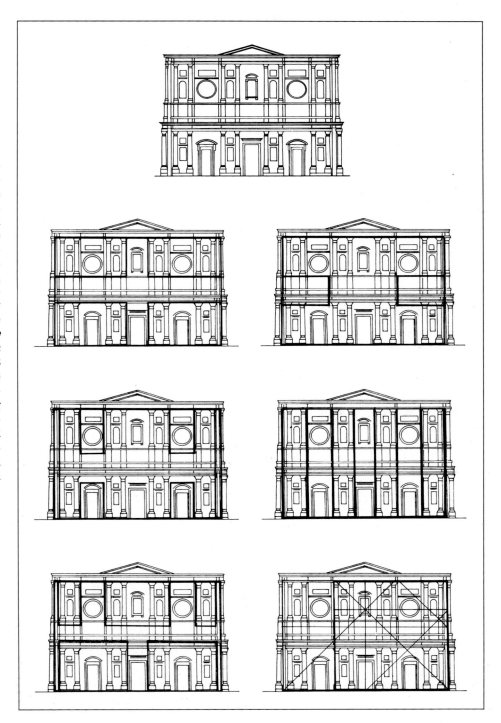

one interpretation to the observer – that is what we call *complexity*.

Supposing the façade were built and we gradually approached it – although the same holds true from a fixed viewpoint – the façade alternates among several formal organizations which dominate in turn. It becomes *a façade to explore* (Figure 62). Colin Rowe and Robert Slutzky have introduced the concept of *transparency* from which they develop an interesting, critical tool for analysing and composing with these phenomena of superimposition.[50]

We meet, however, many involuntary and clumsy complexities (and simplicities) in architecture. The exceptional quality of San Lorenzo lies in the control of the dependency between the elements and the geometries. The balance between them makes the façade complex *without being complicated*, in the same way that the Parthenon is simple without being banal. The mastery of complexity in architecture, as with simplicity, can only be the fruit of assiduous labour. It is not simply a question of talent, as Bernhard Hoesli[51] shows very clearly when he lines up the preliminary sketches of Michelangelo. The first design is still 'clumsy': the geometric subsystems do not yet intersect to form a whole; they are juxtaposed (Figure 110).

Other methods also exist for working with complexity, as for example, *deviation from a norm*. It can result from the introduction of divergences from an established symmetry, or even from an anomaly in a regular pattern, or simply from the distortion of a familiar figure.

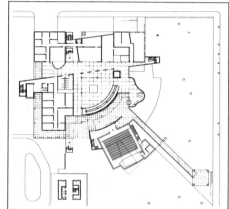

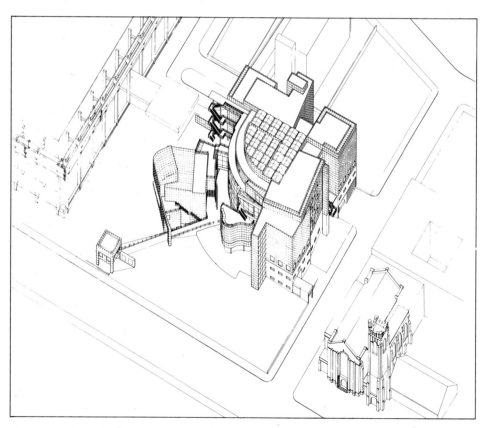

Figure 63 Spatial complexity: Richard Meier, High Museum, Atlanta, Texas, 1983.

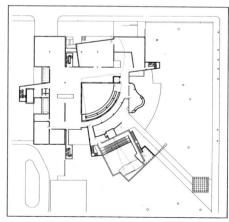

Let us examine, as an example, Richard Meier's High Museum in Atlanta (Figure 63). Where does the cohesion come from in this geometric complexity and multitude of volumes and spatial situations? Here the 'controlled complexity' is no longer restricted just to the façades. On the exterior, a great unity of materials comes from the cladding of square, metallic panels which form a homogeneous texture independent of the geometry and function of the individual volumes. This *continuity of texture* is essential to combine the irregularities into one unit identifiable by the layman. In the organization of the internal space, the de-formations are particularly numerous. The initial orthogonality is broken from one change of angle to another, so insistently that there is a risk of total disorder. Three features of the layout prevent such fragmentation:

– the changes of angle in the end create, at least partially, a new orthogonality between them;
– they almost always relate back to the exterior by transversals;
– the large central space, in the form of a quadrant, acts as a reference throughout the main stages of the architectural promenade.

The cohesion is precarious, intriguing and provocative. It is not certain that this is the best place for displaying works of art, but Meier insists on the ability of the architecture itself to be '*art*'.

This balancing act between obvious order, hidden order and disorder is fragile. This is what fascinates the minds, when such a work reflects not only poetic inspiration, but also skill combined with knowledge of the means for achieving it, as these two examples, several centuries removed, demonstrate.

Contradiction

We can distinguish two types of contradiction in groupings of urban and architectural forms: one accidental and the product of a contradictory origin, the other measured and meaningful, dependent on the process of composition:

(1) *Discordant collision* of two or several formal systems where one diminishes the meaning of the other (Figure 64): it involves a high degree of complexity in which contradictory visual information causes the observer to hesitate between two or more situations which do not add up to form a whole. The lack of co-ordination and the collision of forces and divergent interests then appear to be accidental. We find numerous examples in the everyday architecture of our towns. They are a manifestation of the story of more or less 'egocentric' social and economic impulses.

(2) Contradiction used as an *intellectual game*, as provocation: in this case it is a question of throwing expectations of architectural meaning into confusion by the expression of ironic conflicts (Figure 65). This method plays on dialectic effects; 'formal theses and antitheses' can be seen in the same work. For example a column is placed in the middle of a vault. Between a constructional necessity chosen to solve a given problem (bridging a space without a lintel), and its contradiction (the column), an attempt is made to increase the active and critical role that an architectonic image can produce.

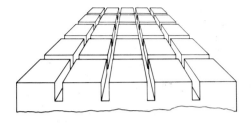

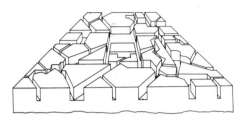

Figure 64 'Order is endangered when the deviations (from a norm or from a rule) are strong enough to upset the pattern of the whole.' (Arnheim)
Two drawings by Dieter Schaal.

Figure 65 Pillar or column: square or round? Les Salines de Chaux, house of the director, Claude Nicolas Ledoux.

Italian Mannerism, which followed the Renaissance, marked the beginning of a poetry of the improbable, the magic game. It reacted against the established rules. Palladio, if he was interested in it, remained none the less 'conservative':

... The violation which in my opinion is the most excessive of them all is that of placing above the doors, on the windows and on the loggias, broken pediments that are open in the middle, since their greatest effect must be to protect the parts of the building subject to rain, our ancient architects having

47

learnt by necessity that these must be vaulted and made in the form of a ridge ...[52]

The purity of the Renaissance was then rejected in favour of an expressive and sarcastic freedom, allowing the caprice of functional discord by the modification of codified elements (Figure 66). We also find traces of Mannerism in the architecture of the nineteenth and early twentieth centuries, aimed at freeing architecture from academic rationalism. We can perhaps agree with Serlio who said, already in the sixteenth century, that novelty is pleasing in so far as it does not erase all the rules.

In contemporary architecture it is Robert Venturi who has set his hand to a re-establishment of the notions of contradiction and ambiguity with a view to freeing himself from the sometimes dogmatic simplicity of modern architecture. He expresses himself through his schemes (Figure 67) and his writings: 'I am for richness of meaning rather than clarity of meaning'.[53] He sets the hybrid against the 'pure', the compromising against the 'clean', the

Figure 68 Drawing by Dieter Schaal and photo by Rolf Keller.

ambiguous against the 'articulated'. Whether architecture is at the same time large and small, continuous and articulated, open and closed, structure and decoration, relates to the links between the parts and the whole. These double choices express a commitment to questioning the simplicity of modern architecture by using a deliberate selection of historical precedents.

Arnheim expresses his scepticism regarding this strategy in the fol-

lowing words:

Venturi invokes contradiction to defend disorder, confusion, the vulgar agglomeration of incompatibles.... An object may be ambiguous in the sense of an alternation between two versions.... But if you say about a thing that it is this and also that and the two are mutually exclusive,... then what is said is nonsense.[54]

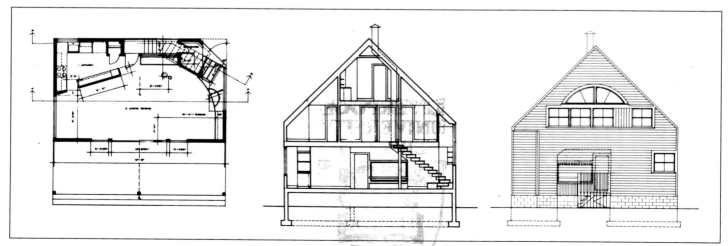

Figure 67 Robert Venturi and John Rauch, Trubeck House, Nantucket Island, Massachusetts, 1970.

48

Chaos

In chaos, no factor of coherence at all is at work. If any subsist they cancel each other out, because no structure, no formal or semantic theme is any more dominant, neither in the individual parts, nor in the whole. There is a conflict or absence of rules. The number of conflicting elements is high. As Arnheim points out, disorder is not homogeneity, even if the latter is at a very simple level, but a disorder between partial orders. 'An orderly arrangement is governed by an overall principle; a disorderly one is not.'[55]

Certain neighbourhoods of our cities have gradually taken on a chaotic form in the course of this century (Figure 68). This disorder reflects their recent transformation into an accumulation of transportation systems, objects and buildings which take only their own utility into consideration, without any common objective of creating a city. Friedrich Schinkel was already warning in 1840: 'No single need produces beauty, circumstantial utility cannot determine form without engendering chaos.[56]

Could chaos itself become a source of creation and life? Nietzche said that chaos was needed for a star to be born. If that is really the case, we can expect to see a very beautiful star. Unless society has completely crumbled away, forgotten its past, been uprooted and lost all capacity for *hope*, its architects and its planners do not have the right to be the accomplices of chaos.

Urban chaos is a state of instability. On one hand, it tends to become organized by signs of occupation. On the other, being accustomed to a city helps us to learn about its more secret order. The inhabitant of the homogeneous kasbah has *an organized centre* – his house – from were he constructs a complex network of relationships which make the apparent confusion intelligible.

Figure 66 *Broken pediment, Carlo Maderna, Villa Aldobrandini, Frascati, 1601–1606.*

49

3.4 Regularity and irregularity

Regular geometric order sometimes has a bad reputation. One complains about uniformity, rigidity, *monotony*, inhumanity. In a contribution to the journal of *Diadalos*, devoted to the theme 'order and disorder'. Ulrich Conrads declares war on order by saying:

> ... If, up to now, disorder has been inimical to architecture – and vice versa – it now acts as a stimulant. And, furthermore, architecture might draw renewed commitment and strength from those special features of disorder which we recognize as the structure of life itself and which, in most cases, cannot be brought into line and into symmetry. Networks and labyrinths would be the appropriate descriptions of this kind of architecture from disorder. And we recall that we have already identified these same architectural structures as the truly habitable ones.

This thesis is based on the concept that the life of man and the organization of nature are much more complex than a regular, geometrical order, implying that a town or building should be a more immediate reflection of this complexity. The argument nevertheless ignores three major issues.

First of all, to orientate ourselves in this world, we need to simplify its complexity mentally and visually to obtain images that we can commit to memory. Without the repetition of leaves that are practically identical, ordered according to the structure of the branches, it would not be possible for us to remember the tree as an entity. We need to be able to join the parts together in larger and simpler units, without having to decipher the detail. The same prin-

ciple is valid for the town, its neighbourhoods, squares, streets, its buildings and their windows.

Let us remember, then, that in order to build rationally from a large number of constructive elements, a certain degree of regularity is a technical necessity.

And finally, building is also an activity of the mind which will often try to surpass imitation of nature or social fact. Simple geometric figures and patterns lend themselves to it particularly well. Life is complex, but the form which contains life is regular (as in ecosystems, the processes of growth and the life of plants, etc.). To manage to respect the complexity of society, while at the same time making use of regularity, is intellectually rewarding.

But what kind and what degree of regularity? On what scale? There is no certainty that a town will imprint itself on our memory if it is perfectly square or circular. The degree of geometric abstraction remains a question which each culture answers in its own manner. This is more or less the ground on which the quarrel between rationalism and the picturesque takes place.

Simplicity

The fascination which simple forms, line, circle, sphere, cube, pyramid, etc., exert on us has lasted for thousands of years – judging by important as well as the most modest accomplishments of architecture and the decorative arts. Looking at the disc of the sun, we hardly question the complexity of its physical reality. Its form and its radiance inevitably evoke the ideas of light and heat.

Lines, surfaces and volumes with simple geometric outlines have for

us – as much as anthropomorphic forms – the power to subsume a complex reality, indeed even to sublimate it, without the distraction of an abundance of variations of detail. We enjoy a moment of satisfaction, of peace and admiration, when at certain times or from certain angles complex structures blend into simplicity. Manhattan – complex in spite of its simple grid plan – resolves itself when seen from afar at nightfall, or in the mist, into a silhouette. San Lorenzo, finally, is nothing but a 'common' rectangle.

The silhouette is merely an example; simplicity, not banality, is a quality to which we aspire just as much in plan as in space. Gombrich thinks that simplicity is intimately linked to Western classical culture. With the Greeks it became a virtue, a proof of theoretical skill without the need to resort to seductive devices.[58] In the East as well, from the King's Mosque in Isfahan to Zen art, we again find this quest for simple encapsulating forms, despite richness of decoration or detail.

The mental satisfaction of simplicity is probably linked to physiological and perceptional preferences rooted within us. In an architectural scheme, both in plan and section, this simplicity will not come to us from the brief. It is the product of patient research which leads to integrating the confused and contradictory elements of reality in the abstraction of a recognizable whole.

The dividing line between banality and simplicity is blurred. The enormous difference lies in *elegance!* Simplicity in architecture and in urban design is only obtained by an elegant solution; one which carries the complexity of elements through to just one image with extreme economy of means and without compromising nuances. 'Elegance

Figure 69 Fragmentary, but legible
none the less, regularity resists the
ravages of time: Olympia, lid of a
sarcophagus.

always appears easy, everything that is easy is not always elegant' (Voltaire). In the same way, in mathematics or in physics, the elegant proof is also frequently the most succinct.

Regularity

Regularity is omnipresent. Our heartbeats, rate of breathing, drips from a tap, a clock, days and nights, the rhythm of the seasons ... we cannot escape it. It is only when the pulse changes that we measure it because continuity is then at risk. Regularity is within us. Hidden rhythms regulate our life.

Monotony? certainly, even torture, if it is the only perception allowed or if perfect repetitive regularity remains the only centre of interest. 'The most effective system of order is uniformity. It is valuable, because it forces us to notice subtle differences. We need to have wide experience in order to recognize small differences. That is where we find the limits of regularity,' says Heinrich Tessenow.[59]

The regular rhythm of Ravel's 'Bolero' is a system of insistent order, but it is there to make the crescendo of the two melodic themes possible. There is no modulation, no development except the conclusion, but each time the themes return there is a new and more intense colouring. In the decorative arts and in architecture it is very similar. From this underlying regularity comes the continuity which guides and reassures us. The measure of the rhythm is not necessarily uniform: it can be ordered by groupings into larger units (Figures 70 and 71).

Where is the dividing line between an accompanying rhythm and a dominant repetition, between order and monotony? It is a question of appreciation in which many factors come into play: place, scale, field of vision, significance of the object, habit, etc. It seems that in large-scale groupings, in which rhythm predominates, and where there is little hierarchy or grouping into larger units, there is, in fact, a risk of monotony.

The regularity of mass production of industrial objects – our chairs, radiators, wash-basins, door handles, nuts and bolts – does not cause any problems of monotony in itself. It is their situation and their context which must, in fact, be questioned. The town, if it were produced as mechanically, without regard for place and use, would no longer be orderly, but schematic.

Regularity does not need to be based on a repetition of absolutely identical elements, or on a perfectly geometric grid in order to be monotonous. A morphological affinity is sufficient, as can be seen in the numerous suburban sprawls of large

Figure 70 On the left the spacings in the rhythm of the windows are purely repetitive; on the right these spacings are altered and grouped under the influence of the edges of the façade (the false and true façade of the Zacherl-Haus by Josef Plecnik in Vienna, 1903–1905).

Figure 71 'The multitude which cannot be reduced to unity is confusion; unity which is not dependent on multitude is tyranny' (Blaise Pascal in Pensées*); Royal Crescent, Bath 1767.*

cities. Regularity is necessary for our orientation in the town and even in the universe and time, but if it has no perceptible limit, no variation, no hierarchical structure introducing a scale other than that which comes from simple addition, then our pleasure is diminished and we are disorientated.

A repetitive structure can, at certain moments, change rhythm, direction or density. These varia-tions, which do not detract too much from the established order, are somewhat like 'a change of mood' which reveals character rather than alters it. These differences question the rules and thus reawaken interest. But we should be suspicious of superficial variety: introducing 'zig-zags' in plan to 'animate' a space or a façade, changing the grid or orientation without reason, sticking on symbols according to taste or fashion, are not acceptable. This sort of fantasy more often destroys than enhances the established order. Interruption or variation of a rhythm, the change of the orientation of a grid, etc., must appear as a *necessity*, an event responding to the site and/or the brief, or even a major articulation among elements of construction.

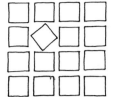

Figure 72 Exception
to the rule.

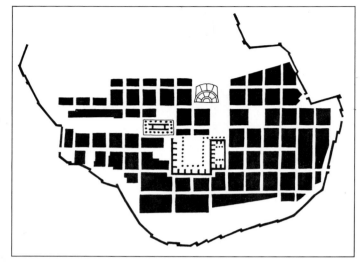

Figure 73 Priene, colonial town of Greek
antiquity on the Black Sea. Regular fabric
interrupted by public spaces and
buildings.

Well-established regularity offers itself as a background to exceptions which will then assume a dominant importance (Figure 72). Our recent warning remains valid: an exception with meaning is better than an exclusively formal game. The door handle is an exception in the regularity of the door, the door is an exception to the façade, the fountain or the law courts to the town, the monastery to the countryside (Chapter 5). In the regular grid layout of Priene, a colonial town of antiquity, the status of exception is reserved for the agora, the sanctuary and the theatre (Figure 73). History has created exceptions in the strict Roman grid plan of the city of Turin simply by varying the width of streets and squares which indicate special places for the most important buildings, without disturbing the pattern. In order to become an exception, 'acrobatics' such as turn-ing a building at 45 degrees are unnecessary.

To justify an exception the meaning does not always need to be related to content. The exception may refer to topographical irregu-larities, historical remains, the con-struction and even the form of the object itself. Handled sensitively irregularity offers the observer an awareness and enjoyment of the rule through the intermediary of its exception. Zen and more generally Japanese art and handicrafts exploit this possibility with subtlety. Japa-nese basket work is not only a highly skilled product but becomes more than that thanks to an inten-tional and measured imperfection.

When we can make this exception coincide with the meaning of the content, the exception is most suc-cessful, because it becomes legiti-mate.

4

MEASURE AND BALANCE

Overleaf
'Undulating' glass panels.
Le Corbusier and Iannis
Xenakis, Convent of La Tourette,
Evreux-sur-l'Arbresle.

4.1 Anthropomorphism and architecture

Harmony in living bodies is a result of the counterbalancing of shifting masses: the Cathedral is built from the example of living bodies. Its concordances, its equilibriums are exactly in the order of nature, they originate in general laws. The great masters who raised these marvellous monuments were men of science and they were able to apply it, because they had drawn it from its natural, primitive sources, and because it remained alive in them.

(Auguste Rodin)[60]

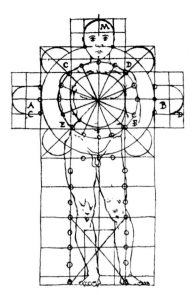

Figure 74 'Humanizing the architectural body' Francesco di Giorgio Martini, end of the fifteenth century.

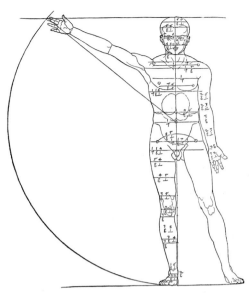

Figure 76 Albrecht Dürer, studies of proportions, beginning of the sixteenth century.

To draw an analogy between the structure of the human body and architecture is tempting, as much for aesthetic as for symbolic reasons. In our subjective representation of the order of the universe it is not the atom but our body which is the primordial element of reference. It is our way to measure big and small, geometric and amorphous, hard and soft, narrow and wide, strong and weak. A healthy human body appears balanced to us. It is a whole to which nothing more can be added; we can dress or decorate it, but cannot add a third arm, nor extend a leg. Our sense of beauty is probably linked to the form of our body.

In the history of architecture attempts to 'humanize the architectural body' (Figure 74) have been as numerous as those which have sought to 'geometrize' the human body (Figures 75 and 76).

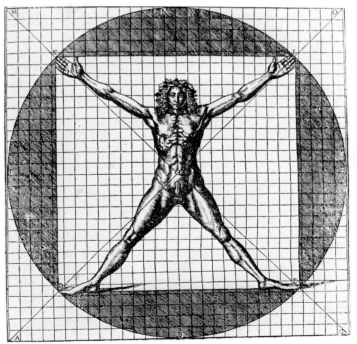

Figure 75 'Geometrizing the human body'; Cesare Cesariano, Vitruvian man, sixteenth century. 'The image is forced ... Cesariano is the first illustrator to stretch man to such an extent that his hands and feet reach the corners of the square. This unusual posture could have given Cesariano the idea of depicting this man as a "savage" with his penis erect and a laurel wreath in his thick hair ...' (Georg Germann in Einführung in die Architekturtheorie).[6]

57

Discovering the rules of proportion between the parts of the human body which would guide measurement in architecture is part of this approach. Even if it is rather 'squaring the circle' to try to divide the human body into whole numbers, or contain it within simple geometric figures, such as the circle and the

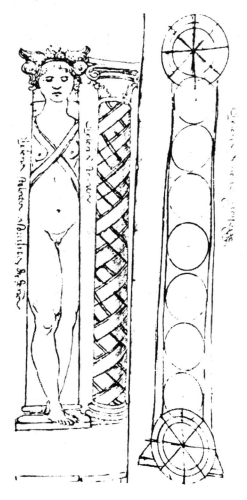

Figure 77 'The female column ...'
Francesco di Giorgio Martini, end of the fifteenth century.

square, we cannot ignore centuries of effort. We shall come back to this later when we deal with proportions.

What interests us for the moment are analogies between the form of the human body and certain architectural elements. The best known example is provided by the three classical orders of antiquity.[61] The subject was of passionate interest during the three centuries of Vitruvianism from the Renaissance onwards. As analogy to the human body, the column can be 'male' evoking strength, solidity and virile beauty: that is the Doric column with a diameter one-sixth of its height. It can be female, a Corinthian column, more slender with a diameter one-eighth of its height, more graceful and decorated with a capital reminiscent of a head of curly hair (Figure 77). Finally, it can be 'female' like the Ionic column, although the analogy is less obvious; should it be the ambiguous hermaphrodite column? Each 'order' is to be used in accordance with the purpose of the temple – of god or goddess. In Ancient Greece examples may be found that replace the columns with human figures: as is the case of the caryatids of the Acropolis or the colossus of the Odeon in the agora at Athens.

Anthropomorphic or literal zoomorphic representation is questionable in architecture (Figures 78–84). When, as lone traveller and layman, the author visited the Acropolis in Athens for the first time at the age of seventeen, he was shocked by the caryatids of the Erechtheion: was it not *grotesque* to make the enormous weight of the stone be carried by these elegant women and thus to 'nail them down'? It would only have taken one of them to step forward for the whole building to collapse. Moreover, do we not feel them relieved by the metal stays that have been added

by twentieth-century restorers?

Vitruvius had already said that these caryatids were a symbol of penitence.[62] The townsmen of Kari in the Peloponnese were said to be allied to the Persians. They were defeated by the Athenians, who killed all the male population and forced the women to wear the same clothes for the rest of their lives. The caryatids are said to symbolize the danger of disloyal alliances. Today we are not sure if the expiatory quality of the caryatids is based on legend or historial fact. Legends are created when humanity has to explain inexplicable facts.

In a wider sense we can again question the Doric and Corinthian orders. Certainly the Doric is heavier, stronger and, by analogy, more virile, the Corinthian more fragile, slender, delicate and, by analogy, more feminine, but these analogies must remain in the mind and not impose a literal representation calculated to distort the primary meaning of the act of building.

Many buildings allude to the image of the human body or to one of its parts in their organization or dimension, without, however, going as far as mimicry. Francesco di Giorgio Martini (1439–1501) was seeking an allegory of the human body not only in columns (Figure 77), but also in town plans, plans of buildings (Figure 74) and church façades. These are perhaps 'speculations', since they are not part of spatial experience, but hidden allusions to the body can have their value in the process of architectural composition. They impose a discipline or a system of reference in design where problems are a priori underdefined.

Analogies between body and building appear even in our vocabulary: skeleton, skin, façade. Do not windows remind us of eyes, and the door

Figure 78 Caryatids of the Erechtheion, Acropolis of Athens, fifth century BC.

Figure 79 Lequeu, representation of a column for the National Assembly (Paris): end of the eighteenth century.

Figure 80 Palazzo Zuccari, Rome, beginning of the seventeenth century.

Figure 81 Oikema, plan for a bordello: 'Believe me, have this passion, it will cure you of all the others.' C. N. Ledoux, end of the eighteenth century.

Figure 82 Mossdorf, Hahn, Busch; competition project for the Chicago Tribune Tower, 1922.

Figure 83 Lequeu, cowshed.

Figure 84 'The duck and the decorated shed' – learning from Las Vegas.

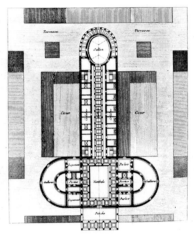

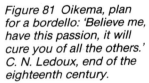

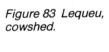

Figures 78—84 Anthropo- and zoomorphism . . . or architectural caricatures?

of a mouth? Robert Slutzky examines these analogies in the architecture of Le Corbusier[63] not only from the point of view of the pilotis as legs and feet, storeys which form body-head-face, the highly articulated roof which he interprets as a crown or a brain. From Slutzky's fascination with *the eye* one can by analogy cite many historic buildings. He points out the Villa Schwob, the tower in Algiers and the convent of La Tourette where such an 'eye' exists. One may wonder whether Le Corbusier consciously acted in this way, since he did not mention it specifically in his numerous writings. That is of little importance, because the truth of a phenomenon of intuition needs no literary explanation.

The voluptuous forms of Art Nouveau and those sculpted by German Expressionism refer to human, animal or vegetable *forms* (section 5.2, Continuity). The protagonists of these movements thus retain the outline of their models. They accentuate or schematize the curves, counter-curves and surfaces which they generate. They reproduce them in the form of fragments in their buildings, furniture and objects, transgressing their original meaning.

Architecture and the human body also come into contact in a more concrete way at an ergonomic level. The relationships between size, form and movement are what essentially characterize 'the human scale', a rather vague term and no doubt charged with various ideological meanings.

When our contact with architecture becomes tactile, it reveals its real sympathy towards us (Figure 85). There are countless examples. Let us take, amongst others, Sangallo's Palazzo Farnese: the plinth is not only a formal element structuring the base of the façade, it also invites us to sit down and to lean against it. The steps and handrails of the Piazza di Spagna in Rome extend the same invitation. The excessively narrow passageways between the library and the vestibule of the dining room of Adolf Loos's Villa Karma at Clarens make us aware of the true dimensions of our body. In the same way Frank Lloyd Wright used variable ceiling heights. The arrangement of openings in Louis Kahn's Exeter Library belongs to the most remarkable window arrangements of the twentieth century. Each cubicle forms an intimate subspace with its own window for reading, whilst the generous bay windows situated above are commensurate with the scale of the larger spaces.

We have seen that the proportions and balance of the human body enter the field of architecture from the point of view of imitation, idealized allusion, sensual allusion and finally the actual invitation to human use. The subject deserves to be treated in greater depth, but that goes beyond the aim of this introduction. Perhaps we may have aroused a wish to reflect on the subject which is too often dismissed by architectural criticism: anthropomorphism as image or metaphor.

4.2 Fascination with number and proportion

Architectural design is always carried into effect by means of dimensions and by the way in which they may be repeated and grouped in order to establish controlled relationships between them. To talk of proportions is to talk of the 'just measure' of the objects which we create. From where can we adduce correct relationships if not from

Figure 85 The plinth of the Palazzo Farnese, A. da Sangallo, Rome.

nature or mental abstraction, that is to say mathematics, and especially geometry?

From antiquity to the Renaissance man sought to combine Euclidian geometry and the forms of nature into a unique and universal system. Nature being considered at the peak of its perfection in the human body, it is that which 'lent itself to geometry' (Figures 86 and 87). There are, in fact, amazing ratios of *equivalent dimensions*, such as the hand which covers the face exactly, and *multiples*, such as the foot which is one-sixth of the upright body, the face structured in three equal parts, the width of the hand measuring four thumbs, etc. As there is perhaps nothing in the world which can delight our senses more than a beautiful human body, its value as an example has never ceased to occupy people's minds. The architect is in search of the rationality of the beautiful and, if his purpose is to teach, this rationality becomes a necessity. The Renaissance sought to find forms, dimensions and universal ratios of dimensions in the human body which would be set up as numeric or geometric principles.[64] The search for cosmic truth permeated these alliances of the body, geometry and number. Whilst the Middle Ages sought this truth in the Bible ('Thou hast ordered everything with measure, number and weight'[65]) the Renaissance referred to philosphers like Plato, Pythagoras and Aristotle. Plato makes a distinction between the beauty of nature which is relative and the beauty of a straight line, a circle, surfaces or simple geometric volumes which is absolute. For Pythagoras numbers represent the laws of the universe. They are therefore beautiful by definition.

Let us remember that, to a large extent, the science of mathematics linked to aesthetics through the intermediary of music originated from Pythagoras and that Vitruvius was the Renaissance's reference for proportions.

The transposition of architecture into 'petrified' music is not without foundation. Alberti refers to the numbers 1, 2, 3, 4 to establish the harmonious intervals of 2:3 (fifth), 3:4 (fourth), 1:2 (octave) among others. The octave, fourth and the whole tone form the structure of the Greek system of tonality. For a more detailed analysis of the logic of musical harmonies in relation to architecture, a reading of the works of Wittkower[64] and Naredi-Rainer[66] is useful. There is a coincidental link between harmonious sounds and physical dimensions. The sound of a taut string divided in the middle corresponds exactly to the distance of an octave and the ear is able to discern with amazing precision its accuracy of deviation. There is a great temptation to relate these measures to vision. However, nothing proves that our visual perceptions correspond to the scheme of our aural perceptions. The works of Alberti are in strict proportion to musical analogy and nobody will dispute their quality. An architect like Alberti would probably have been equally successful if he had used rules other than those derived from music.

The different systems of proportions which have been elaborated and used belong to one of the two following fundamental types: systems *commensurate* with sizes, having a common denominator between them, and *incommensurate* systems in which the different sizes have no common measure.

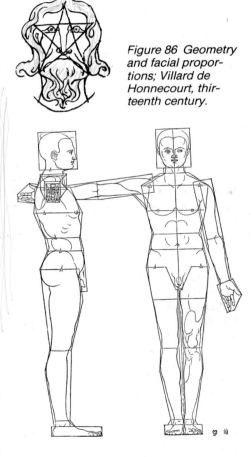

Figure 86 Geometry and facial proportions; Villard de Honnecourt, thirteenth century.

Figure 87 Geometry and proportions of the human body; Albrecht Dürer, beginning of sixteenth century.

Commensurate proportions

The systems inspired by music which we have mentioned are made from commensurate relationships. Commensurate proportions present the great advantage for a design and its implementation of having a smaller *module of dimension*, common to the whole range of relationships. If, moreover, the architect restricts himself to numerical relationships whose common denominator is fairly low, this measure need not be as abstract and small as, for example, an inch. It can be that of a foot, or an element of construction, such as the thickness of a wall or, in the case of the Greeks, the diameter of a column. With ratios such as 1:2, 1:3, 1:4, 2:3, 3:4, 3:5, 4:5, it is not too difficult to combine them into larger units which, in their turn, respect clear ratios of the same type (Figure 88). As part of his design discipline Palladio uses such subtlety as to take into account the thickness of the internal partition wall in order not to distort the clear[67] ratios of space. For his rooms he did not go beyond the proportion of 1:2. He frequently based the dimensions of rooms in plan and section on musical proportions without, however, becoming a slave to them, because it seems that he allowed a certain approximation according to the practical conditions of the design. The substantial difference from the grid plan of the twentieth century lies in the fact that the latter tends to allow *all* dimensions, provided the grid is respected, whereas architects concerned about proportions choose preferential relationships which reappear elsewhere in the scheme and at other scales.

These simple ratios are, even today, still very useful for 'disciplining' a scheme because:

- a ratio of 1:1, 2:3, or 4:5 will always be more apparent to the eye than a ratio of 7:8;
- these ratios can easily combine to form new quantities, which in their turn form clear ratios;
- only one module of dimension needs to be used as a co-ordinating element in the scheme and on site. The dimension of this module can be that of the brick, the column, or an abstract unit of measure, for example a foot, method of production permitting.

The activity of building is by nature collective. Consequently it needs to obey conventions. It was *a priori* not advisable to vary this unit according to the architect's fancy or with respect to a particular design. Unfortunately, nowadays there is no element or dimension of construction which has imposed itself sufficiently to be respected as a conventional instrument.

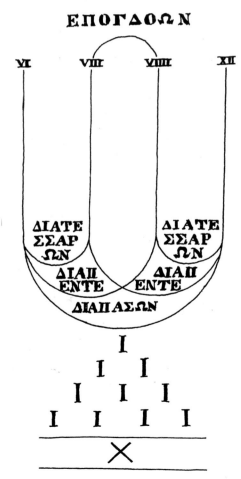

Figure 88 The Tetrachord of Pythogoras; classical musical harmony is based on commensurate proportions.

Incommensurate proportions

Basic geometric figures, the equilateral triangle, the 3:4:5 triangle, the square and the circle, have such properties that the height, the diagonal or the diameter establish ratios of irrational number with the sides. Simple to draw geometrically, they are impossible to measure with precision.

It is supposed that the equilateral triangle is basic to the construction of cathedrals. The Greeks used, in addition to commensurate proportions, the ratio 1:$\sqrt{2}$ and they knew the Golden Section (Figure 89). 'The true reason for the fascination exerted by the Golden Section does not lie simply in its aesthetic quality, but also in its mathematical property of being successively subdivisible to infinity in both directions.'[68]

The Golden Number is very close to a ratio of 5:8. Le Corbusier, basing his theory on the series of the eleventh-century mathematician Fibonacci, takes the credit for reducing the Golden Number to rational numbers applicable to architecture. His *Modulor* is the most innovative and important system of proportions worked out by an architect in the twentieth century. Let us briefly summarize its principles (Figure 90).

A man with his arm stretched upwards is inscribed in a rectangle of 113×226 cm formed from two squares superimposed at the level of the navel. A successive division of the total height into segments, whose neighbouring ratios correspond to the Golden Number, gives the Fibonacci series 226, 140, 86, 53, 33, 20, etc., ('blue series'). A successive division of half of the height, that is to say from the square of 113 cm, gives the second Fibonacci series 113, 70, 43, 27, 16, etc., towards the bottom, and adds towards the top the stature of the 'standard' man, 183 cm = 70 + 113 ('red series'). As the two series start from a ratio of 1:2 (113 and 226), this is continued in the immediate vicinity of the series (with some approximations in the lower figures).

The principle of this series has been known for centuries. Le Corbusier's contribution lies in his success in combining a fundamental, geometric principle with rational numbers *and dimensions of significance for the body and movements of man.*

The Modulor has had only a very limited success until now. It is, in fact, not very practical because one scarcely ever finds multiples of a small dimension in the higher numbers except in the immediate vicinity of the two series. Perhaps a yellow, green, brown or orange series should be added ...? *The module measurement is finally an abstraction of the centimetre.* Obviously this has no concrete relationship either to an element of construction, or to the human body. As building is necessarily a process of addition of identical elements, standardization has not been able to use the Modulor as Le Corbusier would have wished. Even if our principal material was a sort of 'papier mâché', the systematic application of the Modulor would not be as convenient for design as a simpler system like the one used by Palladio. By applying the Modulor to his Unité d'Habitation at Marseilles, Le Corbusier has, however, proved that his method could lead to pleasing proportions for the eye and the body.

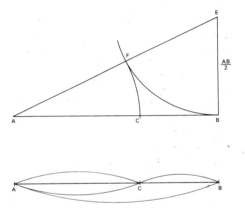

Figure 89 Construction of the Golden Section AC:CB = AB:AC.

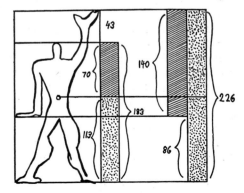

Figure 90 The Modulor, Le Corbusier, 1945–50.

Proportions in difficulty

Today there is hardly any school of architecture giving explicit teaching on proportions. Here and there one finds a lesson, but given timidly, like a theoretical alibi and without concern for its systematic application to design. However, for two thousand years the question of proportions was a central issue for architectural theorists.

At first sight it seems paradoxical that, in this century of science, architecture should have neglected precisely this 'irrefutable' mathematical approach. That is probably due to the *pseudo-scientific* character assumed by the systems of Antiquity and the Renaissance. Mathematically correct, their aesthetic implications are more the result of habit than the result of an intrinsic truth capable of becoming the norm. Statistical experiments on preferences for proportions, carried out more than fifty years ago, showed that there is no peak of aesthetic satisfaction with the ratio 1:2, nor with the Golden Section.[69] The individuality of the artist, which is a twentieth-century ideology, is a second obstacle to the search for a universal system of commensurate or incommensurate dimensions.

The author of this book, for his part, does not make use of any established system of proportions in his schemes or in his critiques. It is first of all his eye which judges. Then he uses simple geometric figures and divisions or multiples of rational numbers, even diagonals, trying to establish coherent ratios between the parts. The fascination of numbers and clear geometric divisions derives from the satisfaction they give to the mind and probably also to those who see the building in progress and at completion. The impor-

tance lies in the establishment of a rule and, as far as that is concerned, there is no *a priori* reason for rejecting those of the ancients. Number possesses this quality, of allowing repetition of the work of art without resorting to plagiarism. The origin of the number can be mystic, symbolic or anthropological (the Trinity, the Cross, the four seasons, the twelve moons, odd and even, squares, anthropometry etc.). What matters, in the end, is the coherence and the balance between the elements.

The erosion of confidence in an 'exact' system of proportions, applicable as a reproducable principle *for attaining beauty* is not, however, the prerogative of our century. Even those who hoped to find a universal rule often suffered uncertainty. The doubt here is, above all, French and not Italian. The following series of critical quotations could be thought-provoking (Figure 91).

'Dürer (1471–1528) who spent all his life searching for the exact proportion finally recognized that the exact proportion which would give absolute beauty did not exist' (Paul V. Nardedi-Rainer).

'Stability and hygiene are more important for a dwelling than the most beautiful proportions and decorations.' (Philibert Delorme).

'... which shows that the beauty of a building still has in common with the human body that it does not so much lie in the exactness of a certain proportion ..., as in the grace of the form which is nothing other than its pleasant modification, upon which a perfect and excellent beauty can be founded, without that sort of proportion being found in it, observed with precision ...' (Claude Perrault).

'Let us imagine in architecture a creation in which the proportions are not observed perfectly; it will certainly be a great defect. But it will not follow that this defect will damage the visual organ to such an extent that we could not bear the appearance of the building; or that this defect would do to our vision what a discord in music would to to our ears ... Proportion, while being one of the aspects of greatest beauty in architecture, is not the first law from which emanate the constitutive principles of the art ... The constitutive principles of architecture are born from regularity ...' (Etienne-Louis Boullée).

'It seems that, in a work of architecture, certain elements must conserve, whatever the size of the building, an almost invariable dimension: from a purely utilitarian angle, the height of a door should have no other measure than the height of the man who will pass through it; the steps of a flight should be adapted to the structure of the man who will have to go up and down them.

This order of considerations was observed by the Greeks most of all during the archaic period, but they quickly lost sight of it; they gradually submitted all the components to the modular law, they enlarged or reduced them as the module increased or diminished. If they doubled the span of the façade, they doubled the height of the doors, they doubled that of the steps. There is no relationship between the intended purpose of the components and their size: nothing subsists which gives any scale to the building.' (Auguste Choisy).

'Well no, architecture is not a science of numbers, and if it was necessary to prove it, I would prove it in one word, the word art ...' (Julien Guadet).

'Systems of proportions are for the past, today they are only used by eclectics. Formulae can never be the basis of creation. For creation it takes purpose and conscious analysis ...' (Moholy-Nagy, Bauhaus, 1929).

Figure 91 Proportions in difficulty.

4.3 Balance

Symmetry

In theories of architecture the term 'symmetry' has not always had the same meaning. It is, in the first place, a concept of order, and as such the foundation of classical architecture. Vitruvius attributes this general sense to it, meaning by that the balance between the parts which form a coherent whole. We shall use it here in the more restrictive sense given to it by the Renaissance; we talk about that particular balance which arises from a 'reflected' disposition of elements on one side, and on the other of an axis, as in a mirror. We have seen that symmetry is a special case of the principle of coherence through the orientation of elements. Gestalt psychology has shown that the factor of symmetry is more powerful than similarity (Figure 92). We tend to combine symmetrical elements into one figure, even if the viewpoint is not situated on the axis. Balance is also evident when the elements thus disposed have no other common factor than their position in relation to this non-physical axis (Figure 93). A symmetrical organization, of which one can see the whole or at least a good part, acts as a magnet in comparison with the asymmetrical. Boullée quotes Montesquieu saying that, '... symmetry pleases us, because it presents obvious facts, and the mind which is trying ceaselessly to understand seizes upon and takes in, with no difficulty, the group of objects which it presents'.[70] Symmetry is evidence. This irrefutable evidence is used by the classic to represent a secular or religious power which declares itself 'irrefutable'. The structural difference between Speer's Reichstag, a building in

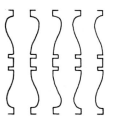

Figure 92 Symmetry more powerful than similarity (from S. Hesselgren).

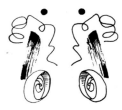

Figure 93 Incongruous elements assembled into a coherent unity through symmetry.

imperial Rome and a temple of Phidias is in the refinement of the proportions and the detail.

With the exception of highly refined examples, one must admit that what is too obvious tends to diminish our interest. What is too redundant, or too consistent with our expectations is not necessarily what gives us greatest pleasure. When everything which surrounds us contains no surprise or other possibility of perceptual grouping, the intellect and sensitivity are dulled. On the other hand, a *complex* symmetrical composition, like that of San Lorenzo (Figure 62), with its superimposition of secondary symmetries and different lateral and vertical relationships, gives an effect of alternation which arouses our interest and keeps our senses alert. Speaking of music, Lévi-Strauss says that aesthetic pleasure is created by the alternation of stimulation

and response, unfulfilled expectations and performances beyond all expectations. In the visual world, symmetry does not attain this plurality with such ease, but is capable of doing so. In architecture the use of symmetry has two theoretical bases of a different nature:

(1) *Symmetry as an aesthetic principle.* For Palladio symmetry is a *sine qua non* of harmony. He sets it up as an absolute rule and never departs from it. In axial symmetry one avoids occupying the centre with a solid element. The temples and palaces of antiquity, except the Minoan, always have a front with an even number of columns so that the middle is an interval-entrance. From Egypt to the Renaissance and until the eighteenth century, bilateral or central symmetry is reserved essentially for religious buildings and for those which seek to symbolize secular power. From the nineteenth century symmetry is used more and more for all sorts of ordinary buildings, small residential houses, blocks of flats, factories, slaughterhouses, transformers, etc. By its popularization, symmetry has lost its value as an exception and, consequently, part of its collective symbolic significance. One consequence of this devaluation is that the twentieth century can just as well resort to asymmetry as to symmetry to achieve buildings representative of authority or religion (Figure 94). Certainly this is not the only reason why new spatial concepts have appeared, but the over-use of axial symmetry has probably played an indirect role in its temporary disrepute.

(2) *Symmetry as a constructive principle.* For Viollet-le-Duc it is the ribbed vault which engenders symmetry. One must stress the rational-

ity of this line of thought and its basis in the laws of statics for simple spans, frames, vaults, domes, etc. But if rational construction requires symmetry of the span and loading, it does not impose a hierarchical symmetry on a group of spans. Moreover, modern methods of construction, notably the continuity of concrete and the possibility of varying its reinforcement, allow us to make rational use of structural asymmetry when the conditions of site, content or aesthetic intention justify it.

Symmetry has a quality of perfect balance but it often provokes a strange uneasiness, even in the works of great masters. What is disturbing is not the symmetry in itself, but rather its axial approach, which is all too often a corollary. *To walk along the tightrope of an axis is impossible; it causes imbalance.* It is perhaps this humiliation of man by architecture which makes us reject it, especially if it is linked to the colossal scale of 'fascist' architecture. However, only thoughts and ideas are fascist. There is no 'fascist' architecture in the same way as there is no 'democratic', 'royalist' or 'Marxist' architecture. Monumentality is not the prerogative of just one form of society.

A majestic Gothic cathedral is built on axial symmetry with a doorway in the centre. We must not forget that the conception of this place of worship does not correspond to the way in which it is used by the tourists of today. It was not originally intended for an axial *approach*. The central doorway and its axis *sanctified an idea* and not the passage of ordinary people: an idea of God, of life, of the death of a saint, the idea of the universe..., the axis as a passage was reserved for

Figure 94 Partial symmetries and overall asymmetry; competition for the League of Nations, Le Corbusier, Geneva, 1927.

Figure 95 The axis reserved for ceremony: 'The pilgrims go in procession to visit the seven churches'. On ordinary days the central door will be locked and the lateral opened.

the procession, a passage symbolizing the idea (Figure 95). In so far as there is not today a similar convergence towards *an idea* whereby the axis would be intended more for the collective rather than the casual visitor, this type of symmetry is again questionable.

Is this to say that every idea of symmetry must be rejected? Not at all: symmetry still offers our eye a satisfaction of balance and the power to create with ease *a unity* standing out from the rest of the environment. But today the sensation of beauty is certainly no longer dependent on symmetry as in the period of the Renaissance which canonized it. On the contrary, the twentieth-century eye has learnt to appreciate balanced asymmetries and subtle deviations from an established order whether they be symmetrical or not. We appreciate both asymmetric *and* symmetric objects.

Analogies can be made between the human face and a façade. If the object is symmetrical, is it not more sensual to see it from an oblique angle rather than 'prosaically' from the front? We look into the eyes of the person to whom we are talking, but we rarely look straight at him, and never for long. Insistence creates uneasiness. Newspapers only show full-face views of criminals sought by the police, never poets or actors! Architectural magazines, on the other hand, contain photographs of 'full-frontal' views of symmetrical buildings, possibly in order to compare them with the elevational drawing to which architects are accustomed. This often misses the real perception of the photographed object. Symmetry is a delicate thing to handle with an axial approach. The axis is not for the everyday, it is reserved for ceremony.

In order to show how difficult it is

to establish rules in this field, I shall take an example which comes from the Renaissance. In this great architectural period, there are remarkable works which produce perfect symmetry, but at the same time they deny the superimposition of the axis and the route one takes through the ensemble. In the Piazza del Campidoglio designed by Michelangelo in Rome in the sixteenth century (Figure 96), the grand flight of steps which leads to the square is in fact situated on the axis, but the topography, the still considerable distance from the steps to the building, and its great width give it a certain autonomy. This flight of steps is necessary to prepare and proclaim the role and particular situation of the Palazzo Capitolino in the urban fabric. As soon as one reaches the square, everything is arranged so that the pedestrian's route moves away from the axis: there are four other accesses in the corners, the main door is right in the middle, but the steps which lead to it rise from the corners. The middle of the square is occupied by an 'idea' (the equestrian statue of Marcus Aurelius) and the texture of the ground has been achieved with such strength and detail that it gains a certain autonomy relative to the building while still respecting its relationship to the axis.

In twentieth-century architecture, symmetry has sometimes been the rule, but more often taboo. For Rietveld, Gropius and Le Corbusier it can be found in their early works. For Mies van der Rohe, Asplund and later Kahn it was an essential principle of composition, especially in their later works. Schools of modern architecture since the 1920s with the Bauhaus, and up to the 1960s or 1970s, have tended to advise against it, even repressed it, as an aesthetic

principle, whilst its constructional value was never doubted. They referred, on one hand, to the development of the plastic arts, and on the other to a tendency for architectural form to take as its starting point the poetic and utilitarian demands of the site rather than the abstraction of a simple geometric order. Today these same schools admit both forms of organization without attributing superiority to one or the other, but also without explaining the factors which increase their chances of success.

For someone who works with symmetry, the job appears easy at first sight. From the beginning his design seems fairly orderly on plan, section and façade. In this sense

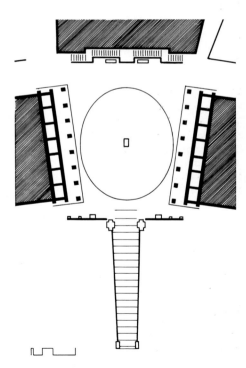

Figure 96 The axis occupied by a statue; the Piazza del Campidoglio in Rome replanned by Michelangelo in the sixteenth century.

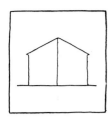

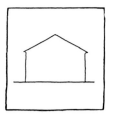

Figure 97 'If we spontaneously follow the demands of axis of symmetry it leads us in the end to draw the line of the axis in the first figure; after that the symmetry becomes completely rigid, it dies, it breaks down, having divided the orginal symmetrical surface into two symmetrical surfaces' (which explains the even number of columns of Greek temples) (H. Tessenow).[71]

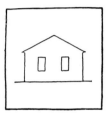

Figure 98 'If we move away a little from the demands of the axis and insert new elements at some distance from it, then our interest in the axis remains, but it is now shared between our interest in the axis and in the new elements and our eye wavers, so to speak, between them. The whole surface is suddenly dynamic and alive' (H. Tessenow).

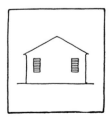

Figure 99 'This now lends itself to improvement by seeking to place the new elements as far away as possible from the axis and if possible accentuating them' (H. Tessenow).

symmetry is also the perfect architecture for developers who are in a hurry. It achieves rapid and more or less successful results. But it has too many consequences to constitute an easy answer. For the architect 'the right balance' is, in fact, no more easily attainable with symmetry than with asymmetry. Between the symmetry of a Michelangelo and the symmetry of a developer there is only a hair's-breadth of difference, but one that makes all the difference in the world.

Are there principles which may be generalized and which lead to a better mastery of symmetry? We refer to Tessenow[71] who shows very simply how tensions within a symmetrical layout can be accentuated or balanced. Speaking of the difficulty of 'leaving the axis', which is one of the displeasing constraints often experienced in symmetry, he explains a principle that has been somewhat neglected (Figures 97–99).

These elementary rules of symmetry are precisely those which must have guided, albeit intuitively, Michelangelo in his final plan for San Lorenzo or, closer to our own times, Le Corbusier for the façade of the Villa Schwob at La Chaux-de-Fonds (Figure 100). In the latter the large central panels and the small circular windows at the edges of the façade, strengthened by the enclosing walls extending on either side, enrich the symmetry with the energy and mystery that were necessary for it to become a powerful presence. Le Corbusier, who very early on abandoned symmetry as a method of composition in domestic architecture, apparently had a good knowledge of its fundamental principles.

There is a second, slightly more complex aspect of symmetry which may be analysed. When a *symmetrical figure is repeated* a second time without hierarchy, we are dealing with three competing axes and are

Figure 100 Deliberate weakening of the axis of symmetry by distancing the motifs (bull's eye windows); Villa Schwob, Le Corbusier, 1916/17, La Chaux-de-Fonds, and Chana Orloffs' house, Auguste Perret, 1927, Paris.

no longer able to isolate the symmetrical image (Figure 101). Gombrich says that 'the balance of a symmetrical design demands as a corollary a firm frame or another means of isolating the configuration. Further repetition threatens repose since it destroys the uniqueness of the central axis'.[72] The image becomes confused and unstable. This is true, but when the lateral symmetries submit to the authority of one central axis, or when the secondary symmetries overlap towards the principal axis, a complex hierarchy is established which can be very coherent, as we can see by studying again the example of San Lorenzo (Figure 102).

A third aspect is worth mentioning. Symmetry *does not have to be perfect*. The human face is rarely completely symmetrical. Secondary departures from symmetry do not affect the general impression of an architectural whole; they can even soften its starkness.

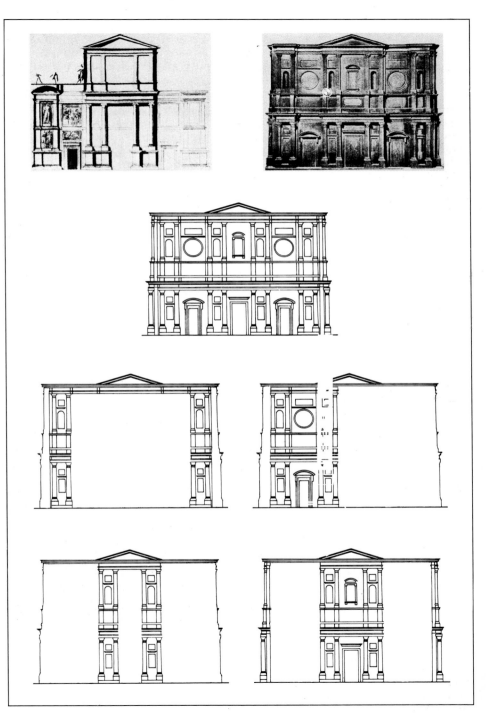

Figure 101 Repetition of symmetries requires a frame for each one in order to avoid confusion.

Figure 102 Multiple symmetries overlap; those established on each of the lateral axes have to all intents and purposes the same weight as the central symmetry. This results in a more subtle balance which permeates the whole of the façade rather than just one axis; Michelangelo's façade for San Lorenzo in Florence.

Asymmetrical balance

We may talk about concepts such as figure/ground and factors of coherence with a certain degree of confidence. In fact they are based on theories drawn from scientific observation.

Although we make daily judgements on objects and compositions of all kinds, it is difficult for us to talk of *balance* in a rational way. Visual balance cannot be demonstrated objectively: it is subject to individual appreciation and yet the degree of divergence may not be so large.

We have seen that in the time of Vitruvius and in Antiquity, to which he refers, in the Middle Ages, in the Renaissance and up to the nineteenth century, it was impossible to conceive of balance and the monumental dignity of architecture without recourse to axial or central symmetry. Having been the preserve until now of painting and sculpture, asymmetrical balance is, in so far as it is a conscious intention of an architectural design, one of the main Western acquisitions of the twentieth century (Figure 103). Earlier applications of note are rather rare in Europe. There is, however, the English landscape tradition, but here it would seem, in fact, that its composition owes something to painting, which it used as a model.

It is a different matter in Japan where asymmetrical balance has been used for centuries, not only in painting, sculpture, ikebana (the art of flower arranging), or in garden design, but also in the art of laying out plans and grouping buildings. The Imperial Palace of Katsura at Kyoto is a brilliant illustration of this from the seventeenth century (Figure 104). While fully recognizing the importance of symmetry for the economy of the wooden structure, this principle is not applied beyond constructional unity.

The underlying rules of asymmetrical balance are more difficult to

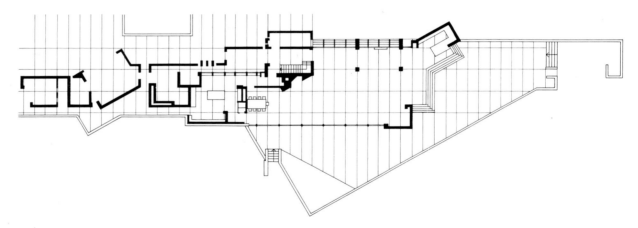

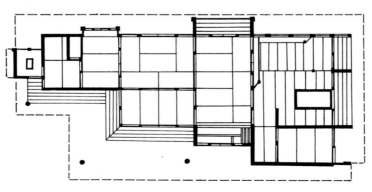

Figure 103 Asymmetrical balance: one of the greatest architects to have mastered it in the twentieth century remains without any doubt Frank Lloyd Wright; the Marcus House project, Dallas, Texas, 1935.

Figure 104 Shoi-Ken, tea house in the garden of Katsura, Kyoto, seventeenth century.

understand and convey than those of symmetry. The horizontal and vertical play essential roles. Our upright position, top and bottom, horizontal or vertical line, the right-angle between the two, are immediately understood and we are able to discern the slightest deviations. These phenomena are easier to perceive with precision than are proportions.

On the other hand the whole of our discovery of the world, from infancy to adulthood, is linked to the experience of *gravity*. In a wider sense we make daily use of the asymmetrical principle of leverage: to open a tin, pull out a nail, move a weight (Figure 105).

Horizontality/verticality and gravity/leverage are probably fundamental factors which govern the balance of a composition (Figure 106).

In a façade, and above all in a section, the principle of gravity intervenes immediately, since we are well aware of the forces of terrestrial attraction which all buildings try to defy. The flux of forces expressed, transmitted to the ground by a bridge by Robert Maillart, or by a ribbed vault, provide an immediate image of the action and reaction of the parts (Figure 107). These types of construction arouse in us an awareness of the beauty, precision and balance of nature. At a higher level of abstraction, we perceive a state of equilibrium or disequilibrium in all groupings of objects on a plan or in space. Let us take the example of windows in a façade. The wall, which is first of all a constructional reality to guarantee static balance, adopts a secondary role in our perception. It becomes background and framework for a game of imaginary weights and counterbalances (the openings) between which tensions are to be balanced. The principles of horizontal, vertical and gravity are

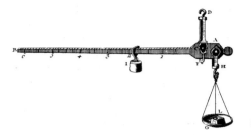

Figure 105 Leverage and balance.

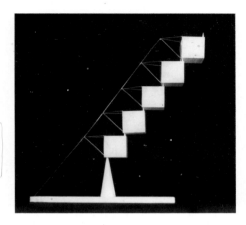

Figure 106 Balance pushed to the limits of credibility: a sculptural game, Santiago Calatrava, sculpture, 1984.

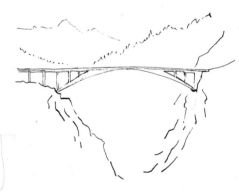

Figure 107 Balance of forces and gravity; Salginatobelbrücke, Robert Malliart, 1929/30.

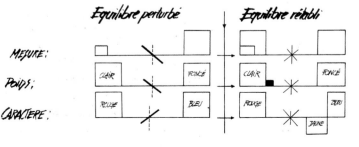

Figure 108 Asymmetrical balance according to Paul Klee, Pädagogisches Skizzenbuch, 1925.

71

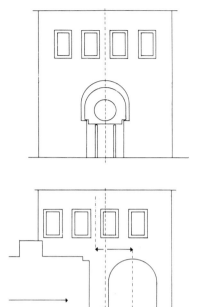

Figure 109 Above, the idealized situation and its theoretical solution with axial symmetry; below, the real situation: the four windows, the arch and the kiosks are positioned as they have been added, in random fashion. The archway and the windows have nothing in common.

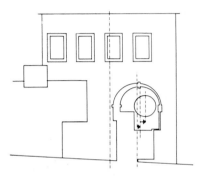

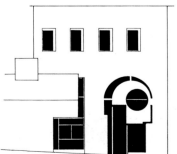

Figure 110 Architects restore balance to the whole façade by intervening only in the geometry of voids and solids defined by the existing archway: on one hand by the insertion of a concrete panel with an off-centre oculus in the upper part and; on the other, with a rebalancing of the wall mass. The archway has thus found its place in relation to the windows and edges of the facade. They are part of one composition of balanced tensions. The differences in the three fixings of the panel accentuate these relationships. Transformation of a house in the old town of Lausanne by Atelier Cube (G. and M. Collomb, P. Vogel), 1983.

so deep-rooted in us that they continue to exert an influence. That is what led Paul Klee[73] to talk about asymmetrical balance (Figure 108).

Rudolf Arnheim analyses this phenomenon under the title 'balance' in his work '*Art and Visual Perception*.'[34] There are hardly any recent works which have increased our knowledge of the phenomena of visual balance. At least for the moment, we will proceed by trial and error. Knowledge of a few principles can nevertheless accelerate this process. We present an example of it by examining a façade to be transformed in order to show how certain interventions can restore its balance (Figures 109 and 110).

The phenomena of balance also come into play on a horizontal plane or in space. Objects carefully set out on a table, an artist's still life, or the buildings around a square create relationships of balanced or unbalanced tensions similar to those we have just outlined. Colin Rowe's urban designs are most remarkable demonstrations of balance.

The opposite of balance is not *dynamism*, but imbalance, instability, uncertainty, confusion. Frank Lloyd Wright's houses are not unbalanced, but they emphasize the approach route and the principal directions of the site. Imbalance results where the distances between the acting forces have not been accurately balanced by the play of appropriate 'counterbalances'; remember the image of the lever arm.

5

FABRIC AND OBJECT

Overleaf
The wall and its object-window.
Palazzo Zuccari, Rome.

5.1 Town and monuments

The building fabric gives an image of continuity, of expansiveness stretching 'to infinity', the *object* is a closed element, finite, comprehensible as an entity. Objects concentrate visual attention; they stand out against a background. This concept can be transposed to the town where certain structures appear as objects (object-buildings) because they stand out from the urban fabric. This is organized according to the laws of proximity, similarity, repetition and common orientation of elements.

The same phenomenon occurs inside buildings where certain elements – columns, doors, windows, niche, fireplace, altar, etc. – appear as isolated elements *which can then be identified and even named*, while the rest of the environment is characterized by greater homogeneity.

In practically all pre-industrial societies, ordinary dwellings and urban places of work are accommodated in buildings which together form a relatively homogeneous fabric. Once this regularity has been established, any breaks in it assume special importance. In principle they are reserved for monuments or

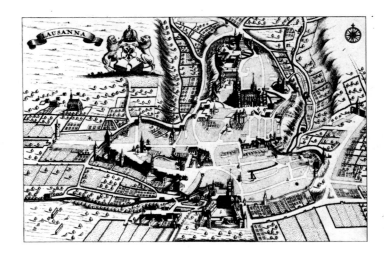

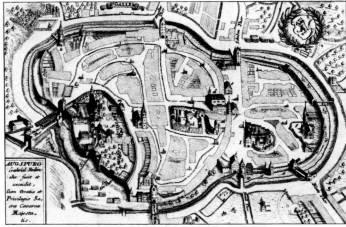

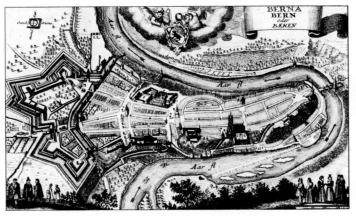

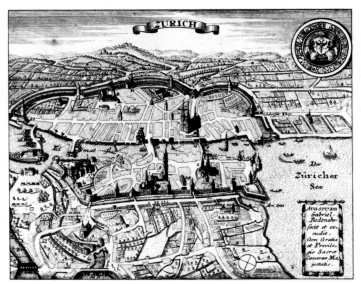

Figure 111 These engravings, from an eighteenth-century atlas of Swiss towns by G. Bodenehr, are significant: gates, churches, convents and fountains (public symbols par excellence) are shown isometrically, whereas the rest of the town is indicated as fabric.

public landmarks: the temple, castle, market.

In the historic centre of Berne 'object-reading' is allowed only for the cathedral, town hall, town gates and the fountains. The other buildings join together to form the fabric and it is only when one is close to them that one starts to recognize new units identifiable as such. *A hierarchy is thus established* (Figures 111 and 112).

The plan of Rome drawn up by Giambattista Nolli in 1748 is a remarkable typological document which shows very clearly this complementarity between texture and object or between town and monument (Figure 113). It makes it possible to distinguish relationships of scale and spatial organization between external space, internal public space and the mass of the urban fabric of residential areas and work places (shown in black). It also shows how the buildings intended to have the value of an object or a monument are integrated into this fabric of the ordinary and the everyday, and in what way they structure the town. Alberti says that the site on which a temple is erected must be solemn, noble and splendid and that it must be exempt from profane interference. He considers the object for a place of worship and specifies that in front of its façade a spacious and dignified square should be laid out.

For certain sacred object-buildings in Rome it is only the front façade which takes on this object role – announcer of an extension of the public space towards the interior and vice versa, while the other three sides are embedded in the general fabric. We are concerned here with an object-façade. Despite the demands of urban density, *the fabric yields*, even if only slightly, to retain a widening of public space in front of the buildings or object-façades.

In the two examples cited, Berne and Rome, the urban object is linked to an idea: the temple to worship, the gate to power, the fountain to the idea of a place of exchange of news and gossip. These concepts go beyond the primary function of the object and imply tradition in the form of an allegory, expressing a profound truth about collective life. The prerequisites for a monument are fulfilled.

In a certain sense the school, university, museum, train station and even the bank have acquired enough collective importance during the

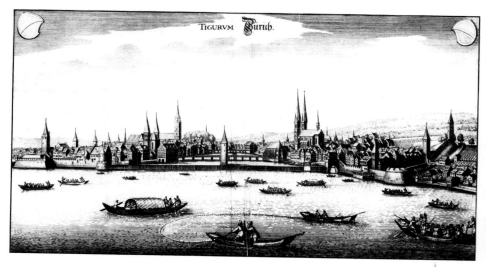

Figure 112 '... The roofs of the private houses shall be designed in such a way as not to rival in any way the majesty of the temples ...' (L. B. Alberti); Math. Merian, Zürich seen from the Lake, 1642.

Figure 113 Fabric, object-buildings and object-façades; plan of Rome by Giambattista Nolli, 1748 (excerpt).

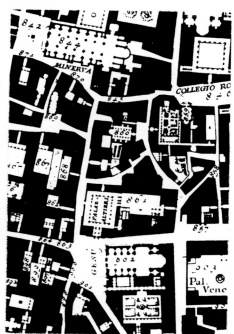

Figure 114 *Object on the square – fabric along the street; Mario Botta, State Bank of Fribourg, 1977–81.*

twentieth century to supersede traditional institutions. The object-building tends to become a symbol of the institution. Mario Botta's State Bank of Fribourg (Figure 114) shows an interesting articulation between object and fabric. It is not the whole of the bank which is treated as object or monument, but only the volume which faces the square in front of the station, whereas the two wings facing on to the street mesh with the urban fabric. This example reflects a new sensitivity to the site and the town as fabric. If this head office had been built during the 1960s, on the same site, the entire building would probably have been treated as an object to the detriment of the urban fabric.

Since the monumental character of buildings is linked to the idea of permanence, there is a great temptation to refer to conventional codes. We then tend to use codes from the past, which leads Peter Eisenman to say that '... the monument has been eclectic by definition since the six-

teenth century ...'.[74] That explains the tenacious resistance of great public institutions to adopting the language of modernity. The competition for the League of Nations in 1929, won by Le Corbusier, but commissioned to other architects in the purest eclectic tradition, is a good illustration of this battle between the moderns and the eclectics over what is appropriate for a monument.

A fundamental problem of twentieth-century urbanization is that it has led to the multiplication of objects and the neglect of fabrics. There are too many buildings which present themselves as 'objects', indifferent to the public or hierarchical role they play in the values of our society. The reasons can be many: public health laws, publicity value or professional vanity – but they can scarcely be an indicator of the road that should be followed in the future (Figure 115). As building objects have multiplied, they have thus lost their value as exceptions. Nowa-

days, planning rules and repetitive methods of production confer an object-status upon buildings whose content and significance are ordinary. These buildings are repeated not so much as types adapted to the site, but as models reproduced almost identically. It is in this way that modern architecture has sometimes sinned, neglecting the lessons of the historic urban fabric.

Curiously there has not been a parallel phenomenon with the interiors of buildings. On the contrary, there has been an evolution away from the consideration of objects towards the consideration of space. Paradoxically, the Modern Movement has conferred upon buildings the object-status and upon interiors that of a fabric providing spatial continuity (Figure 116).

Fabric or object? The question may be asked about any architectural project and the answer cannot be arbitrary. If one considers each new building as a spatial transformation of the town, the decision

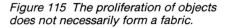

Figure 115 *The proliferation of objects does not necessarily form a fabric.*

5.2 Composition of the object: articulation and continuity

Buildings are the volumetric combination of a large number of elements. They are joined together in larger units which, in turn, modulate the relationships between parts and the whole. Since buildings are of composite structure, the manner in which the joints between elements are highlighted or played down gives rise to strongly differing aesthetic characteristics. In general, we can distinguish two methods of composition of the object: *articulation and continuity*.

Certain periods in history have favoured articulation, others – more rare – continuity. The art of building in the Gothic period is probably the one which has been the most successful in combining the two methods. The clusters of small columns, modest capitals and the ribs of the vaults correspond very well to an articulated language. At the same time, there exists enough dynamism in the soaring energy of the columns and their extension into ribs and vaults, that the continuity of the overall form takes precedence over the autonomy of parts.

In a quite different way the interior of a Baroque church exploits the double play of articulation and continuity. Curves and counter-curves, pilasters and columns, niches and bulges are linked together in a scale of continuity. Articulation is unique; it is reserved for emphasizing a strategic break; the meetings of the walls, belonging to the earth, and the ceilings, vaults and domes belonging to heaven.

In order to clarify these two concepts of articulation and continuity, it is useful to refer to specific examples.

Articulation

(Figures 120, 122, 124, 126, 128.)

Articulation between elements accentuates the autonomy of parts. It strengthens the particular role of the different constituent building elements. The interruptions form accents and rhythms, the location, form and size of which should be carried out with the greatest care in consideration of the whole. Constructional logic is not sufficient justification, aesthetic sensibility must come to the aid of construction.

The meeting point between two or several elements is underlined by a void or by another element specially designed to this effect, as for example the capital which articulates the column and the entablature. It is evident that in this definition the simple 'collision' of two elements may still not be considered as an articulation. An articulation requires a recognition of the limits and the meeting of the two elements.

The *means* by which we can create an articulation are various and can come into play simultaneously: of material, of architectural element, of function or meaning.

Contrary to sculpture, articulation in architecture requires a reference to one or several of the means listed above: it cannot be a question of caprice. Articulation makes it possible to express construction, function and relationship to the site. In this way the building becomes more explicit; it expresses its own nature.

Continuity

(Figures 121, 123, 125, 127, 129.)

Continuity, or 'fusion' between elements reduces the autonomy of the parts. It reflects the largest element of the whole of the object. Continuity replaces the relative autonomy of the elements by a progressive transformation of form. The resulting form contains potential sensuality similar to that of the human body. It appeals to the tactile sense. Each undulation of the continuous line hints at what is to come.

The object then appears to have been formed from a single mould. That is the case, for example, with large reinforced concrete shells. Often the constructional reality is more composite than it appears, as in the vernacular villages of the Cyclades. In this case, it is a facing which reduces or eradicates the joints between the elements and creates a continuity of volumes, contours and surfaces. Achievement of this continuity is something of a technical feat. The use of continuity certainly has the advantage of reinforcing the coherence of the object. Sculptors regularly use this device by limiting the number of articulations to strategic places. Contemporary building based on continuity has more difficulty in being accepted. The examples presented are unusual. The reasons may be of a cultural nature. Having been accustomed for centuries to the constructional and intellectual rationality of the town consisting of articulated structures, we have great difficulty in imagining it modelled in clay. These structures of continuity stand out like strange objects.

Figure 120 Articulation: Henry Moore, Elephant Skull, Plate 19, 1969.

Figure 122 Plinth-column-entablature articulation; change of element of construction: vertical structure – horizontal structure. Temple of Neptune, paestum. Classical architecture from antiquity to the Renaissance and up to Neo-classicism is a composition by means of articulation. Moreover, we have no trouble in naming the conventional elements such as 'plinth', 'column', 'capital', 'pediment', 'entablature'.

Figure 124 Articulations between vertical and horizontal elements; autonomy of the elements: line/plane, structure/infill, etc. Gerrit Rietveld, sideboard, 1919.

The de Stijl movement always maintained the integrity of geometric elements. There is neither 'collision', nor confusion since the straight lines and the planes extend virtually beyond their meeting points.

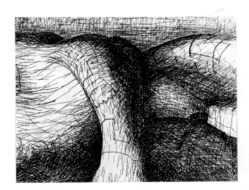

Figure 121 Continuity: Henry Moore, Elephant Skull, Plate 6, 1970.

Figure 123 Fusion between elements: If Gothic art reduced the importance of the articulations in favour of continuity, German Expressionism of the beginning of the twentieth century sought perfect continuity. Erich Mendelssohn, Einstein Tower, Observatory in Berlin, 1917.

Figure 125 Reality and the constructional imprecision of the 'collision' between incongruous elements is avoided by a layer of mortar and unifying whitewash; Hydra, Greece, 1984.

Figure 126 Articulation of a threshold by the recessed joint and change of material: roughcast-concrete-marble; change of element: floor-step; change of meaning old-new and 'end of journey'. Carlo Scarpa, Museo Castelvecchio, Verona, 1957–64. The perfection of this articulation is not only a play of forms and materials. This particular attempt ennobles a narrow passage which leads the visitor from the museum back to his point of departure. It is a sort of final coda to his journey.

Figure 128 Articulation of the plinth or base, windows and roof; as with Carlo Scarpa, articulation is created here by a change of material. It is used in order to accentuate the most important elements in the building. Hosios Loukas, eleventh century.

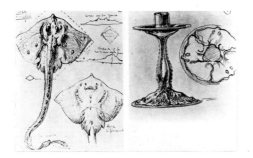

Figure 127 Zoomorphic continuity: Art Nouveau with its plant- or body-inspired continuity raised the fusion between elements to an aesthetic principle. Eugène Grasset, variations on the theme of the Thornback Ray, 1890. A wavy line drawn freehand can easily appear indecisive. One of the best exercises for learning to draw satisfactorily is still drawing from observation and from the nude. No part of the profile of the human body appears unbalanced to us.

Figure 129 The method of building rubble walls, whose porosity is filled and covered with mortar and lime, gives rise to continuous forms. It appears as if it were a clay sculpture that had been hand moulded. Sifnos, Cyclades, Greece.

Figure 130 Articulation and continuity at the same time; Baroque reserves articulation for significant breaks: the meeting of terrestrial walls and ceilings which symbolize sky and heaven. Saint Nicholas of Mala Strana, Prague, 1702.

5.3 The object: faces, corners, relationship to ground and sky

We have seen that the objectbuilding is closed, that it is isolated from its context, that its exterior can be walked around and that, because of this, the treatment of its faces, its corners, its meeting with the ground and its termination towards the sky is of prime importance in shaping its identity. The concepts of articulation and continuity are also applied here. The four types of corner – articulation by a corner element in relief, by a negative corner, by a sharp edge which is no more than a line, and by a rounded corner, find their equivalents at the base and in the cornice. It is evident that in Figures 131–134 lateral combinations (for example 131c – 132b – 133c) are possible. In order to clarify the question, we shall discuss the visual effects of each homogeneous series.

In the dynamics of the attractions and repulsions that an object exerts on its surroundings, there is a matter which is of great importance to the architect: the relationship with gravity and especially with the ground.

Whilst the lateral relationships between objects can be open to free interpretation, and may even be a matter of indifference, the meeting of the building with the ground is inescapable. It indicates that these objects are amongst us, with us on the earth, detached from the sky.

There is not, however, only one possible relationship. A building can give the impression of 'springing from the ground', of 'sinking into the ground', or being 'placed on the ground' or 'hovering above the ground'. How does one choose and put into effect one or other of these forms of expression?

Figure 131 Positive articulation: relief.

The accentuated edge, or corner in relief, is an indicator which grants a privileged status to this feature of the building. Cornerstones, for example, are often emphasized. They are not only markers and stabilizing elements for construction, but their treatment also emphasizes the end of one face and the beginning of the other: *the cornerstones belong to both faces*. They tell us about the thickness and stability of the wall and provide a lateral frame to each face. This classic method has been used on buildings since the beginning of masonry construction, sometimes taking the form of a corner pilaster, of a more careful corner treatment, or a simple decoration painted on the rough-cast. In all these cases the importance of the corner is recognized and delineated.

Articulation in relation to the ground, with the aid of a plinth, is a second classic principle. It celebrates the meeting of a building of simple geometric form with the irregularity of the ground. An intermediary element of great stability provides *a seating* for the building. The building puts down roots in a precise location: one cannot 'move' it like a glass on a table. It is for this reason that the base of the Parthenon belongs to the ground, rather than to the building. Moreover, it must receive and prepare the building. The plinth has a double relationship of dependence: one relative to the object supported which must be specific and precise in its composition, and the other relative to the junction with the ground which is ineluctable and more generic; in classical architecture the same plinth is applicable to other similar situations.

The importance of the plinth as an intermediary element is recognized with great acuteness by sculptors. Brancusi is perhaps the twentieth-century artist who has taken the greatest care over the design of the base. He has often made it a contrasting element to the sculpture (Figure 136). For him the base belongs resolutely to the sculpture.

Figure 135 In its interior the Baroque church exploits both articulation and continuity. On the exterior, it makes positive use of articulation: plinth, intersecting horizontal strata, corners in relief, cornice; Church at Noto, Sicily.

Figure 136 *Complementarity between base and object, Brancusi, The Fish, 1922.*

Figure 137 *The eclectic plinth; Am Steinhof Church in Vienna, Otto Wagner, 1903–1907.*

Figure 138 *Horizontal plinth: a simple gravel border edged with concrete paving stones, where grass would, in any case, have difficulty in growing.*

A second method consists of incorporating the idea of the plinth, or rather of *the base*, into the building itself by including the whole or part of the ground floor. In the Am Steinhof church (Figure 137) Otto Wagner takes up a theme that has been current since the Renaissance, by marking this transition between the raw earth and a highly refined building with a more rustic treatment of the cladding, reminiscent of the coarseness of earth and rock. In the cases where the whole of the ground floor receives this treatment, as in Alberti's Palazzo Rucellai, the '*piano nobile*' is located one floor above ground level, the rusticated base not being a suitable place for it. But Otto Wagner enters his building in the upper part of the base, whilst increasing the rustication of the lower part.

The examples that have been chosen could lead to the erroneous conclusion that plinth or base is always a substantial element. This is not so; if it is a simple building, the recognition of the junction with the ground can be a modest profile, or even the more precise handling of a strip of ground (Figure 138).

Capping with a cornice and a roof handles the delicate transition between the rainwater on the roof and the vertical faces and openings which need protecting. It generally belongs to the building and not to the sky, thus avoiding the visual ambiguity that would otherwise result from apparent verticle protraction. According to the importance of the building, this upper termination can include the whole of the top floor. There are some exceptional cases in which the extension towards the infinity of the sky becomes a sought-after symbol. The helical spire on Borromini's Sant' Ivo della Sapienza is a pertinent example (Figure 59).

The combination of the requirements of the junction with the ground and the upper conclusion of buildings led Palladio to the famous tripartite division of his country villas. The base with the services, the '*piano nobile*' with the stately rooms and the attic storey with the bedrooms; utility and form combine in one coherent architectural concept.

Figure 132 Negative articulation, the recess.

The recessed corner is one method of emphasizing the junction of the façades by clearly separating them from each other. They then appear as more or less autonomous elements. The importance of the recess gives an indication of the thickness or habitable depth of the façades (Figure 139).

This inversion of the corner towards the interior was already used in the Renaissance when two pilasters formed a corner without actually turning it. Each pilaster belongs to one façade, but the idea of a terminal pilaster goes further than that of the negative corner. In fact the articulation of the corner by its 'absence' has been reconsidered in the twentieth century by many. This is probably linked to two phenomena: firstly the façade, having become non-loadbearing, has lost its material thickness; the apparent

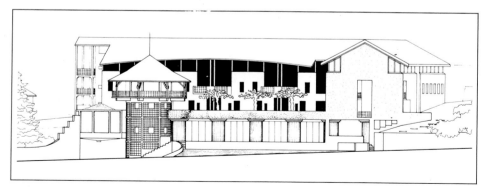

Figure 139 Negative articulation: 'independent' façades, Louis Kahn, Phillips Exeter Library, New Hampshire, 1967–72.

Figure 140 Negative articulation: recessed junction, partial pilotis and cutaway top floor, Casa Frigerio at Como, Giuseppe Terragni, 1939–40.

Figure 141 Negative articulation defines the building in its relationship to the roof and the sky; Pierre von Meiss, competition, 1982.

thickness then becomes a question of choice: Mies van der Rohe expresses the construction, whereas Kahn subjects it to an intention arising from the brief. Secondly, designs inspired by modern art introduce the principle of *dislocation* of the corner in favour of a virtual extension of the façades beyond their real limits or of an interpenetration of the two faces forming the corner with the surrounding space. Giuseppe Terragni's Casa Frigerio at Como, with its set-backs, the slight projection of the balconies on the return façade and the loggia and canopy as the upper termination on only one of the façades, is without any doubt one of the most brilliant examples of this form of articulation of corner and cornice[75] (Figure 140). Another example is the Villa Stein at Garches analysed in masterly fashion by Colin Rowe and Robert Slutzky in 'Transparency'.[76]

It is not only negative articulation or dislocation of the corner which is popular in the twentieth century: building on pilotis is explicitly pronounced by Le Corbusier to be one of the aesthetic principles amongst his five points of modern architecture. The base is replaced by a void and sometimes this void is, in its turn, 'placed' on a base, as in the buildings of Mies van der Rohe. The building hovers above the ground, clearly detaching itself from it. The void and the pilotis act as intermediary between building and ground.

Negative articulation between wall and roof has been applied for centuries in northern Italy, for example. The junction of two systems of construction, stone wall and timber frame, provides the opportunity for a different use of the storey under the roof (drying of foodstuffs and laundry, ventilated attics, bedrooms) (Figure 141).

The sharp edge

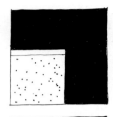

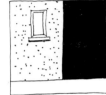

Figure 133 The sharp corner as a single line.

Figure 142 The sharp edge, the pure line of intersection between ground, walls and roof; Giuseppe Terragni, S. Elia daynursery, Como, 1939.

The rejection of classical conventions, such as the corner in relief, the plinth, cornice and ornament in general, and the search for elementary geometries by the Modern Movement, have led to the reduction of volumes to their simplest expression. The corner and the parapet are defined by the abstraction of a line produced by the meeting of two planes, or the fine filigree of shadow cast by metal trim. The absence of a corner element can also be seen in some of Palladio's villas when they are not capped by a pediment extending over the whole width of the house, but the corner is emphasized nevertheless by the composition of the windows and the returns of the base. Mies van der Rohe is a master of articulation of the corners of thin façades, but his subtleties are more perceptible from close to than from a distance. In the twentieth century the simplicity of apparent volume is not only elevated to an aesthetic virtue, it also results from the method of construction in rendered brick or from the adoption of the principle of skeleton structure, which makes it possible to remove the load-bearing function from the façade. From the moment when the façade becomes no more than an envelope – a curtain-wall for example – the corner and the cornice no longer need to be of the same solidity. With present thermal requirements the façades are almost always 'clad' whether they be load-bearing or not, and whether they be built from new or traditional materials.

This method of building will influence the appearance of buildings of the future; the concept of 'wrapping' leads to the sharp edge or to continuity; articulation becomes a luxury or a decorative feature without a constructional basis.

A sharp edge at the junction of the wall with the ground may give the impression that the building is 'growing' from the ground or that it is 'sinking' into the ground (Figure 143). This penetration into the ground can become a theme of the composition, especially when the emerging elements suggest other hidden elements as in Pierino Selmoni's sculpture of the Giant (Figure 144). In the streets of Amsterdam or Delft, on the contrary, brick, used as a unifying material, links the ground and the facades. One thus has the impression that the ground has been 'folded up' in order to become a wall, whereas the volume of the building does not seem to extend underground.

Figure 143 The chapel rising out of the ground; Le Corbusier, Convent of La Tourette, 1957.

Figure 144 Visible parts indicate the presence of hidden parts; sculpture of 'Giant' by Pierino Selmoni in front of Mario Botta's school at Morbio Inferiore, 1979.

The fusion of planes

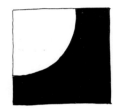

Figure 134
The fusion of planes.

The gradual bending of a wall on plan or in section causes the fusion of the object's surrounding surfaces. The sphere is the most extreme example of this. An obtuse or rounded corner, which is to say the continuity of the envelope without change in its texture and without articulation of break, gives an impression of 'massiveness'.[77] Light models these objects by casting an evenly graded shadow and accentuates their enclosed form. To understand this phenomenon it is sufficient to take the example of the choir of the Abbey of Vézelay. Its large piers, formed from clusters of linked columns articulated by their multiple lines of light and shadow, do not seem any more massive than the round columns of the hemicycle of the inner row which are, neverthe-

less, much more slender (Figure 145).

The chapel adjoining the church of the Convent of La Tourette is an example of the massiveness of an object-building. The absence of corners in fact bestows upon it a greater 'visual weight' than on the much larger church itself. The impression of mass is increased still further by the tilting of the walls, which gives rise to a feeling of great stability and of being rooted in the ground. The body of this small building thus acquires the weight of a rock protruding from the ground (Figure 143).

The theme of continuity between ground and object occurs in many medieval castles and towns. Clinging to the rock, the built form appears to be a crystallized excrescence of the rock itself.

Since we shall not return later to questions of the massiveness or lightness of buildings, let us make a digression here. The treatment of corners and openings (doors, windows, etc.) constitutes a useful tool for giving an impression of 'massiveness'. If they resemble deep recesses, they emphasize the massiveness. If, on the contrary, a window is placed level with the face of the wall, its surface character takes precedence over its thickness (Figures 299 and 300). The relative size of the openings is equally decisive for the character of the mass. In Gothic cathedrals it approaches the point at which the construction is reduced to a skeleton. Relatively small openings, on the contrary, emphasize massiveness.

Figure 145 Different weights, different dimensions: large piers with clusters of slender columns appear less massive than the round columns; the Abbey of Vézelay.

First Interlude
FROM OBJECT TO SPACE

Overleaf
The opening organizes its space. Sant'
Andrea, Mantua, by Leon Battista Alberti.

Spatiality of objects

To discuss the spatiality of objects we shall use the analogy of *radiance*. A free-standing sculpture or building exerts a radiance which defines a more or less precise field around it. To enter the field of influence of an object is the beginning of a spatial experience. The extent of the radiance depends on the nature and size of the object on one hand, and on the context on the other.

An obelisk 'appropriates to itself' a significant radio-concentric space. It is erected in the middle of a square, but a square of what size? If this obelisk were to topple over one would not want it to touch the surrounding buildings; one might therefore suggest the radius of the square should be at least equal to the height of the obelisk.

A similar radiance emanates from a cylindrical building. The baptistry of Pisa Cathedral refuses to be

Figure 146 Free-standing radiating object. Baptistry of Pisa Cathedral.

touched by any other building (Figure 146). Bramante's tempietto is imprisoned in the courtyard of San Pietro in Montorio like a ring in a jewel case, but it does not touch the walls (Figure 147). It is equally hazardous to 'wedge' a spiral staircase against the wall of a room or to link an amphitheatre to other buildings. They require clearance; if this is only slight, it can create a desired tension between the elements, but it should not be omitted altogether.

A concentric object at a point which has several equivalent axes of symmetry (square, octagon, circle …), emits *a priori* a 'spatial radiance' of equal intensity in different directions, rather like a lighthouse. The sites and briefs of buildings which would justify such a balanced radiance tend to be exceptions, reserved for temples and unique buildings in a dominant position. In practice, the asymmetry of urban and rural sites requires nuances of spatial effect. The sides, left and right, are often similar, but for the front facing the street, or the back facing the courtyard, the demand for space varies considerably in comparison with the other sides. It does not, however, mean that we should remove elementary geometric figures from our architectural vocabulary, because we can change the basic form into a hierarchy of forms by additions and transformations, as can be seen from the example of the cylinder-sphere of the Pantheon in Rome (Figures 148 and 149).

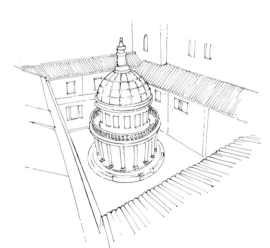

Figure 147 Object in its jewel case – radiance contained. Tempietto of San Pietro in Montorio in Rome, by Donato Bramante.

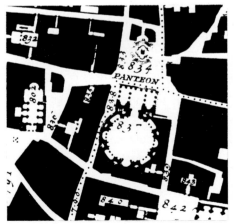 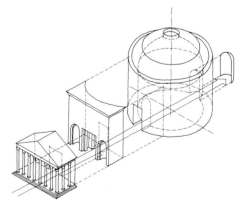

Figures 148 and 149 From radial to frontal radiance: the Pantheon, built in Rome in the second century by Hadrian, is a circular and spherical building par excellence. This reduction of the cosmos needs a colossal portico in order to be taken from its universal plane and linked to the town, to a square and to its people (plan by Nolli and axonometric by Jürgen Joedicke).

the face, the human face – face of the building, in short, frontality. The direction and intensity of this radiance of the 'face' transposed to the building have been particularly well understood and evaluated by certain Italian Renaissance and Baroque architects, as for example at Vigevano. Baroque architects completed the last side of the Piazza Ducale with a cathedral whose facade has forsaken the reality of the internal space of the church in order to control the urban space better. To this end, the facade has no fears about extending beyond the limits of the church itself (Figures 150 and 151)!

It is not easy to give a precise definition of the 'radiance' of a monument, a building or an object-facade. One method which the architect sometimes uses is to 'suggest the extent' of this radiance by giving it a concrete form and limits. In this way the design of the paving in the Piazza del Campidoglio in Rome makes visible the radiance of the statue placed in the centre (Figure 152). In the same way the walls and balustrades in the garden of a Renaissance palace mark the limits of the territory controlled by the facade (Figure 153). The existence even of such an artificial limit decided by the architect reinforces the power of the composition; the radiance of the facade is structured in stages without vanishing into infinity; it is contained and concentrated in a limited space. The object is therefore not only an 'emitter' of radiance, but also a 'mediator' between the observer and the surrounding space.

The spatiality of an object reaches its peak when it is pierced, when it can be crossed and thus links the observer to other elements in the environment beyond the object (Figure 154).

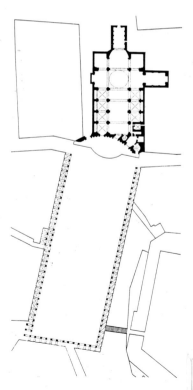

Figures 150 and 151 When the Palazzo of Vigevano became the summer residence of the Sforzas, an antechamber was carved out for it in the medieval fabric, surrounded on three sides by a colonnade, the fourth being taken up by the ramps of the principal acces to the palace (1492–94).

Nearly two hundred years later (1676–84) it was decided to erect the cathedral of Sant Ambrogio on this fourth side. The geometry of the plot having an awkward relationship to the square, the architects decided to give the façade an independence in favour of its urban role. Its frontal radiance takes in the whole of the square. In order to achieve this, the facade even overlaps a neighbouring building.

In our historic towns the plots tend to be rectangular and it is on the small side facing the *front* that we confer a special role of controlling public space with the facade's radiance. There is an underlying anthropomorphic significance: the facade,

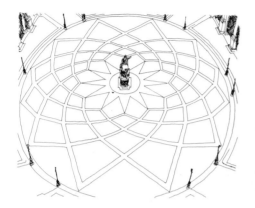

Figure 152 Spatial radiance made visible: texture of the ground surrounding the equestrian statue of Marcus Aurelius in the Piazza del Campidoglio in Rome.

Figure 153 Ballustrades, walls and statues which contain spatial radiance, graduating in stages.

Figure 154 Object traversed by space! Henry Moore, Sheep Piece.

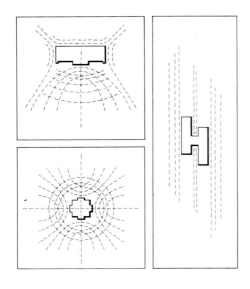
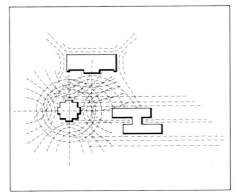
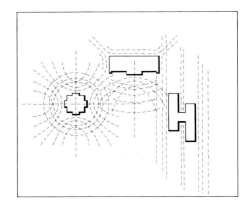

Figure 155 Approximate spatial radiance of three buildings according to their geometric characteristics. The first layout, combining three volumes, causes conflicting fields. In the second, the fields are co-ordinated and contribute to the formation of a well-defined and coherent space.

Relationships between objects

Objects are rarely isolated; they are in the company of other volumes or limits. Space is born from the relationships between these elements.

The geometry and organization of each object bestow a *direction* and *amplitude* upon the radiance. The direction is legible in the geometry of the volume and the modulation of its façades. The amplitude is a question of appreciation. When several objects are grouped, the fields of radiance are superimposed. This superimposition creates a field as a result, which could give a new recognizable figure or could lead to a confused and conflicting structure. The series of diagrams (Figure 155) illustrates how we can manipulate several volumes in such a way that their sum is more than a simple addition, and how we can help them to form a unity when they are arranged in a dispersed manner.

The spatial interaction of objects which we have tried to show with

this series of simple diagrams can be found everywhere in reality. Urban architecture has left us exemplary evidence of this, some of which is subtle and refined, some imposing and noble, like Saint Mark's Square in Venice, and some more modest.

Let us examine Saint Mark's Square (Figures 156, 157 and 158). Historically it is not the product of a single design. Yet its genesis is of little importance for the purpose of a discussion of its spatial characteristics. The 'L' shape is one of the most difficult layouts for a square and the least liable to succeed. This shape presents the disadvantage that each branch has its hidden counterpart. Moreover, one of the branches opens on to the lagoon, which at first sight weakens its spatial definition. Two object-buildings form the basis of the shape, the church of Saint Mark and the Doge's Palace. The other sides are defined by the colonnade or 'hem' of a fabric in order to recognize the edge of the square.

Thanks to the introduction of three additional objects – the Campanile and two free-standing columns – and to the project of the church, the 'L'-shaped square finds a masterly solution. The Campanile is positioned in the inner angle of the 'L'; *it articulates* the two directions by giving each branch a relative autonomy whilst at the same time announcing the presence of the other. Seen from the west, it hides the Doge's Palace whilst hinting at continuity. It confirms the intersection of the two branches whilst defining the intersection more clearly as part belonging to the church. On the other hand the role of the two fore-standing columns as a virtual end and gateway to the square before the opening of the quay on to the lagoon is essential. Thanks to these three elements, the square finds its solution, or almost. There remains the problem of the exterior angle of the 'L' which necessarily takes greater importance and must be recognized in one way or another.

Figure 156 Saint Mark's Square in Venice.

Figure 157 Articulation of the square seen from the lagoon.

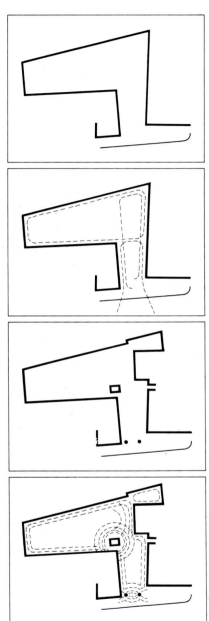

Figure 158 The space of this incongruous square is articulated with great mastery thanks to the Campanile, to Saint Mark's Church with its small square, and the two free-standing columns on the lagoon side.

It is the projection of Saint Mark's Church and its detachment from the leg of the 'L', giving on to the small entry square to the north – a negative articulation – which resolves this corner as a threshold to the square.

If we now return to the concept of 'radiance', we discover that the radiance of the principal object-building, the highly articulated church, is contained by a deep square. The Doge's Palace, which faces on to a comparatively narrower arm of the square, presents a very smooth façade treatment, producing an intense radiance, but contained and parallel to the building rather than perpendicular. The fact that there is a pair of columns is decisive. If there were only one, it would exert a concentric radiance whereas, with two of them, their effects combine, defining a dominant field of action between them. The Campanile, vertical and isolated, produces a somewhat radio-concentric influence which corresponds very well to its role as *fulcrum*. A second reading of the articulation of this square can be made from the subspaces which are defined by the projections and recesses. There are few squares as complex as this, which are as balanced and in which each object and each limiting element is located with such accuracy in the place best suited to it.

The architect can anticipate the feelings engendered on passing through a space by correctly positioning radiant objects and space-limiting elements. By measuring the width and the relationship of the 'open passages' and of significant radiant objects, he manages to orchestrate a succession of convergences which avoid, at the same time, boredom and excess. Analysing Mies van der Rohe's Barcelona Pavilion

(Figure 159), Arnheim shows how the object modifies understanding of a complex and dynamic space:

the life-sized nude, conspicuous as the only organic shape in a building formed of rectangular slabs, stood in a corner that otherwise would have escaped the visitors' attention. It stood on a terrace in a small pool, which was visible through the glass partition of the large internal space, and it was backed by low walls. The sculpture pool was accessible through a narrow corridor that would have led pointlessly to an empty corner without the statue as its vis-

ual focus. By giving a special accent to the far corner of the building, the architect stressed the strongly confined rectangularity of the whole.... This example shows, not only does the setting determine the place of the object, but inversely the object also modifies the structure of the setting.[78]

The geometric shape of the Pavilion is a rectangle, an intrinsically symmetrical figure. Mies manages to play down the basic shape by several displaced and superimposed rectangles, causing a dynamic of spatial tensions and compressions. The fascinating ambiguity is thus reinforced by the asymmetry and the eccentricity of the most radiant object.

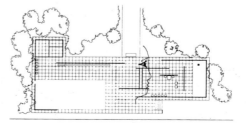

Figure 159 A single object articulating the whole of a fluid space; Mies van der Rohe, Barcelona Pavilion (1929) with the sculpture of a nude by Georg Kolbe.

6

SPACE

Overleaf
Invention of a new window space. Giuseppe
Terragni, Sant'Elia Day-Nursery, Como.

Aristotle defines space as a container of things – a sort of succession of all-inclusive envelopes, from what is 'within the limits of the sky' to the very smallest, rather like Russian dolls. Space is, therefore, of necessity a hollow, limited externally and filled up internally. There is no empty space; everything has its position, its location, its place.

In fact, for the architect the space or the gap between ground, walls and ceiling is not nothingness, quite the contrary: the very reason for his activity is to create the hollow in order to contain. He will give it a concrete form to offer that hospitality and relative freedom of movement which people require.

Painting, sculpture and music also have their spatiality but this is defined from the exterior, offering only the possibility of *mental* penetration. Architecture is the art of the hollow; it is defined both from the interior and from the exterior; *walls have two sides*. We *penetrate* it with our body and not only with our mind. Any critique or architectural history must take account of this double aspect of hollow and solid in buildings. A work of architecture which is designed or considered only from the exterior ceases to be architecture and becomes a stage set. Conversely, the reduction to just the spatial characteristics eludes the concrete signs and symbols underlain by its material nature.

Ancient treatises on architecture hardly talk directly about space. Their theories bear more on the physical elements of the buildings and on their formal justifications than on the hollow space which they define. The debate on space only developed at the beginning of the nineteenth century with the German philosopher F. W. J. Schelling in *Philosophie der Kunst*. It grew to-lishes relationships, enabling him to interpret an implicit limit.

The architect knows that not all the points on the limiting surfaces do play an identical role. The edges of isolated surfaces and the intersections of two or more limiting surfaces (angles or corners) constitute principal cues for orientation and comprehension.

A cubic space, for example, is limited by six planes. Without needing to focus, the eye uses angles and corners as more precise cues for understanding the space. The material existence of these planes is not indispensable for the perception of space. By 'eroding' these planes to leave no more than the essential cues (angles and corners), or by reducing these cues even further to just edges or boundaries, we continue to distinguish an 'inside' and an 'outside'.

The elements defining the space in which we are do not form an 'image', but exert a field of unequal, but more or less balanced, forces. The strength of this field is increased when the limiting forms are complementary or converge towards one point, instead of being autonomous[83] (i.e. centrality).[84]

As human beings we do not consciously need to register in a linear fashion *all* the fragments present in order to obtain an overall idea of the space which we are visiting or in which we are living.

We have seen in Chapter 2 that we also use other senses apart from vision, such as hearing and touch. The resulting over-all idea is not the objective fact of space as it is, but space experienced, passed through the subjective filter of perception conditioned by our previous experiences, our language and our culture.

In figures 160 and 161 we are wards the end of the nineteenth century with historians such as Riegl, Wölfflin, Schmarsow. August Schmarsow introduces his work *Barock und Rokoko* by insisting on the priority of space in architecture:

... Man imagines in the first place the space which surrounds him and not the physical objects which are supports of symbolic significance. All static or mechanical dispositions, as well as the materialization of the spatial envelope, are only means for realizing an idea which is vaguely felt or clearly imagined in architectural creation ... Architecture is 'art' when the design of space clearly takes precedence over the design of the object. Spatial intention is the living soul of architectural creation.[81]

It is the twentieth century which has the most developed architecture as a non-figurative art. Space is part of it. New building techniques have made it possible to imagine an architectural space which is characterized by its fluid relationship with other spaces.[82] Moholy Nagy goes as far as saying that 'spatial composition is not, in the first place, a question of materials.'[83]

6.1 Elements of spatial definition

Architectural space is born from the relationship between objects or boundaries and from planes which do not themselves have the character of object, but which define *limits*. These limits may be more or less explicit, constitute continuous surfaces forming an uninterrupted boundary, or, on the contrary, constitute only a few cues (for example four columns) between which the observer estab-

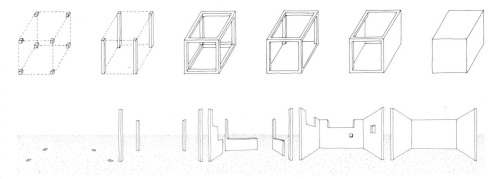

simulating the genesis of a space
defined by cues which at first leave
it implicit and then gradually make
it more and more explicit. This
shows the potential of more or less
apparent planes and edges which
the observer re-establishes between
the concrete cues.

The colonnade defines explicit
space although the amount of void is
greater than that of solid. By the
alignment of the columns we perceive a limit which separates whilst
acting as a filter. Alberti says that
'*colonnades are nothing (but) a
perforated wall*' (Figure 162).[85]

By studying several simple layouts of vertical elements on the
same square plan - four columns,
two parallel walls, a 'U'-shaped
wall, a cell - we obtain very different
spatial fields (Figure 163). These
characteristics are illustrated in
detail in Francis Ching's *Architecture, Form, Space and Order*.[86]

Instead of defining space by a wall
which surrounds it, we can also use
a series of pierced parallel walls.
The limit of the principal space is
then defined by the edges of the
walls which between them produce
an implicit plane (Figures 164–166).

*Figure 162 '... Colonnades are nothing
but a perforated wall,' (Alberti); Temple
at Bassae dedicated to Apollo
Epikourius, 420 BC.*

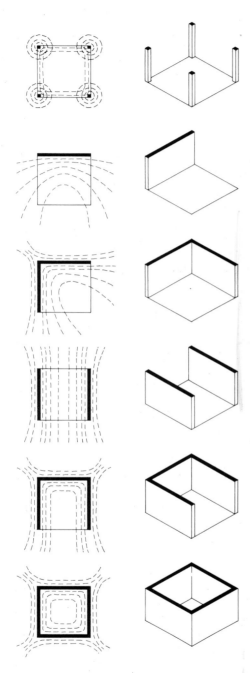

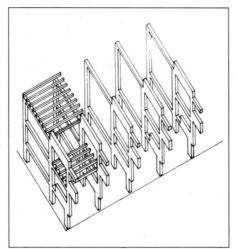

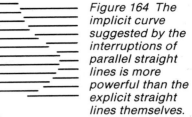

Figure 164 The implicit curve suggested by the interruptions of parallel straight lines is more powerful than the explicit straight lines themselves.

Figure 165 The main space traverses a series of perpendicular walls and layers of space.

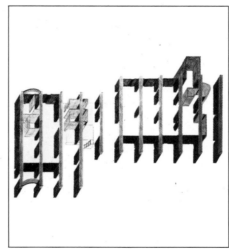

Figure 163 Different spatial fields on the same square plan by means of varying the vertical elements.

Figure 166 Since the Romanesque churches, but especially in modern architecture, the principle of regular parallel interrupted walls and spaces has been used to create the main perpendicular space. It is one method of forming architectural space; axonometrics of Rudolf Schindler's Lovell Beach House (1925), and of Le Corbusier's Sarabhai house (1955) and a picture of the courtyards of Livio Vacchini's Saleggio School (1975).

6.2 Depths of space

Figure 167 Lake Geneva, the mouth of the Rhône and the Alps: in the foreground the graduated texture offers a clear reading of the relative depths, whereas in the background the change of depth is less gradual. There the spatial layers between the hidden and the visible seem very shallow.

The most common and effective indicators of the perception of depth are, on the one hand, *the effect of perspective, with, notably, a gradient of texture*,[87] and, on the other, *the phenomenon which tells us that an object which partially hides another should be in front of it*[88] (Figures 167–171).

Figure 167 shows the two phenomena on the same picture torn in two. The effect of depth in the lower

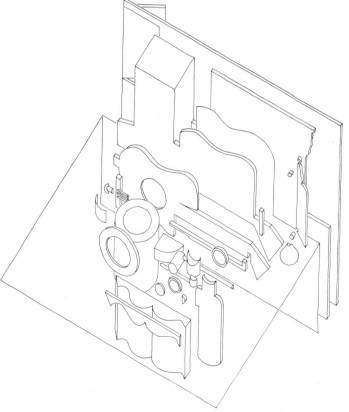

Figure 168 Attempt at spatial decomposition of a painting by Le Corbusier (B. Hoseli in Kommentar . . .).[51]

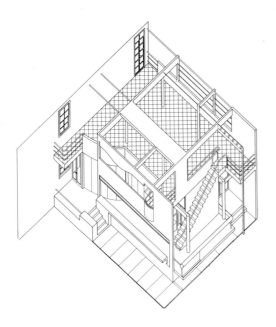

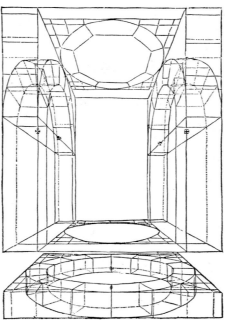

Figure 169 Two façades with multiple close-set planes – an invention of modernity, Michael Graves, Benacerraf house addition, 1969.

Figure 170 Sebastiano Serlio, Libro Secondo, della prospettiva (1545).

Figure 171 Perspective and texture as gradients of depth; Claude Nicolas Ledoux, Salines de Chaux at Arc-et-Senans, director's house, 1773–79.

part is the result of the texture gradient caused by the waves of the lake, whilst in the upper part there is no longer any perspective, but a simple superimposition of planes one in front of the other: clouds, the mountain on the right, those on the left and finally those in the distance. There is hardly any 'real' depth.

For important representative interiors, urban squares and avenues, classical architecture accentuates deep perspective not only by its vanishing lines, but also by its profile of mouldings which adds a gradient of texture (Figure 171).

In painting, one or other of these two phenomena are used as a method thus producing the illusion of *deep space* or, on the contrary, of *shallow space*. Painters from the Renaissance to the nineteenth century do not conceal their preference for perspective and deep space. Painters of the Middle Ages and, in another manner, painters like Juan Gris, Braque, Le Corbusier and more recently Robert Slutzky are masters of this shallow space in which superimposed planes appear compressed, very close to each other and often ambiguous in terms of their actual position. It is not, therefore, surprising that modern architects have also attempted to compose spaces and objects by using these methods.

Working with frontal planes whose respective distance is small and ambiguous, certain architects of the Modern Movement exploit not only the effects of shallow space, but also the phenomenon of transparency[89] which results from the disappearance and fragmentary reappearance of one plane behind the other (Figure 169).

This principle of several layers of superimposed shallow spaces, in the façade, is extolled by Guiseppe Terragni in the Frigerio house at Como, by Le Corbusier in the Villa Stein at Garches, or again by Carlo Scarpa in the articulation of the walls and windows in the Castelvecchio at Verona.

6.3 Densities of space

For the architect space does not only have depth; *it is also more or less dense*. When a greater density appears appropriate, he seeks to modulate distances by intermediary and closer 'stages of depth'. This is generally the case when we work with shallow space, but we can also create density with a deep space: the Mosque of Cordoba with its *'forest' of columns* is a deep space of extraordinary density. On the contrary, the design for extension of the Bibliothèque Nationale, by Boullée, characterizes the absence of density, universal space, deep and empty (Figures 172 and 173). In the same way we could have compared the density of Scharoun's Philharmonic Hall and the void of Mies van der Rohe's National Art Gallery, both in Berlin.

Spatial density is due not only to the physical staging of depth, as at Cordoba. It can be sufficient to *suggest* subdivisions implicitly by the modulation of floors, walls or ceilings so that the same unitary space appears relatively 'full' or, on the contrary, relatively 'empty'. Let us compare Brunelleschi's Pazzi Chapel, with its well-filled and modulated depth, with the terrace of Luigi Snozzi's Kalmann house with its tension of just one movement between two extremes (the interior and the end of the terrace). The imaginary inversion of these realities makes the argument more explicit (Figures 174–177).

There are no inherent advantages in dense space compared with 'empty' and unitary space. What is important is that the architect makes his choice of means in accordance with the site and, of course, the brief, but also with his design concept. By observing examples of history, he will perhaps discover that 'empty' and unitary spaces are able to create an extraordinary tension between the location of the observer and the limits of the space, which then approximates to a reproduction of the universe – a bridge between the real and the unreal. On the other hand, a strongly rhythmical and modulated dense space appears more reassuring and more earthly.

Figure 172 Dense space: interior of the Mosque at Cordoba.

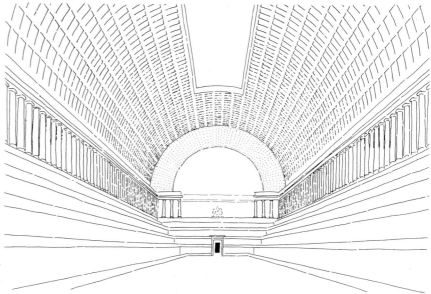

Figure 173 'Empty' unitary space: design for the interior of the reading room in the Bibliothèque Nationale; E. L. Boulée, 1785.

6.4 Openings of space

One of the fundamental oppositions which makes it possible to distinguish types of architectural space is that they can either be closed, introverted, concentrated upon themselves, or open, extrovert, centrifugal. Whereas mass is more or less concentrated, space is more or less closed. The degree of enclosure does not only depend on the quantity and the size of the openings. When we wish to create a space which tends to open to the exterior, we are trying to make it less explicit. There is therefore a direct relationship between notions of explicit and implicit space and the degree of opening or

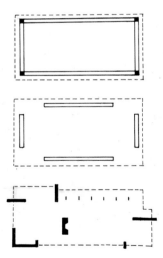

Figure 174 The modulation of the floor and walls increases the density of space by subdividing its depth; Filippo Brunelleschi, Pazzi Chapel, Florence, fifteenth century.

Figure 175 Elimination of modulation and tendency towards a homogeneous, unitary space.

Figure 176 Continuity of the ground and the walls creates tension between the observer's viewpoint, the end of the terrace and the framed landscape in the distance. Luigi Snozzi, Villa Kalmann, Locarno, 1979.

Figure 177 Introduction of modulation and tendency towards a filled subdivided, dense space.

Figure 178 These didactic diagrams by Allen Brooks, show Frank Lloyd Wright's contribution to a new spatial conception: first of all eliminating the corners, he continues by distorting the initial spatial geometry, displacing or turning segments of the geometric envelope by 90 degrees in order to organize the spatial continuity to his liking.

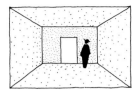

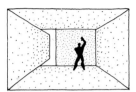

Figure 179 The intact corner is 'introvert'; the missing corner is 'extrovert'; the element – wall, ground or ceiling – which belongs to the two spaces, achieves continuity.

closure. We can use the principles of one in order to achieve the other (Figure 178). The opening of a space is obtained by the reduction of its degree of definition (for example elimination of a corner) and by the presence of elements belonging to both the interior and the exterior (for example, extension of a wall towards the exterior) (Figure 179).

The door and the window are the two classic methods of handling an opening in a structure of load-bearing walls: a place for passing through, a 'picture' framing an exterior view, and a source of light and air.

The position and the relative sizes of these openings, their form itself, structure the space and help define the nature of the envelope, for example, ·· kness.

The larger these openings become the more they designate 'an absence of wall', especially if it is a corner opening. The notion of pierced wall diminishes; the space opens out. Reinforced concrete, steel and glass have made it possible to extend the

Figures 180–183 Carlo Scarpa combines in one building a whole range of articulations of openings in relation to the wall in which he inserts them. He adapts each solution – hole, window, glazed bay, free façade, wall that leads, spatial interruption or continuity – to a particular situation in his museum layout.

architectural vocabulary by the elimination of the dependence between structure and opening. The spatial limit no longer necessarily corresponds to the load-bearing structure. The space and the façade are 'liberated' and offer the possibility of a new dynamic. The instruments of this architecture are the glazed bay, the ribbon window, the corner window and the glazed wall which introduce a new spatial dimension consciously exploited by the Modern movement.

The differentiated and carefully studied treatment of the openings in Carlo Scarpa's Castelvecchio Museum in Verona shows how this 'discovery' of the twentieth century is, in its turn, applied to the transformation of an old building (Figures 180–183). Scarpa makes ample use of a very rich register of means by adapting the type and treatment of each opening to its local situation without, however, losing the coherence of the whole.

Notions of interior and exterior are not necessarily linked to those of covered and uncovered. Human beings are inclined to consider the environment in an egocentric manner. The famous notion of Bergson 'hic et nunc' (here and now) suggests an interior wherever you are. When we are *in* town or *in* a garden, we consider them as interiors. Conversely the interior acquires its intensity by the presence of limits relative to an exterior.

The architect uses methods of juxtaposition and interpenetration to regulate interior–exterior relationships and to articulate transitions as inside–outside, man–nature, private–public, element–context ... He establishes intermediary zones of transition which belong to both (Chapter 7).

6.5 Spatial juxtaposition and interpenetration

The elements of spatial definition and the openings characterize the *types of spatial relationships*, indeed the degree to which the space remains autonomous or is more or less linked to other spaces. We can pick out two basic types: juxtaposition and interpenetration (Figures 184–187).

Juxtaposition insists on autonomy. Our language includes a large number of terms which are, in principle, only applied to a relatively well-defined and closed space – room, bedroom, cell, hall, corridor – all linked to an idea of 'privacy' and of exclusion from other spaces. The connection with other neighbouring spaces is made by doors or windows, narrow and controlled passages in a wall. The corners are intact. Such a space, when it does not coincide with the envelope of the building, implies the existence of other similar spaces (the series by addition or division). The way in which to order or distribute the spaces then becomes an important structuring factor of the

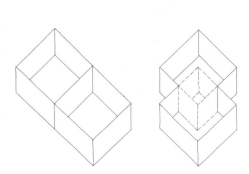

Figure 184 Juxtaposition and interpenetration.

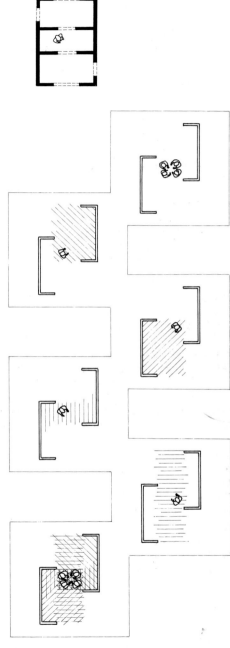

Figure 185 Spatial juxtaposition and interpenetration.

whole: a succession of rooms, uni- or bilateral corridor, central hall, etc. (see also 6.6 Geometry of plans, sections and spaces).

The methods of construction of past centuries, which were more often based on a system of load-bearing walls or of other ways of making materials work by compression, have generally led to cellular groupings with an explicit definition of juxtaposed spaces (Figures 186 and 188).

Spatial interpenetration creates continuity from one space to the other from the moment when an important element of definition, a wall, ceiling, floor, appears to belong to two or more spaces.

The plane which separates one space from the other is then less substantial and produces an implicit division. The conditions for implicit closure are achieved with a relatively high degree of ambiguity and a minimum of means such as a lintel, a column, the framing of a large

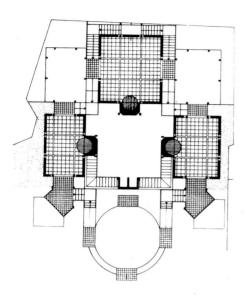

Figure 186   Spatial juxtaposition (student exercise).

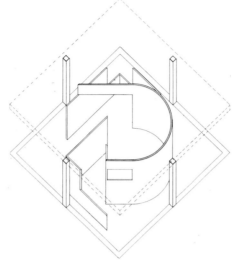

Figure 187   Spatial juxtaposition (student exercise).

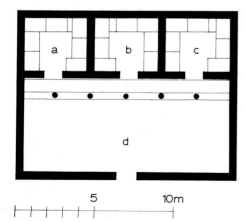

Figure 188   Spatial juxtaposition: the constructional constraint of load-bearing walls; Megara Hyblaea, house in the district of the old Agora (drawing by Paul Auberson).

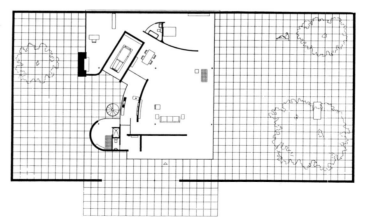

Figure 189   Spatial interpenetration: liberation of the structure; plan of a courtyard house with garage, Mies van der Rohe, 1934.

110

glazed opening, the top of a wall, the difference in texture of a surface, or object. The *role* played by the various means gives rise to different interpenetrations of the space.

The theme of spatial continuity evokes a dynamic principle, of passages and stops with planes which guide and lead us to wonder what is to follow by the use of ambiguity between the hidden and the visible, the present and the future (Figures 187 and 189).

The above-mentioned opposition could lead to the belief that architects in the past did not defy the constructional limits of traditional load-bearing systems and never tried to work with implied limits and spatial interpenetration. They did, however, for the construction of monumental buildings, especially for places of worship, compose spaces with the idea of interpenetration. But contrary to the successive innovations of the Modern Movement, which introduces a spatial dynamic ('plan libre'), they chose a rather static interpenetration based on hierarchy. Palladio could, for example, demarcate the principal room of a house by an intermediary zone, defined by the walls, four columns and their lintels, but the space would remain that of *one* room. More than any other period Baroque 'mocked' constructional limitations in order to attain its aesthetic and spiritual ends. It led to the first 'spatial liberation'. It is a freedom from rules and conventions from the static state of space, elementary geometry and even from opposition between interior and exterior. Its means are the continual and complex play between convexity and concavity, continuity and break which structure the space beyond its proper limits (Figures 190 and 191). To achieve this effect the architects

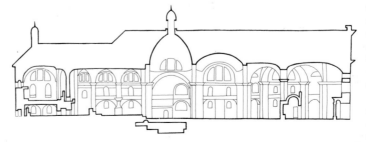

Figures 190 and 191 Liberation from constructional constraints by the Baroque which dissociates the design of the structure and envelope from that of the inner shell for a space of fantasy which has the characteristics of theatrical decor; the abbey church of Einsiedeln.

of the Baroque de-composed walls and roofs. These elements are no longer considered as 'solids' with two faces. Conceptually, and sometimes even constructionally, there are two shells – one internal and one external – each one able to respond to particular formal requirements. It is only at the openings that the two shells are stitched together again by the treatment of the window recesses, without any apparent incoherence.

Baroque space has particularly distinguished itself because 'it has been able to show, in numerous ways, the interdependence of cells or niches at the front, at the back and on the sides without each one of them appearing as a fragment, but by giving them a perfect unity'.[90]

The technical means, developed towards the end of the nineteenth century, contributed towards the second 'spatial liberation'. Steel and reinforced concrete have made possible the mutation towards a space more closely fitted to the characteristics of man's activity and will.

It is in the mastery of this new freedom that we find the great spatial and architectural inventions of the twentieth century. The almost limitless possibilities have marked the rise of a new poetry. Frank Lloyd Wright, with his destruction of the box by the dissolution of the corner in order to anchor his buildings in the near and distant landscape, the young Mies van der Rohe and the Dutch de Stijl movement, obsessed with independent planes defining a portion of space as a sort of special event in infinite space, Le Corbusier, with his painter's vision, searching for compression, superimposition and the phenomenal transparency of space[91] – all figure amongst the inventor-pioneers of dynamic and asymmetrical architectural space in the twentieth century (Figure 192).

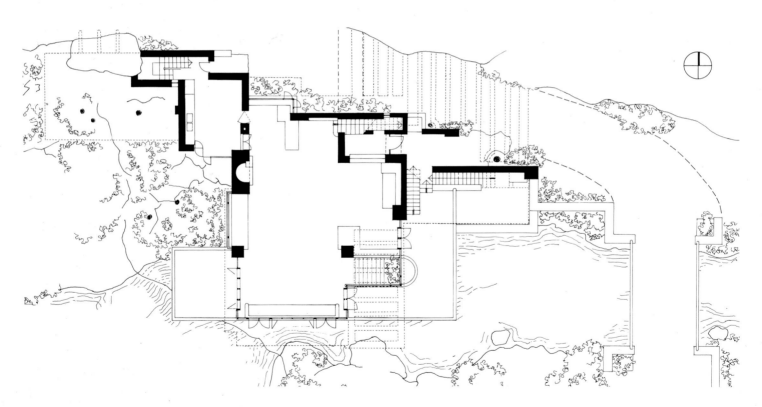

Figure 192 The 'destruction' of the box: Kaufmann house, Falling Water, Frank Lloyd Wright, 1936.

112

6.6 Geometry of plans, sections and spaces

The demands of rationality, compactness of the grouping of spaces, and structural regularity make geometry a prime necessity to discipline architectural design. We shall examine the role of geometry from two points of view:

- *The spatial characteristics of certain elementary geometric figures*: square, cube, circle, octagon, cylinder, sphere, triangle, prism, pyramid.
- *The assembly of rooms*: the principal forms of organization for grouping series of spaces, ensuring their accessibility and fitting them to a load-bearing structure.

Once the lines of force of each geometric figure have been determined, the architect immediately considers means which could be used to exploit its intrinsic geometric characteristics in order to adapt it better to the circumstances of a specific site and brief. The 'transformation' of the square or circle is only possible after understanding the characteristics of the elementary figure.

Spatial characteristics of elementary geometric figures

The square contains hidden fields of radiance: they stem from its corners, periphery, diagonals, medians and centre. This recognition allows us to know where to intervene in order to reinforce or alter its intrinsic characteristics (Figure 193).

The fields of radiance in these two examples of the open square show a very different interpretation of the basic figure (Figures 194 and 195). In the case in which the corners are

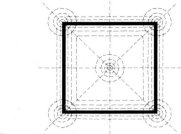

Figure 193

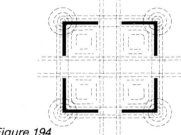

Figure 194

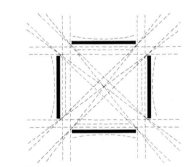

Figure 195

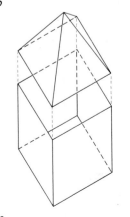

Figure 196

explicit, there is an implosion of the space. The implicit subspaces are, in their turn, squares which reinforce the primary form by their similarity. Where the corners are implicit, there is an extension towards the exterior. The primary form is less determinant. These complementary examples underline two themes of centrality by their centripetal or centrifugal character. We discover that the example with the openings in the middle of the walls accentuates centrality, compared with the simple closed square.

The vertical extensions of the square are the cube, the tetrahedron or the prism. The principles evoked in two dimensions are equally applicable to the third dimension (Figure 196). But perception is not objective, and the perfect cube will tend not to be equivalent in all three directions. In spite of that it is often preferable to respect the given geometric rules rather than to carry out uncertain optical corrections.

The building on a square plan has often fascinated the architect by its great compactness; with its four orientations at right-angles, it

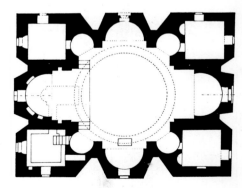

Figure 197 *Nearly square centralized plan; Armenian church of Saint Ripsime, Vagarshapat (Echmiadzin) 618–630 (drawn by J. Strzygowski, 1903).*

113

adopts a universal dimension (Figure 197). The building is never square because its functions demand it; it is square in spite of them, whilst accommodating them often with elegance. That is a *rationalist* approach as opposed to more pragmatic attitudes in architecture.

Transformation of the square: real situations rarely justify an interpretation and a reinforcement of the square in the sense of its own specific constituents. We then have the possibility of transforming it by introducing elements which give it an orientation: for example by a series of parallel walls which impose a hierarchy on the various directions or – in the case of the first floor of this lakeside house – by the clustering of the rooms and the 'erosion' of the original form by the placing of the openings and enclosing elements. In both cases – even more so in the first than the second – the centre loses its importance (Figures 198 and 199).

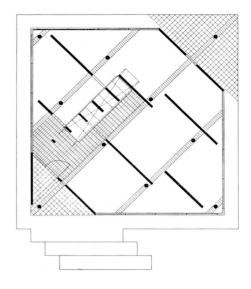

Figure 199 *Transformation of the square form with its synthetics to system arranged in a hierarchy according to the site and the brief: on one side the sun and the lake stretching into the distance and on the oppposite, north side the road and the mountain with its vineyards which, in their turn, face the lake. Pierre von Meiss, house on the shore of Lake Geneva, first floor, 1977–9.*

Figure 198 *Transformation of the square by a series of parallel walls (student exercise).*

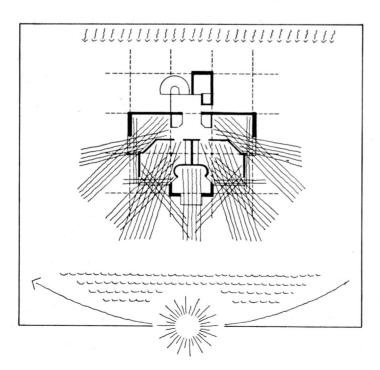

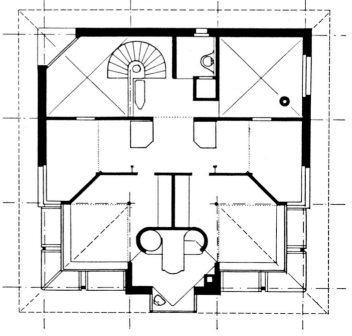

114

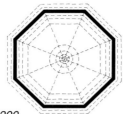

Figure 200

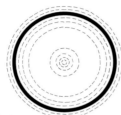

Figure 201

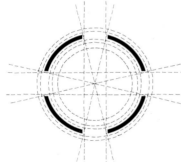

Figure 202

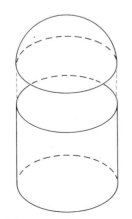

Figure 203

The octagon and even more *the circle* no longer have four precise corners balancing the centre. Only the centre and circumference remain; centre and periphery are the complementary opposites (Figures 200 and 201).

When one makes symmetrical openings in the circle, as we have done with the square, one does not, however, obtain an implosion. The subspaces do not form new figures similar to the original figure. They are sectors of a disc whose geometric identity and legibility are compromised (Figure 202).

The three-dimensional extension of the circle is found in the cylinder and the sphere, or more often the hemisphere or dome, which accentuates the centrality of the internal space and the object character if seen from the exterior (Figure 203). The universal character of these volumes hardly needs to be emphasized, and one wonders whether such spatial layouts should not be reserved for exceptional buildings whose public significance really deserves it. The project for the cenotaph of Newton by Boullée, a monument dedicated to the glory and universality of science, perfectly illustrates this correspondence between the intrinsic qualities of the form and the meaning that is conferred on it (Figure 204).

Transformation of the circle. The circle requires 'vulgarizing' if it is to abandon its monumental destiny in order to become an everyday space, feasible for living in. The means at our disposal are the same as the square: parallel walls, trans-

Figure 204 The sphere, reproduction of the universe; plan for the cenotaph of Newton by E. L. Boullée, 1784.

fer of the hierarchy towards other points than the centre, creation of fragments, etc. (Figures 205 and 206).

Concentration and centrality are common to the circle and to the square, which suggests their combination. Between the two is the octagon as an effective means of transition. It has been used as an interface in many sacred buildings (Figure 207).

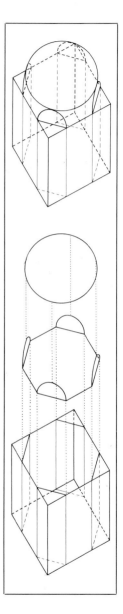

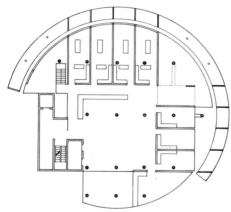

Figure 205 Transformation of the circle by a series of parallel or perpendicular walls, and annihilation, even substitution of the centre; Le Corbusier, project for the Chancellery of the French Embassy in Brasilia, 1964–65.

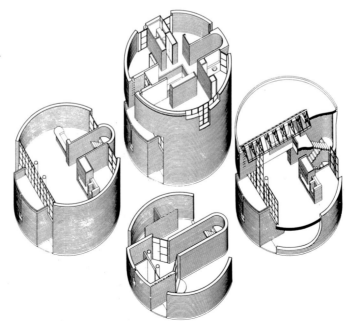

Figure 206 Transformation of the circle by producing front, back and sides; 'Casa Rotonda', Stabio, Mario Botta, 1980.

Figure 207 The octagon as an interface between the square and the circle; Hosios Loukas, Greece.

The equilateral triangle has only a hidden centre, because it lacks diagonals and the bisectors have no precise reference to the middle of the opposite sides. In this sense the triangle is less centralizing than the octagon or the square, whilst at the same time defining an extremely closed and even 'claustrophobic' space because of its acute angles (Figure 208).

If only the angles remain and if the middles of the walls open up, the centre is re-established by the intersection of the oppositions between angle and opening (Figure 209).

If the angles are missing and if only the middle of the sides is maintained, the notion of triangle almost disappears; it appears to be an implied hexagon. By angling the edges of the walls differently, one can reinforce the suggestion either of the hexagon or of the triangle (Figure 210).

The spatial corollary of the equilateral triangle is the prism and the pyramid (Figure 211). Their application to architecture is unusual because the handling of interior spaces with acute angles is not an easy matter. The subdivision of the equilateral triangle, by a grid at 60 degrees, on the other hand, makes a hexagonal grid appear, which presents the advantage of obtuse angles which are easier to occupy. The hexagonal grid nevertheless has the disadvantage of staggering edges.

A discussion on elementary volumes brings out the importance of relationships between *centre and periphery* and, in the case of transformations, between front, back and sides. These fundamental themes of architecture also occur in more complex geometries.

In churches with a central plan, the centre is an imaginary point in the space; everything turns towards it; walls, recesses, subspaces and ceiling. On the other hand, Frank Lloyd Wright often occupies the centre of his houses with the solid mass of the hearth: fireplace and kitchen; the centre becomes a solid nucleus. Space is organized from this starting point and progresses towards the exterior, but it cannot easily be contained within an elementary figure.

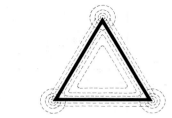

Figure 208

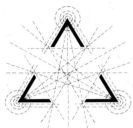

Figure 209

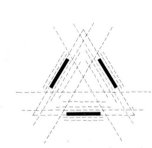

Figure 210

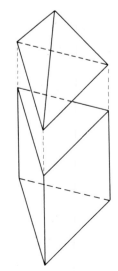

Figure 211

Assembly of rooms

Buildings generally combine many rooms whilst at the same time constituting a relatively simple and compact overall form. The search for regularity of the structure and of the system of distribution to the rooms is characteristic of all rational architectural organization. We shall restrict ourselves to the consideration of a few basic principles.

Linear organization is perhaps the most frequently used and most elementary form of grouping of spaces; it implies a system of linear distribution: the street, the corridor (Figure 212).

For obvious reasons of economy, the structure of load-bearing walls in a linear organization is frequently perpendicular to the linear extension which in its turn influences the position of the divisions, the nature of the openings and the possibilities for alteration and extension. These load-bearing walls may correspond to the separations between rooms, which impose a disciplined regularity of spaces whilst offering greater design freedom in the façade. When, conversely, the façade and walls of the corridor are load-bearing, there is greater flexibility in the subdivision of spaces and, if need be, to their alteration.

A linear organization ought to have a beginning and an end, and it is up to us to give form and direction to these particular places, in the same way that the middle of a centralized organization of space can hardly be considered like any other location in that space.

Centralized organization introduces a maximum of compactness and implies a hierarchy. Centrality dominates the secondary spaces which surround it (Figure 213). Remarkable designs have used smaller spaces on the periphery to contain the major central space. A hierarchy is thus established; the interior commands its subsidiaries and vice versa as in Louis Kahn's Unitarian church at Rochester.

The circle, the cupola and the square with an orthogonal bi-directionality of the structure match best the intrinsic characteristics of a centralized organization.

Radial organization, or a fan, is a form of combination between centrality and linearity, in the sense in which several series of spaces in a line radiate from a centre or a spine. The latter assumes an exceptional place in the hierarchy. It becomes to some extent 'the origin' of the whole (Figure 214).

It is a form of organization which is not very common and fairly difficult to deal with, particularly because of its inherent problems of

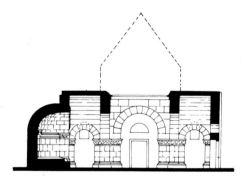

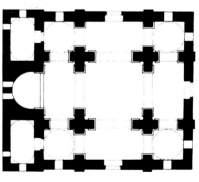

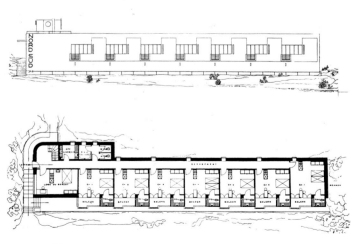

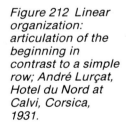

Figure 212 Linear organization: articulation of the beginning in contrast to a simple row; André Lurçat, Hotel du Nord at Calvi, Corsica, 1931.

Figure 213 Centralized organization: maximum compactness in which everything contributes to the creation of the major central place; Resapa, Syria (drawing by Cyril Mango).

orientation and the often 'residual' spaces which it leaves between wings. One orientates oneself in relation to the centre, but it is almost impossible to know in which wing one is. On most sites the implicit extension of radiating branches creates problems of transition to the surrounding morphology. Few briefs can sustain such an unequivocal hierarchy; large hierarchical and cellular organizations, living in isolation are arranged on this principle: prisons, hospitals, administrative headquarters, student hostels, etc.

When the radial organization is compact and, instead of radiating corridors serving cells, there is no more than a grouping of adjacent spaces, we find a particular form of organization which is still centralized. When this results in mere segments of a circle, the resulting individual rooms are not always satisfactory. Frank Lloyd Wright and Alvar Aalto, on the other hand, manipulate brief and site with genius; a diagram with little potential is turned into an end result with superb qualities.

Organization in the form of a

crown. The house with a peristyle is a principle of linear organization with neither beginning nor end. Its economy lies in obtaining an additional space at little expense. The 'gift' of this geometry is the central courtyard (Figure 215). When the corridors of this type of organization remain unilateral in order to become colonnades enclosing the courtyard, orientation is facilitated. Moreover, the entrance of the crown must be differentiated if one wants to avoid the infinity of this linearity. A rectangular courtyard would be a better guide than a square courtyard.

Organization on a grid plan assembles elements or groups of elements in a criss-cross of routes (orthogonal for example) (Figure 216).

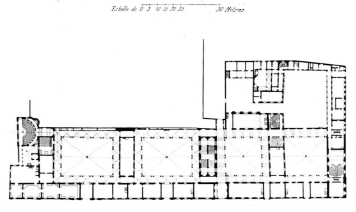

Echelle de 0 5 10 15 20 25   30 Mètres.

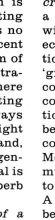

Figure 214 Radial organization: excessively hierarchical and restricting, because linear structures emanate from a single centre; former Mazas prison, Paris, nineteenth century.

Figure 215 Organization in the form of a crown: since antiquity its prototype has been the courtyard house. University of Pavia, ground floor plan (as at 1825).

Figure 216 Organization on an orthogonal network, a priori non-hierarchical, accommodates a large number of elements in an orderly and comprehensible system; Candilis Josic Woods, Berlin University, 1963.

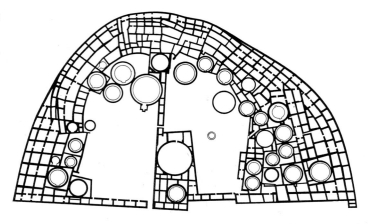

Figure 217 Beehive organization: 'organic' cluster by proximity of similar elements. Pueblo Arroyo (from a drawing by A. van Eyck, in Forum 3, 1962).

This principle can be applied particularly to large-scale groupings. The grid is not suited to assembling individual rooms, the internal organization and purpose of which remain open to other spatial arrangements already discussed. It is not surprising that the founders of colonial towns, from Miletus to Turin and Manhattan, chose this layout, since a clear order had to be rapidly established preceding the particular requirements of its future occupation. A hierarchy is introduced into the homogeneity of the grid, either by a change in dimension (the agora at Priene in antiquity, or certain widenings of the streets in Turin), by an oblique (Broadway in Manhattan), or by a change in orientation of the grid (Athens). When the grid is rectangular rather than square, it allows a directional differentiation which helps our sense of direction.

Cluster (Figure 217) assembles elements by proximity. It is topological, that is to say independent of form and dimension. It suggests an additive growth by historical 'accident', rather than the intentional design of a human settlement. Durand, for example, does not give it a mention, as it stems from the 'unplanned'. In the sixties and seventies this form of organization prevailed in the creation of numerous large residential schemes. Architects intended to break with the 'machine à habiter', 'monotony', 'repetition resulting from technology', 'large scale' ... in order to create 'lively' spaces and volumes. Lively? ... One thought it possible to produce artificially the picturesqueness of history without history. History does not lend itself to approximate simulation, unless one resorts to methods of romantic illusion. Under different circumstances, some pre-industrial societies had adopted this form of clustering for their community. For Indians living in pueblos this form of habitat corresponds to their vision of the world.

The 'plan libre' is not anarchy or a negation of order. This twentieth-century technique of spatial composition exploits the interpenetrations between spaces rather than the juxtaposition or the alignment and piling up of cells. This concept reaches beyond what was imaginable at the beginning of the nineteenth century when constructional constraints and organization of the plan rarely betrayed their partnership. Whilst Hennebique was the first to offer reinforced concrete to conventional spaces, Le Corbusier is one of its most daring exponents. Questioning traditional space he develops a new concept in plan and section by dissociating structure and envelope from spatial organization (Figure 218). The increased complexity of this spatial language and the relationships between elements would be disorienting, if it were not compensated for by the mastery of a principle of hierarchy in spatial continuity. Before Le Corbusier, and without reinforced concrete, Frank Lloyd Wright was already experimenting with this kind of space which would no longer be the slave of the enclosing load-bearing structure.

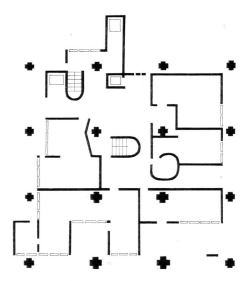

Figure 218 The 'plan libre'; liberated from constructional constraints, rooms are assembled obeying functional needs and formal concepts of the designer. Le Corbusier, Governor's Palace, plan of level 3, Chandigarh, 1953.

6.7 Light and shade

'The sunlight did not know what it was before it hit a wall'
Louis Kahn

Light comes to us from things

Architectural space exists by the illumination of objects and enclosing surfaces, though echo, tactile qualities and smell help as well. Arnheim attributes to lit objects the value of light *sources:*

Things are less bright than the sun and the sky, but not different in principle. They are weaker luminaries. Light ... is an inherent virtue of the sky, the earth and the objects that populate them and their brightnes is periodically hidden or extinguished by darkness. To claim that these are children's and primitives' misconceptions eradicated by modern science, would be to close our eyes to universal visual experiences which are reflected in artistic presentation.[92]

Following this line of thought, architectural design can be considered as *the art of placing and controlling light sources in space.* Our usual instruments, the plan, section and elevation, do not completely take account of this aspect; even the scale model is disappointing. At the time a plan is drawn up, light is often one of the least controlled phenomena and, in consequence, one of the least taught subjects. It is only thanks to long experience and careful observation of real situations that we manage to build up our 'catalogue' of references enabling us to proceed by analogies.

Quantity and quality

The level of illumination can be sufficient or insufficient for certain activities such as walking around, reading, drawing, etc. The comfort thresholds are relatively well known, but the scope of adaptation of the eye is considerable, and context plays an important role beyond these thresholds. Brightness is, in fact, very relative; it depends on the distribution of the light, on the process of visual adaptation, and on the quantity of light reflected by objects and surfaces.

Perception of a space remains relatively constant, even if the level of illumination increases objectively tenfold or more. This is true beyond the capabilities of ocular adaptation. Within certain limits a constant effect is maintained; the space will be lighter or darker, but not fundamentally different.

Perception of the same space will change, on the other hand, when one changes the brightness or illumination of *some* of the objects or elements which define it, whilst keeping the others at the same level. In everyday speech we talk about a 'change of atmosphere' which denotes a qualitative change in which the *quantity* of light is of only secondary importance. Thus a room lit by daylight from its windows is not the same space as when it is lit artificially at night; skylights which tone down contrasts, or side lighting which accentuates them, give quite different perceptions of the same geometric space; a black ceiling will, for example, appear slightly higher than a white ceiling.

When we move from one room to another the settings which follow each other can present different atmospheres in terms of their light-ing, more or less contrasting; perception of them is relative. Alberti says: '... ivory and silver are white, but placed next to swan's down they seem pale ... everything is perceived by comparison.[93] The architect conceives a sequence of spaces not only as a succession of spatial events, but also in terms of comparison of different ambiences of light. The effects of back lighting are uncomfortable and violent contrasts often unpleasant. To move from full sunlight into the semi-darkness of a Romanesque church induces a kind of shock, which emphasizes the opposition between sacred and profane. When there is a porch and a narthex, these form an intermediary stage which makes the transition easier and more solemn. Once we are inside, the brighter light of the central space or of the walls opposite the entrance is a reassuring welcome. 'Architecture is the skilful, correct and magnificent play of volumes in light; shadows and highlights reveal their forms ...' says Le Corbusier. Thanks to changing light, the petrified immobility of the building suddenly comes to life. The east, south, north and west-facing rooms, even if they are geometrically identical, appear quite different according to time of day and season.

Light and space

The terms which characterize openings, such as 'bay', glazed wall, 'hole' in the wall, 'slot', 'corner window', etc., are not of much use for the study of spatial ambience in terms of light. We shall tackle the question starting with four typical conditions of illumination – light-space, light as an object, light from a series of objects and light from surfaces –

whilst at the same time being aware that numerous combinations are possible. Since light comes to us from things, we shall not make the usual technical distinction between the actual light source (a lamp, a window) and light reflected by the illuminated object or surface, which, in turn, become weaker sources. This integration of the phenomena of source and reflector into one concept is essential for spatial composition by means of light.

Figure 219 Light-space.

Light-space is an imaginary space which is created when a portion of space is well lit while the rest is left in semi- or total darkness (Figures 219 and 220). The limits are imaginary but perfectly perceptible. If the observer is situated outside the lit area, he sees it as 'a transparent box within a large box'. The small illuminated box concentrates his attention. If he is within the small illuminated box, the space in the semi-darkness appears of indeterminate size to the point of ceasing to exist.

The light-space is very useful in architectural design. It makes it possible to *present scenes* as in the theatre, the circus, the museum, a shop window at night, in the open air, etc. It also enables the person who is in the illuminated area *to isolate himself and concentrate better,*

just as when, with our individual work- or reading-lamps, we are in a large office or at home and the rest of the space gradually vanishes.

Since the coming of electric light, such spaces can be created and transformed instantaneously and at little expense if compared with mechanical alterations of spatial lay-outs. In the daytime, a shaft of sunlight through an opening into a relatively dark room can have a similar effect, but now the 'little box' moves, following the sun's course. Its effect is more often a marvellous accident than a calculated intention.

Light as an object, the single window, the isolated stained glass window, an object or a person spotlit in a dark space, a candle in a room, establish a relationship of dependence between source and space sim-

Figure 220 Le Corbusier, chapel of the Convent of La Tourette (drawing by Larry Mitnick).

ilar to that of figure and ground. When looked at directly, the source fascinates and dazzles at the same time, on condition, however, that the size of this source is relatively small in relation to the spatial envelope (Figures 221–223). When one turns one's back on the source, spatial perception is completely altered, because the walls, the floor and the ceiling in turn become weak light sources whose surface is immense and enveloping.

Figure 221 The light-object.

In terms of design, it can happen that we try to work with a unique, concentrated source for practical or symbolic reasons, at the same time wishing, for one reason or another, to avoid this alternation of glare and uniform lighting. In this case the source must be placed well above eye level (e.g. the Pantheon) or even concealed (indirect side lighting). It is not by chance that glare is used for intimidation and torture. Each architectural project must be re-examined from this point of view before building, in order to avoid this kind of aggression. Too often glare makes the most important and highly valued things disappear.

Light from a series of objects, series of windows, spotlights, candles, tends to establish balance and a possibility of inversion between the figure character of luminous objects and the background character of the spatial envelope which they illuminate.

A regular series of windows, or wall lights, or even a strip window, make an active contribution to the *delineation of spatial limits*. A larger or smaller window on the axis, or a series of lights suspended on the centre line of the room, help to clarify the spatial geometry. A freer arrangement of the light sources requires understanding of the principles of balance (Figures 224 and 225).

Figure 224 Light – series of objects.

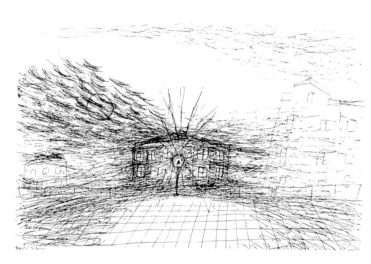

Figure 222 Paul Klee, Moon and Lantern, 1911.

Figures 223 and 225 Le Corbusier, chapel of the Convent of La Tourette.

Figure 226 Surfaces which give light.

Light from surfaces; the walls ceilings and floors may be lit by invisible slots. Spatial limits thus become light sources with a noticeable gradation from light to darkness (Figures 226–228).

One does not observe the same phenomenon with the surface of the illuminated ceiling in a department store or an office, because the absence of gradation eliminates the quality of throwing figures into relief. The dominant presence of the ceiling, due to its glare and to the absence of contrast, is tiring. Lighting engineers resort to additional light sources to restore necessary contrast. It is only during recent years that a technique has been found to 'put these ceilings back in their place', thanks to ceiling lighting with mirrored reflectors.

The corollary of the luminous ceiling is, in daytime, the skylight which, if one looks carefully, is practically never used for places where people stay or work for a long time, with the exception of factories where functional requirements make other solutions difficult.

The large glazed wall, in turn plays down contrast but, by being vertical, it does not do away with it altogether. Its role as a spatial extension very often takes precedence over its purpose for illumination. According to its size and orientation, it can create problems by an excess of light and heat.

These brief considerations on light and space are both important and incomplete. Sometimes it is possible to break these elementary rules in order to obtain the most appropriate atmosphere for the purpose of the building. In a place of worship, lighting from behind the altar can invite meditation (Figure 229). What is important is that the study of light be considered as an essential part of the different stages of the design and its execution. Large-scale models are very useful. Photographs are deceptive because the sensitivity of film is not comparable to our subjective perception.

Figure 227 Le Corbusier, chapel of the Convent of La Tourette (drawing by Larry Mitnick).

Figure 228 Le Corbusier, Convent of La Tourette.

Figure 229 The walls become light! – curtain wall in alabaster defining a sacred place, Switzerland, Franz Fueg, 1964–66.

Shadow

Shadow is light's counterpart. It is the gradation between lit surfaces and surfaces in shadow which supplies information about the three-dimensional form of a body. When the contrast is strong, due to light coming from only one direction, information about the object is reduced (Figure 230). If that is not always desirable, as in the case of the Moore sculpture illustrated here, we must emphasize, none the less, that there are particular situations, such as the display of a bas-relief, where it is precisely what is sought; in the same way that a façade assumes an exceptional intensity during those moments that the sun strikes it from the side.

If the contrast is reduced, or even balanced by lighting from several sources, the three-dimensionality is increased (Figure 231).

If the lighting is uniform, coming from all sides, the object becomes flatter (Figure 232). Each context and object can be lit in such a way as to enhance its three-dimensionality and establish a balance between contrast and homogeneity. In situations in which the exhibited object is the *raison d'être* of the building as, for example, in a sculpture museum, the study of lighting from several sources is essential; the presence of a principal lateral source is desirable. It will be counterbalanced by secondary lighting. Carlo Scarpa's museum of Canova plastercasts at Possagno (1957) is a good example.

Skylights produce a particular kind of natural lighting which has been frequently used by architects ever since technical advances made them possible. Some ascribe intrinsic qualities to them, capable of 'reinforcing' somehow the architectural value. But it must be recognized that skylights are often poorly used, badly positioned and of the wrong size, and thus do no more than reduce contrast and increase the quantity of light and heat.

A skylight placed in the middle of a low room cannot, in any way, despite appearances, resemble the sun, because its proximity prevents it being considered as a source producing parallel rays. The atmosphere of the room tends to become 'pale', dusty, sometimes even sad or, more rarely, solemn. When this same opening has a direct relationship to the structure or to a wall, and *the light can descend by means of a vertical receptor*, a direct link is re-established with the space, and contrasts are re-introduced (Figure 233).

We have spoken up till now about the object's own shadow. *The cast shadow* is, from the subjective point of view of perception, 'an emanation from the object' rather than of light.[95] The object casts darkness, reproducing or deforming, depending on the angle of incidence and the

Figures 230–232 Henry Moore, Piece–Interlocking, 1963/1964.

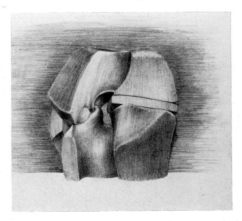

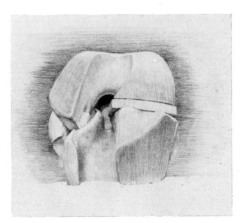

Figure 230 Parallel and directed light: reduced information on the three-dimensional form of the object.

Figure 231 Light coming from several sources and reflections; the play of shadows increases the three-dimensionality of the object.

Figure 232 Uniform light: the absence of shadows weakens the three-dimensionality of the object.

Figure 233 Light from a skylight strikes a vertical receptor; Herman Hertzberger, Montessori school, Delft.

Figure 234 When the light is too overpowering, shadow provides a respite (Morocco, 1960).

features of its shape on other surfaces and objects.

Shadow, like light, used consciously as a line, can be used to delineate, even to emphasize the forms and edges of bodies and space. The shadow cast by the outline of a cornice emphasizes the upper termination of a façade. Window frames produce an elegant line when positioned flush with the façade whereas the shadow line from a deep recess emphasizes the apparent weight and thickness of the structure. The recessed joint between a timber frame and the wall defines the articulation.

In conclusion, let us remember that, on a practical rather than aesthetic level, light and shade regulate the use of a space more often than do its size and form. The presence or absence of contrast, as well as the definition of space by the quantity and quality of illumination of the space, appreciably influence its potential and the wellbeing of its occupants (Figure 234).

6.8 Floor, wall and ceiling

At first sight one could be tempted to describe spatial limits simply in geometric terms. Imagining an empty room enclosed by planes of homogeneous colour and texture, one would, on the other hand, easily see that these planes do not have the same value. In architecture there are basic differences between *the floor, the walls and the ceiling*. These are spatial locations within the space. Humans on the Earth orient themselves first of all in relation to gravity. Vertical and horizontal do not, therefore, have the same force. 'To go up', 'to be at the top', 'to look down', 'to go down into a crypt', are more significant movements than turning and looking to the left or to the right, moving forwards or backwards.

The floor has first of all a pragmatic meaning, much more than the walls and especially the ceiling. One must be able to move around on it and place objects on it. Gravity confers on it a role linked to the idea of support of life and objects. Variations in texture can give it a specific importance but, as a general rule, it must remain horizontal in order to guarantee versatility and the possibility of movement which we expect from most architectural spaces. In this context differences of level and staircases are very important. The ground is therefore less manipulable than the walls and the ceiling - because of this fact it has a stabilizing character, unifying different parts of space.

We walk on it; Western man hardly ever uses it for sitting or lying on, touching with his hands or the rest of his body. It could be that his preference for carpets betrays an 'attempt at reconciliation', the re-

Figures 235 and 236 The pragmatic floor: depository, place of rest and exchange (Morocco 1960 and Japan 1983).

Figure 237 The floor is not always pragmatic. On your path you come across perhaps a gravestone carefully carved to the memory of the dead. You walk on it with discretion, perhaps even with respect, you enter into tactile contact with eternity. This ground is therefore no longer a simple horizontal plane for feet and posterior, it becomes a symbolic place.

establishment of an essential relationship between the body and the built floor (Figures 235–237). We should remember that there are two sorts of artificial ground: the covering of the earth - our paving stones and tombstones - and the floor, the ground of an upper storey, lighter and more artificial. The materials used and their design are a response to location and means of support.

Figure 239 The wall serves as a poster: by modulation it specifies space, here it defines the space of the door; Monemvassia, Byzantine-Venetian church.

Figure 238 Walls separate and protect to enable occupation. They guide our movements and where they open up they link. When these openings are large and repeated, they amplify the space. Barcelona Maritime Museum, created within the Renaissance dockyards.

The walls and the vertical structure are there to carry the ceiling and roof, guide our movements, enclose our activities, our objects and tools, accommodate us and lead us from one place to another (Figures 238 and 239). Walls separate and structure architectural space; they demarcate, protect and by this fact enable us to inhabit. *To dwell*, according to Martin Heidegger, ... means to be at peace, to be brought to peace, to remain in peace. The word for peace, *Friede*, means the free, *das Frye*, and *fry* means: preserved from harm and danger, preserved from something, safeguarded.'[96] One rarely touches walls, just as when one walks round a table for example, an 'object-peripheral' gap remains. The walls are 'opposite' our eyes. Their modulation, their texture and their ability to accept the display of messages, play a basic role in determining the character and the atmosphere of a place. Between walls and ceiling are 'high walls' which accept a sublime and untouchable role (Figure 240). According to their design, they may belong more to the wall or more to the ceiling.

Figure 240 A wall inclines slightly towards the interior to acquire ingeniously the characteristics of the ceiling: images out of reach, Alvar Aalto, Finnish pavilion at the New York World's Fair, 1939.

The ceiling is the floor's counterpart. Together with the roof it is pragmatic, due to the role of giving shelter and to the necessities of construction (Figure 241). But the ceiling may accept more metaphysical meanings. Being far removed and most often out of reach, it is the favourite place for stuccos, frescos, mosaics - a means of expression of dreams, ideals, the sacred (Figure 242). Graffiti - which are a spontaneous means of expression - are rarely found on ceilings. Amongst the pioneer architects of the twentieth century, there are very few who have bestowed upon the ceiling the sublime role of which it is potentially capable. When it is treated with care it is usually through the aesthetic effect of a beautiful structure: the exposed frame. That is a perfectly justified solution for Toni Garnier's abattoirs, in which there was no other theme to symbolize than the wonder of a great meat machine. Other places suggest a more subtle role for the ceiling. Rare are those who, like Alvar Aalto, have always subscribed to the importance of a 'ceiling design': Aalto's ceilings give meaning to space.

Figure 241 The aesthetics of ceiling structure: the great builders of covered markets and railways stations, Garnier, Nervi, Waschsmann, Piano, have opted for a ceiling 'decorated' with the filigree of the structure.

Figure 242 The ceiling, a repository for our legends: Andrea Palladio, Villa Maser, Bacchus room, frescoes by Paolo Veronese.

Second Interlude
FROM SPACE TO PLACE

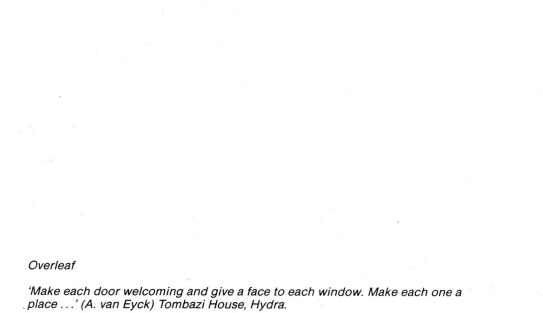

Overleaf

'Make each door welcoming and give a face to each window. Make each one a place . . .' (A. van Eyck) Tombazi House, Hydra.

The void exists as long as you don't throw yourself into it.

O. Elytis[97]

... Space seized by imagination cannot remain indifferent space to the measuring and thought of the surveyor. It is to be experienced. And it is to be experienced, not in its positiveness, but with all the bias of imagination ...

G. Bachelard[98]

... Whatever space and time mean, place and occasion mean more ... Space has no room, time not a moment for man ... Make of each door a welcoming and give a face to each window. Make of each a place, a bunch of places of each house and each city ...

A. van Eyck[99]

We start to go beyond the essentially visual approach to architecture in order to probe into existential concepts. To be close or far away, to enter or leave, to be in front or behind, inside or outside, to feel safe or not, to be together or alone, near water or fire, in the library or at the market, no longer refers just to the structure of forms. We are moving away from questions of proportions and balance, of form and abstract painting, certain of the principles of which have served us well thus far. These principles are not sufficient for the experience of architecture, which is a reflection of the joys and toils of humanity. Architecture makes visible the inhabited world.

Where place is concerned, space and time assume a precise, unique value; they cease to be a mathematical abstraction or a subject of aesthetics; they acquire an identity and become a reference for our existence: sacred space and secular space, personal space and collective space,

nature and town, street and house, ruin and rebuilding.

The building protected by its enclosure, its walls, its roofs, gathers within itself a specific world of the functional and the emotional, of work and leisure, of traces of past and present events.

Space changes with the movement of the sun, place changes with the movement of human beings. The harbour, the public square and the market, for example, are places for the exchange of ideas and goods, places for meeting familiar and unknown faces, places which sleep and wake with the movement of the hours and days of the week.

Recesses, loggias, alcoves and other subspaces opening onto a major space make temporary and spatial isolation possible whilst still belonging to a wider collectivity. A place has its roots and its his-

Figure 243 'Space, Raum, means a place cleared or freed for settlement and lodging. A space is something that has been made room for, something that is cleared and free, namely within a boundary, Greek peras. A boundary is not that at which something stops but, as the Greeks recognized, the boundary is that from which something begins its presencing.' (Heidegger)[96]. Our Lady of Tinos, Greece.

135

tory; it is anchored in time and in a precise spot on the earth. A place has its 'dome', its sky and perhaps even its 'star'. By building we fix special relationships between earth, sky and time.

As a technique at our service, architecture must satisfy our needs; it has to be useful and economical. As art, it assumes, sometimes successfully, sometimes arrogantly, the right to neglect the useful and practical in the name of philosophical principles beyond the everyday and the ordinary. To create a place is nevertheless to observe and accept the ordinary as a major poetic source.

The illustrations accompanied by captions, quotations from a text of the German philosopher Martin Heidegger[100], link architectural space to human activity, thought and history. In the immensity and confusion of the environment, certain portions of space assume the value of place. They are identifiable, can be pointed out by others, and suggest ways of behaviour. Some places are intended for our movements and exchanges, others encourage withdrawal and isolation. The place always suggests an action or a pause, even if only mental. Its forms are associated with events which it accommodates or which it has once accommodated, and with other similar places and events.

What was order and spatial interval is now charged with values. The principles discussed in previous

Figure 244 'That for which room is made is always granted and hence is joined, that is, gathered, by virtue of a location, that is, by such a thing as the bridge. Accordingly, spaces receive their being from locations and not from "space"' (Heidegger). Harbour at Hydra, Greece.

chapters do not, on the other hand, lose anything of their relevance. The means for building an architectural place are always physical, but they are not sufficient by themselves. We build urban fabrics, subject to asking ourselves about their purpose. Architectural form must therefore refer to 'the idea of place' and not only to aesthetic principles, utility, or geometric and constructional rules. More exactly, we try to unite them in order to sustain the idea of place. The importance of the mastery of aesthetics and construction is seen in what Alberti calls '*commodity*'. By this he means a way of treating forms and spaces which respect the objective purpose of a place and the subjective attribution of this place to the patron commissioning the work. Thus for Alberti a fortress must be severe and solid, a temple must possess such beauty that one could not but marvel at it and the location of the altar must be sombre....[101] These values can change in time, but at the moment of building we seek those which correspond to our own time.

When Kahn was working on the plan for a conference hall for Venice, he understood very clearly that he

Figure 245 In the spaces provided for by locations there is always space as interval, and in this interval in turn there is space as pure extension. Spatium *and* extensio *afford at any time the possibility of measuring things and what they make room for, according to distances, spans, and directions, and of computing these magnitudes. But the fact that they are* universally *applicable to everything that has extension can in no case make numerical magnitudes* the *ground of the nature of spaces and locations that are measurable with the aid of mathematics' (Heidegger). Lesbos, Greece.*

was going to make a place where people look at each other, and not a cinema.[102] For the Centre of British Art Studies he chose the qualities of 'collection space' to underline the intimacy between the book, the painting and the drawing. Our role is therefore to create opportunities so that these places become possible. It is not the architect who decides on the value of places, but *he can, by allusion based on observation, reflection and research, provide a framework* which has the best chances of accommodating man's specific situations. The spaces which he builds will offer a greater or lesser potential for stopping, passing through, being happy, meeting, being moved, stimulating associations of ideas, and even dreaming. Architecture supports man's actions without being coercive or, at the other extreme, neutral.

Some spaces have great difficulty in becoming places. Let us take the example of the 'neutral' spaces of large open-plan offices where the large, free area claims to allow each working unit to establish itself with maximum flexibility. In spite of the contribution of numerous specialists in the area of social sciences, it has turned out to be difficult to build a 'home' in the absence of a structuring order of stable architectural

Figure 246 'The location allows the simple onefold of earth and sky, of divinities and mortals, to enter into a site by arranging the site into spaces'. . . . 'Things like such locations shelter or house men's lives.' . . . 'The making of such things is building' . . . This is why building, by virtue of constructing locations, is a founding and joining of spaces' (Heidegger). Le Corbusier, Convent of La Tourette, Evreux, France.

cues. Herman Hertzberger created a real alternative in 1972 with the Central Beheer offices at Apeldoorn. He substituted a structured space for a vague space by arranging numerous implicit divisions suited to designating possible places for work and leisure. He created a spatial hierarchy, focal points, high and low spaces, balconies, which contribute to the distinction between one place and another. It is sufficient to talk to the users to understand how the identity of place and the identity of human beings have become interwoven in this place.

Hertzbergers' example shows that important questions must be asked about the purpose of the scheme and the opportunities which it offers for the creation of places. The production of buildings has never been as efficient, rapid and significant in quantity as during the last thirty years and, at the same time, it really seems as if we have lost control of our methods. Although our task is to design the context for everyday life, we have never been so incapable of creating places in the town or within the dwelling. Of course, there are exceptions; Alvar Aalto and, after him, van Eyck, Siza, Botta, Galfetti and others have known how to orientate methods of production in the right direction. But, too often, we destroy more places than we create, whether interiors or exteriors.

Contemporary society reacts in different ways to the economic and utilitarian forces which have brought more devastation to our towns than the bombers during the Second World War. As a result we have the nostalgics who try to fix, preserve and sometimes even reproduce the appearance of an architecture of the past, without the slightest confidence in the living forces of our time. But in the margins luckily exists also a movement of thought which is seeking to rediscover the importance of the site and its history, for the transformation and creation of new places.[103] The idea of place originates from *conventional* activities and behaviour linked to concepts of memorable spatial situations, light, form and texture. The new interest in that typology, which tries to link life to the fundamental and structural characteristics of a built fabric, implies research on the nature of these conventions.[104]

In order to become a convention, a place needs temporal *stability* and recognizable physical characteristics which suggest particular socioculture experiences.[105] It is in this way that we recognize links between form, place and history. Architectural space acquires its double role by its perennial nature: its role as witness of history and its role as opportunity for the future. As Aldo van Eyck puts it so well: *'The places one remembers and the places one anticipates become confused in the time lapse of the present. Memory and anticipation constitute in fact the real perspective of space and give depth to it,'* (A. van Eyck).

Figure 247 *'Man's relation to locations, and through locations to spaces, exists in his dwelling. Only if we are capable of dwelling, only then can we build'* (Heidegger). J. P. Oud, residential area, Rotterdam.

7

PLACE

Overleaf
Light-space appropriated
Cyclades
Photo Ino Ioannidou and Lenio Bartzioti, Athens.

7.1 The site

The discussion on site as place could be held in a phenomenological[106] or poetic[107] way, but we have chosen a more concrete approach because it is our transformation of the site which is embodied in architectural design.

The site as a place is always linked to human history. The site which we choose or which is assigned to us to erect a building is perhaps already *a place* in the country or in the town. This place will be destroyed, reinforced or transformed by our intervention. If the site is *between* places, without really being a place itself, it can become a place, at least for its future inhabitants. If it is intended to house an institution, its role as a place assumes a public dimension. Let us observe it carefully and study its history before designing; it is our duty and our opportunity, because, in its origin, its formal structure and its meanings, we find the most powerful stimulants and the most enriching material for design: geometric lines, remains, fragments of nature and of human efforts.

Teaching in schools of architecture in the four corners of the world, for thirty-odd years, has dedicated an important part of its curriculum to site observation and justification of the design on this basis. It is perhaps in this area that the schools have best assumed their critical role in relation to current practice which obeys more the laws of the real estate market, little suited to taking account of the specific character of a site. Besides these laws of the market, there are several technological factors which have contributed to the reconsideration of form and the meaning of the site.

Figure 248 Birth of a place; Dutch polder.

- The methods of transforming the topography have become monstrous. Huge movements of earth to erect the fortifications of a city in the past necessitated the solemn decision of the sovereign as well as considerable sacrifices by the people. Today any developer can erase the irregularities of a site in a few days and at little expense. We are thus present at the birth of the 'bulldozer landscape'. And why not? There are some examples, although too few, where these tools have really been used to build *a new site*, desired by or desirable for people (Figures 248 and 250). But more often it is a question of *disfigurement* which even erosion has difficulty in healing (Figure 249). Property lines and the internal rationale of the building process are very weak arguments for the radical transformation of a topograhy.

- The techniques of artificial control of the internal climate by the addition of energy, in the form of central heating or air-conditioning no longer restrict one to a careful choice of site and judicious orientation according to sun, wind and humidity. Nevertheless, it has only taken two oil crises and a nuclear accident for our way of thinking to be, if not shaken, at least alerted.

- Water, electricity, telephone, public and private transportation make distant sites accessible and easy to supply. The physical proximity of the city, its institutions and its

Figure 249 Scars inflicted by mechanical excavation: preparation for a suburban housing area in California.

Figure 250 Subtle terraces formed by the sweat of man; the Péloponèse.

places of work, is no longer a prerequisite for convenience and even less for survival. The disintegration of our towns is evidence of this. Means of transportation, especially the private car for which access must be guaranteed to every building for obvious reasons of comfort, have transformed the urban landscape. High speeds require alignments which are sometimes insensitive to local topography and history.

- The speed with which we are able to plan and construct new settlements ready for occupation leaves little time for planning and little room for those in times coming to seek out and adapt places which reflect daily reality. Recent suburban extensions are equal in population and area to entire towns of the past which took centuries to build. The builders of the old towns, by experiment and trial and error, had the opportunity to define gradually places of collective importance. Perhaps one day we shall have the opportunity to

give these suburban areas urban dignity by transforming them into what van Eyck would call 'a bunch of places'.

These are reasons which have made the site-related issues negligible since the nineteenth century, and it is not just property speculation as one might think. The latter has only seized opportunities that were presented to it by the market and production capacities.

Architecture of the past - whether vernacular or prestigious, the anonymous farm worker's house tucked away in a hollow sheltered from the winds, or the temple on a promontory - was hardly in any danger of neglecting or ill-treating the land on which it was erected (Figures 251 and 252). If Vitruvius spoke about 'correcting the nature of the site by art' he never implied its obliteration. If he speaks about laying out roads 'according to the most advantageous aspect of the weather', he means avoiding paths exposed to strong winds. What contemporary road layout plan would take this aspect into

consideration, even for a moment? Alberti and Palladio talk at length about the importance of the quality of water in choosing the site for a town or a house. We are no longer allowed to locate buildings indiscriminately: *alliance with the land is sought*. The same authors advise the choice of a site with easy access, a site that is not too damp, which will be identified by examining old stones and plants found on it, the choice of a well-ventilated situation, but protected from strong and damaging winds, of a stable climate, sunny in winter. These are qualities of hygiene and comfort for which modern technology provides efficient but not harmless substitutes.

The technical limitations of the past contributed to an appreciable coherence of the built environment and of its universal relationship with nature. That does not mean, of course, that we should abandon the

144

Figure 251 The site – sheltered place, Bernese farms.

Figure 252 The site – exalted place, Acropolis at Athens, sketch by Le Corbusier.

acquired comfort and economy which contemporary technology offers us. Without these constraints we must however, if we want to re-establish peace between what we build and Mother Earth, discover other means of making the town into 'a bunch of places'. The most promising ways are an understanding of the land as morphology and as history, leading to an architecture which, instead of 'camouflaging' or ignoring, exalts the fundamental characteristics of the site.

Kevin Lynch, known above all for his book *The Image of the City*,[108] previously wrote the book *On Site Planning*[109] whose didactic relevance to the subject has not been equalled since. He succeeds in making us aware, for example, of the topography of the natural site and in encouraging us to work out its transformation. However, he remains pragmatic and not very forward-looking in terms of the methods to be used.

Vittorio Gregotti completes this pragmatic awareness by research in other directions and by other methods.[110] These have since found an audience in schools and sometimes

in the practice of an elite; they could be developed more generally when our society, disenchanted by the setbacks of technology, attempts to reshape its territory.

In fact, if material constraints are no longer sufficient to result in a harmonious pattern of land use, the constraints will have to be of an *ethical* order. Gregotti recognizes the urgency of developing methods of reading not only site or town, but even the whole country and its natural and built form in order to guide its transformation. Some of the principles which he suggests, especially the definition of coherent groupings or 'fields', bring us back to Chapter 3 on 'Order and disorder'. The methods of reading range from the identification of the formal structural characteristics of groupings and subgroupings, to the analysis of the historic process which has influenced their creation, and from the inventory of materials to their characteristics of form, texture and colour.

In order to achieve this, '... we must change the tools at our disposal; maps, aerial photos and topographic models are only props; they

do not show values, nor the objective weight of the elements,[111] that is to say they tell nothing about the place and the effect it exerts on our life.

However, understanding of the site is not sufficient. The art of design requires the ability to interpret the meaning of the brief by linking it to the underlying opportunities of the site. Two projects recently carried out in the Lake Geneva area – one by Atelier Cube (Marc Collomb, Guy-Emanuel Collomb and Patrick Vogel), the other by Vincent Mangeat – show how strongly differing programmes and formal languages on relatively uninteresting sites have succeeded in defining and enhancing them as places (Figure 253 and 254).

THE PLACE

How to introduce a building to house archives on the vast site available? The answer does not flow from rules fixed in abstraction but from a succession of questions aimed at the site and the brief.

The triangular outline of the building arose from the growing series of units for storing documents. It echoes the shape of the site which is also defined by approximately three sides. The building's parts are differentiated, some are north-facing, completely closed off from daylight for better conservation of historical documents of the canton of Vaud: the others are south-facing, widely open to the sunlight for the archivist and visitors.

Owing to its off-centre position near one of the corners of the site, the building establishes close relationships between the archive depository and the existing industrial area, the workplaces and the forest along the watercourse to the south. A dialogue is set up between the constituent elements of the site. The rest of the meadow remains, keeping its identifiable character as an independent place, a visible reminder of the site before its construction.

Atelier Cube

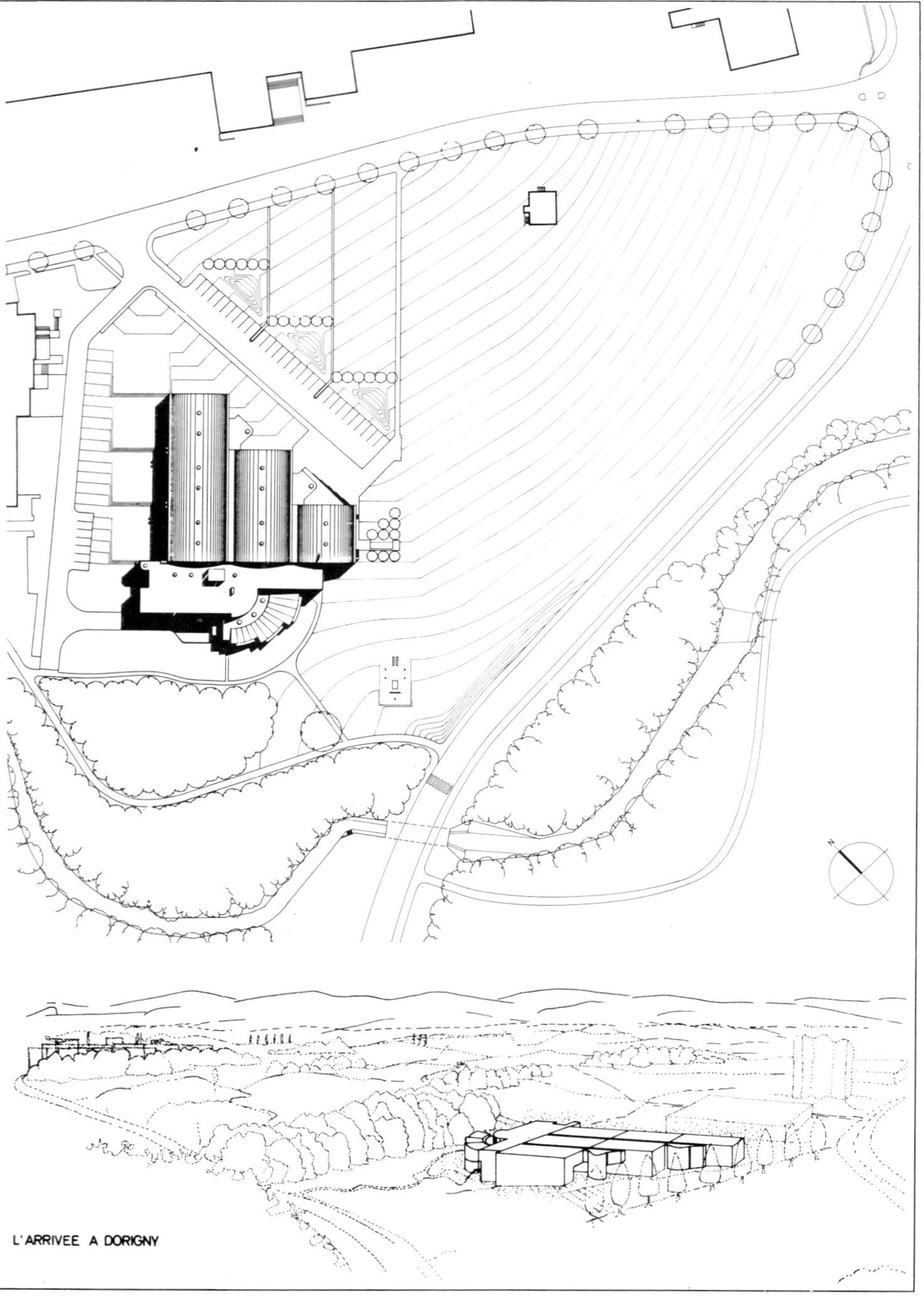

L'ARRIVEE A DORIGNY

Figure 253 Atelier Cube (Guy and Marc Collomb, Patrick Vogel). Archives of the canton of Vaud, Lausanne, 1980–84.

146

SYNTHESIS OF A PLACE AND A PROGRAMME

This project aims above all to demonstrate and embody the significant convergences inferred at the same time from topography and the shaping of the theme.

The topography is expressed here in a small, asymmetrical valley of varying width. It being impossible to cross downstream, it can be crossed and built on upstream; 'the bridge building'. The two basic ways of constructing such a place have been handed down to us by history and both reveal the inhospitable character of the place. The first thing was to build the bridge at the spot where the valley can be crossed.

The banks, the bridge and the valley draw from the brief characteristic features which make clear the expected convergence of the topography and the 'form of the theme'. All the more public parts are therefore in the bridge/building, the classrooms in the buildings on the banks and the courtyard in the valley bottom.

Vincent Mangeat

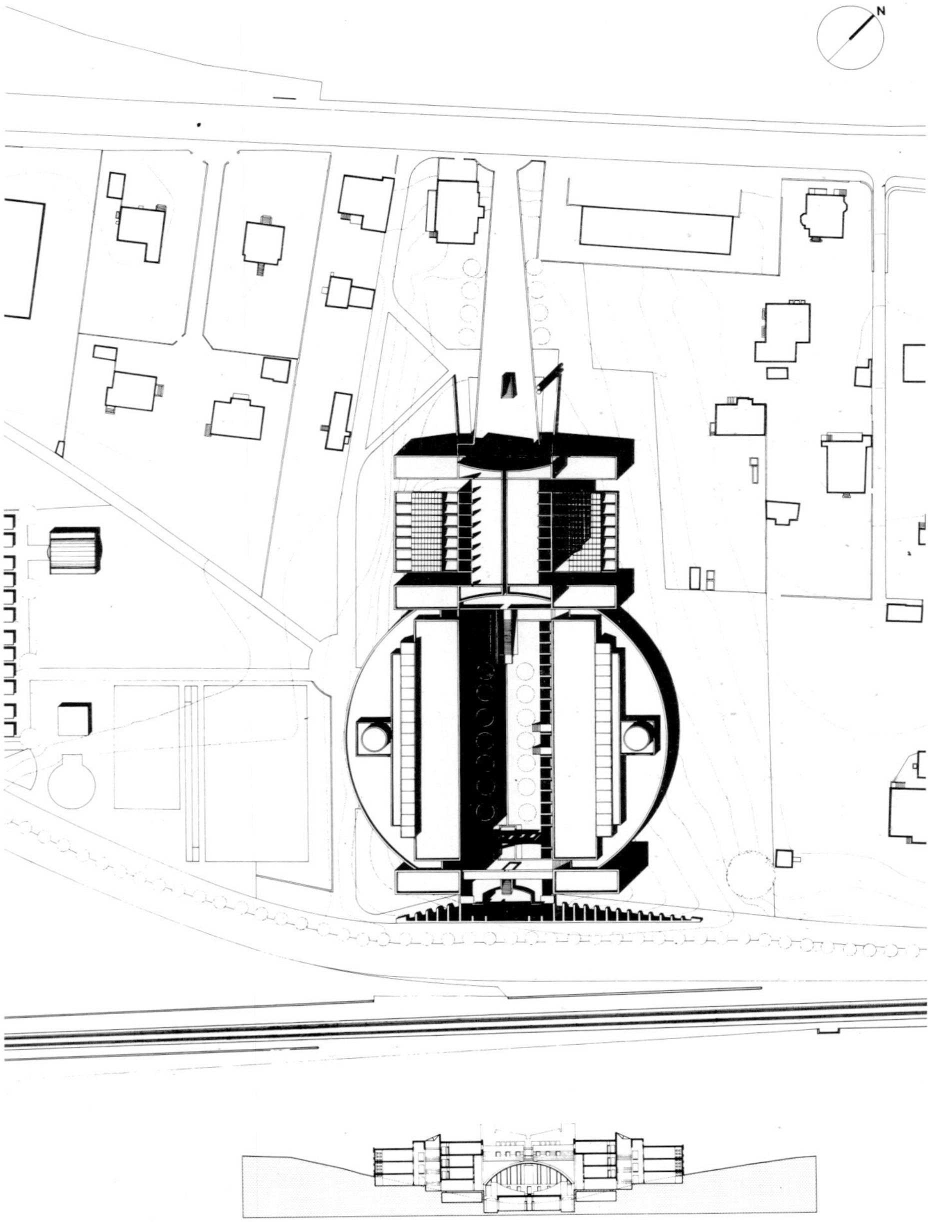

Figure 254 Vincent Mangeat, High school and school of business studies, Nyon, 1984–88.

7.2 Limits and thresholds

To build means first of all to create, define and limit a portion of land distinct from the rest of the universe and to assign a particular role to it. *The limit* creates the interior and the exterior (Figure 255). Each durable place is marked by limits: the bedroom, town hall, market square and sometimes even the whole town. We refer to limits in order to know that we are inside and 'at home' in this world. The man who clears a piece of ground quickly marks the boundaries of his conquest. The limit of a place implies control by a person or a group on what happens inside, in his or their place.

Each relationship between two places or between an interior and an exterior proceeds from two aspects of dependence. It provides both separation and connection, or, in other words, differentiation and transition, interruption and continuity, boundary and crossing. *Thresholds* and spaces of transition become 'places' in their turn: 'places in which the world reverses itself.'[112] Steps, eaves, gates, doors, balconies, windows ..., are all regulators of this inversion (Figure 256). They control the permeability of a limit, confirming spatial discontinuity whilst at the same time allowing one to cross it physically or visually. It is the threshold which reveals the nature of the limit. The door or window reveals the wall, its presence and its thickness. But thresholds are, even more, indications which proclaim the nature of the places to which they give access or which they represent.

Thus thresholds have three roles which they assume to different degrees:

Figure 255 To build is to limit, to create an interior distinct from an exterior. Once the limits are established – plot boundaries, enclosures, walls and domes – men defend them; it takes disasters to demolish them. It is therefore crucial that those who build them do it with great attention in order to place them in such a way as to avoid conflicts and suffering ....

Figure 256 The threshold, this place where the world is reversed; Bath, eighteenth century.

A utilitarian role: passage for the door, light and ventilation for the window – this role is always present. Functional, perhaps, but that is not enough to designate this a place where the world is reversed: 'What is a door? A flat surface comprising hinges, a lock establishing an extremely tough barrier. When you go through such a door are you not divided? Split into two! Perhaps you no longer notice it. Think simply of this: a rectangle. What horrifying poverty of expression. Is that the reality of a door?'[113]

A protective role: controlled passage for the door, *selection* of the view and choice of being exposed, or not, to observation from outside. The adequacy of this arrangement depends first of all on the difference between the external and the internal world. This difference has two aspects, one physical and the other social. Thus, in order to preserve our privacy, we prevent the entry of a dangerous, aggressive, noisy, ugly or simply too anonymous outside world. According to urban situations, priority is given to the protective aspect, as is the case with doors with many locks in New York City flats, or the triple glazing on a block of flats on a noisy road.

Social practices, on the other hand, govern the extent of protection according to the cultural characteristics of the inhabitants and the purpose of the buildings. Windows, doors and entry devices are not the same in Islamic countries as in the West. Sometimes these devices change by the importation of images from elsewhere or by building practices which have their own justifications. The 'international window', which is replacing the lattice-work screens characteristic of Jeddah before customs changed, is an uncomfortable example of this (Figure 257).

A semantic role: meaningful passage for the door, eye for the window – the character and values of the world which are to be found 'behind' are indicated by architectural elements or by the presence of objects. The signs of a place underlie, according to the prevailing social conventions, specific behaviour on either side of the limit.

Even in societies in which the standard of living is almost the minimum, we can observe that the threshold is not only utilitarian or protective. Particular attention and extra work are devoted to the entry space and to the door. Historically the transition space is probably linked to the existence of a ritual. The first forms of worship of a god or a chief presuppose preparation. From the moment that worship is linked to a place, the threshold is created as a means for this preparation. In his work *The Sacred and the Profane* Mircea Eliade speaks about the ritual linked to the threshold of the house:

A ritual function falls to the threshold of the human habitation, and it is for this reason that the threshold is an object of great importance. Numerous rites accompany passing the domestic threshold – a bow, a prostration, a pious touch of the hand, and so on. The threshold has its guardians - gods and spirits who forbid entrance both to human enemies and to demons and the powers of pestilence. It is on the threshold that sacrifices to the guardian divinities are offered. Here too certain paleo-oriental cultures (Babylon, Egypt, Israel) situated the judgment place. The threshold, the door *show* the solution of continuity in space immediately and concretely; hence their great religious importance, for they are symbols and at the same time vehicles of *passage* from the one space to the other.[114]

The door and its immediate surroundings have not only been the privileged place for giving expression to beliefs, but also evidence of the prosperity and social status of the inhabitants. Let us observe, for example, the inscriptions and decoration on farm doorways: sometimes a biblical quotation carved above the door attests to the belief of the inhabitant, whilst heraldic symbols, dates, forms and mouldings of the frames allude to the architectural codes of other houses belonging to a higher social stratum. They are social signs and manifestations of

Figure 257 From the window belonging to place and society to the 'international window'; Jeddah, 1965.

hopes and discreet or advertising images, controlled by the person who uses the interior space, the inhabitant-owner.

We shall examine some cases of transition from the exterior to the interior which present, each in its own way, a particular combination of *commodity, protection* and *semantic value.*

The first example is taken from research work which took place at the Ecole Polytechnic Fédérale in Lausanne between 1976 and 1982.[115] In apartment blocks in French-speaking Switzerland, until about 1930, the front door abutted directly

Figure 258 A no-man's land between inside and outside, between private and public.

onto the pavement. One entered abruptly into an interior *collective* space where - particularly in the nineteenth century - all sorts of activities and objects had overflowed from the flats. This space served as a transition between private and public domains, lit by daylight, at least in the stairwell. From 1930 onwards, a private path was often laid, with some planting, between the pavement and the front door of the building, thus creating an external transitional space between the street and the front door of the apartment block. Later, and particularly after 1950, apartment blocks were provided with a garden which surrounds and isolates the building.

A threshold *exclusively* governing commodity and protection exists, in the form of the landing, in front of the door of those who live in high-rise buildings. Let us consider access to the apartment in many recent blocks: one is led into an underground garage, into a little metal box - the lift - and comes out again at the -nth floor on a landing, without the slightest reference to the exterior and - in high-rise buildings - without even the visual reference of a staircase. The lighting is artificial, but first of all we have to find the luminous time-switch which makes it work. We are surrounded by bare walls and plain doors whose eyes - the spy holes - remind us that we are perhaps being observed in this cage (Figure 258). We have got used to it, but habit is not yet a custom. On our way between the public and private we have gone through a succession of locks, breaks and boundaries which have created a gulf between the dwelling and the street, the neighbourhood, the town. In fact it is more than a gulf, because these intermediary spaces are visible neither from the public domain

nor from the private space. Do they belong to the town or to the dwelling? - neither one nor the other; they decline into a 'no-man's land', they belong to nobody. This break prevents the inhabitant showing himself to the public; it inevitably leads to the abandonment of a sense of responsibility for what happens in front of one's own front door, sometimes with dramatic consequences. The more wealthy employ a security guard to watch over and look after this dark and anonymous passage.

When we pursue our observation to the *interior* of the apartment, we note that in the old rented buildings a well-defined hall prevents one from seeing into the living spaces. More recently there has been a change; the possibility of building large, fluid and open spaces economically, has often eliminated the separate well-defined hall by combining it with living spaces. This layout also subscribes to economic rationalization by doing away with 'those corridor spaces which serve no purpose'. 'Open-plan' housing could have induced a new life-style, but experience shows that, for the moment anyway, the bourgeois way of life attaches great importance to a well-controlled sequence from public to private. To create this transition space and acquire an entrance hall, we are ready to make considerable financial sacrifice.[116]

Neglect of the threshold as an important element in a housebuilding programme was vehemently denounced by some post-war architects such as Aldo van Eyck and Herman Hertzberger.[117,118] Robin Hood Gardens, built by Alison and Peter Smithson in 1970 in London, is an example in opposition to the common practice at the time. It is a source of hope since it promotes the humanization of a large-scale building by respecting apparently minor and individual facts of everyday life (Figure 259). The building is tall (eight storeys), the site densely developed. It has rather poor links to the urban fabric, but within these options - what a contrast! From the car park one reaches ground level *before* taking a lift or a staircase in contact with the public space to reach the covered access galleries, still in contact with the city. They are sufficiently wide to become an extension of the flats, an 'elevated street' belonging to and cared for by those who live on it.

Not all thresholds are situated between town and building. Le Corbusier's Convent of La Tourette and a house by Frank Lloyd Wright pro-

vide us with two strongly differing examples of transition, this time between 'nature' and building, by enhancing this dialectic event. At the Convent of La Tourette, the combination of moat/bridge/doorway is necessary neither to mark the entrance (it would be sufficiently obvious from its position under the pilotis) nor to give shelter from inclement weather (one does not stop there). In fact it articulates the end of a long access route through a small forest to this special place which is the entrance to a convent, 'a ship' moored in this secular and physical world (Figure 260). The protective and above all the semantic roles of the threshold are both sublimated here.

Frank Lloyd Wright proposes another ethic, probably drawing its substance from Rousseau and Thoreau. The protective role of the threshold is abolished and the ideal union between two worlds, nature and dwelling, is sought. The poet Georges Perec talks about this intimate threshold between man, the building and nature when describing, as follows, the access to one of Frank Lloyd Wright's houses:

It is obviously difficult to imagine a house which does not have a door. I saw one one day, several years ago in Lansing, Michigan, USA. It has been built by Frank Lloyd Wright: one began by following a gently winding path on

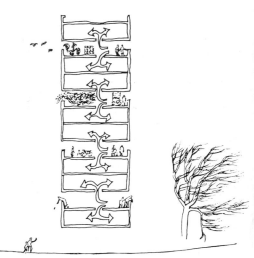

Figure 259 A high-rise building with high density, but humanization of the transition space. Golden Lane Study, Alison and Peter Smithson.

Figure 260 The entrance to the convent, 'a sacred ship' moored in this secular world; La Tourette, Le Corbusier.

the left of which rose progressively, and even with extreme nonchalance, a slight slope which, at first oblique, gradually approached the vertical. Little by little, as if by chance, without thinking about it, without at any moment being able to state that one had positively noticed something like a transition, a break, a passage, the path of continuity became stony, that is to say that first there was only grass, then there began to be stones in between the grass, then there were a few more stones and that became like a paved and grassy footpath, whilst on the left, the slope of the ground began to resemble, vaguely a low wall, then a wall without any doubt. Then appeared something like a roof with a sky-light practically indissociable from the vegetation which climbed over it. But in fact, it was already too late to know if one was outside or inside: at the end of the path the paving was jointed and one was in what is usually called an entrance which opened directly into a quite gigantic room. . . . The rest of the house was no less remarkable . . . because one had the impression that it had sunk into the hill like a cat which snuggles into a cushion.[119]

The last example is dedicated to the threshold without passage: *the window and the balcony*. Some preliminary attention to the *asymmetry* of thresholds is imperative. The threshold, offering the possibility of crossing a limit, is linked to movement. These passages are directional in the sense that they originate in one space and lead to a different space. One might think that the direction would simply be reversed in the case of an *exit*. The church porch would become the

threshold of the sacred towards the secular town. However, the two directions are not equivalent. All the decoration of the porch and the doorway is directed towards the exterior and the church remains *the destination space* which one *leaves* without the street necessarily becoming a new destination space. It is therefore often the 'entrance' which one designs rather than the exit. In domestic architecture the situation is more subtle, but on the whole comparable. The house can be considered in its own way as a 'centre of the world'; it is, in the first instance, a destination space.

The window reverses this priority of destination. It is the point of departure of the gaze which tends to lead rather from interior to exterior. It is because of this view to 'elsewhere' that one feels at home. The space of the window is a potential privileged place in the room. Its transparency, the direct light and sun which enter it, invite and encourage particular activities: to sit near the window and follow the comings and goings outside without being seen, see the postman arrive, observe nature and the weather, read or do tasks requiring accuracy, grow some plants. . . . The window is therefore not merely a lighting device, it may become a precious place between the inside and the outside. Some contemporary architects, like Kahn, van Eyck or Hertzberger, have thus given considerable thought to the theme of the window in terms of place. In his Montessori school in Delft, Herman Hertzberger insists that each classroom must also be capable of being 'a house'. In the hall, in front of the classroom doors, he has provided a brightly lit threshold evoking the idea of an 'outdoors' by top lighting. Next to each door there is a window suggest-

ing appropriation of the space by conferring an identity on each class by an exhibition of favoured objects, plants, pictures, ornaments and craft work (Figure 261). In the same way the main window looking on to the exterior is designed, to be associated with other windows, in the Dutch tradition of making a small garden out of every large window. When a place makes reference to our movements and rituals, it has more chance of becoming memorable.

What has been said for the window also applies in principle to loggias and verandas with slightly less privacy. Balconies are of a somewhat different nature. They offer practically no privacy and involve much more the double game of seeing and being seen (Figure 262).

Figure 260 The entrance to the convent, 'a sacred ship' moored in this secular world; La Tourette, Le Corbusier.

Let us conclude by summing up that thresholds and spaces of transition are places of exchange between opposing, and sometimes even conflicting, phenomena. This polarity confers upon them a duality between their autonomous existence and the principal spaces which they articulate and to which they are subordinate. Our observation of these phenomena and of a few examples shows an aspect of architecture which rarely figures explicitly in a brief given by the client. The architect's responsibilities are therefore even greater. The site, limits and thresholds are places in which the architect manoeuvres with relative freedom in practising the art of design. Each site must be understood in terms of places, limits and existing thresholds as a guide to our intervention. Each project brief must be fulfilled and transcended by these considerations in order to become a design for the creation of places. The site and purpose of the building are its major sources.

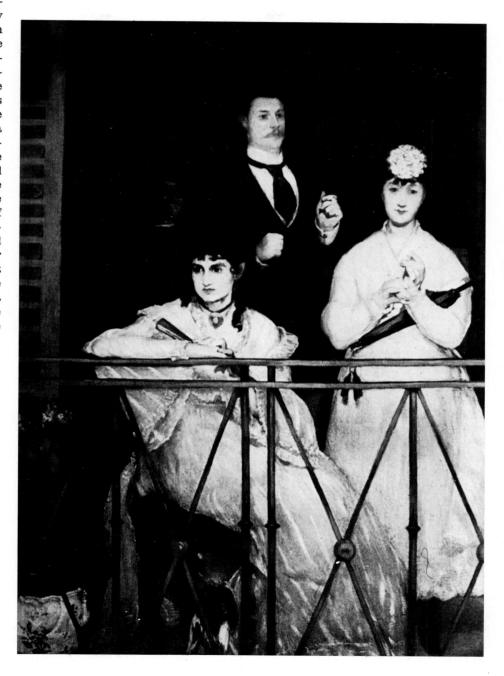

Figure 262 The balcony as threshold: 'Seeing and being seen'; painting by Edouard Manet, The Balcony, 1868/69.

7.3 From one place to the next: path and orientation

Cosmic, territorial and temporal orientation

Figure 263 Cosmic orientation.

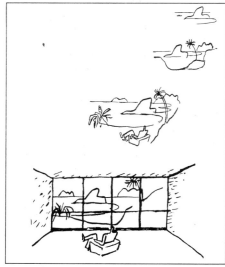

Figure 264 Territorial orientation.

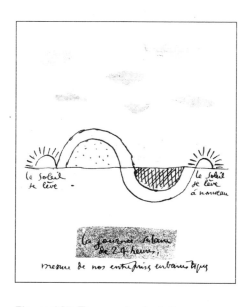

Figure 265 Temporal orientation.

'*To satisfy his inner sense of orientation, man needs to situate himself in space*'.[120] Disorientation causes anxiety. To stay in one place or to move from one place to another we need references. The subject transcends the limits of this book. It can merely offer an introduction to these aspects. Inspired by the form of a literary text[121] I shall adopt the stance of '*notes for another book*'.

I shall write first of all about *sky and earth* and about their opposition which gives us the primitive feeling of being on Earth. I shall show that high and low, vertical and horizontal, light and darkness are consequences relevant to architecture. I shall talk about the universal application of this basic experience with place. I shall quote Bachelard.

Then I shall talk about the importance of the *path of the sun* for our sense of orientation, because it bestows cardinal *directions* upon places and on the relationships between them. The word 'orientate' comes from the word 'orient' – the east – the place where the sun rises which is a fixed reference for space and time. I shall say that it does not only serve as a guide to a few remote nomadic peoples because the levant,

south, occident and their 'navel' – the north – still enable us today to position ourselves. They facilitate our journeys; they guide the layout of our interiors in relation to differences in light and temperature.

Then I shall combine the two phenomena by quoting Cassirer[122] to arrive at the mythical figure of seven: the four cardinal directions, their middle or their intersection (where I am) and the vertical axis with top and bottom.

After that I shall talk about time starting with the *seasons*, showing how spring, summer, autumn and winter control the rhythm of our clothing. Bodies are *rediscovered* in the heat, in both senses of the term. The sensual place of the 'self' is perhaps more remote in winter than in summer. By speaking of the seasons, I shall insist on the special indication of time and the universe offered by the rhythm of vegetation. Perhaps I shall suggest a very simple planning law: 'from each house and from each place of work one must be able to perceive the rhythm of the seasons and the weather'.

I shall not forget to speak about *the alternation of day and night* which is our most immediate rhythm. It provides the opportunity for two very different spatial experiences which our projects often fail to take into consideration. In more detail, one can distinguish morning, noon, evening and night.

I shall also write about *the presence of the past*, about old stones and the traces of streets which are evidence of the confrontations of our predecessors with the site, their spiritual values, their sense of comfort, and the economy of means at their disposal. The stratification of time made visible endows a synchronic view on culture and its transformations. I shall certainly talk about the city of Rome as it is today. It has been the most successful in this simultaneous actualization of history. The presence of the past embodies the hope of continuity and renewal of the town and thus of life itself.

I shall speak about the unexplained past which we are constantly rediscovering in new places and at different moments. Memory is latent; it awaits its moment of creativity, or, as Italo Calvino puts it in *Invisible Cities*:

... even if it was a matter of the past it was a past that changed gradually as he advanced on his journey, because the traveller's past changes according to the route he has followed: not the immediate past, that is, to which each day that goes by adds a day, but the more remote past. Arriving at each new city, the traveller finds again a past of his that he did not know he had: the foreignness of what you no longer are or no longer possess lies in wait for you in foreign, unpossessed places.[123]

In another chapter I shall talk about *close and distant*, about foreground and background. I shall say that the simultaneous presence of the two facilitates localization and our movements in the wider environment. To be at home and see the distance, then not to see it so that it does not become an omnipresent intruder, is a factor to be taken into consideration in the design of a plan and the openings of a building. The reference to distance does not, however, have to be explicit. I shall therefore talk about the viaduct, the station or the airport, which conjure up distant destinations. I shall probably also mention the cemetery which suggests temporal distance or the length of *our* time ... I shall not forget either to show that a distant view from our house is an appropriable thing, which explains our distress when urban changes do away with it.

It will then be time for me to talk about *plains and hills, valleys and mountain ridges*, in short, about topography and its role as a gradient, establishing scales of depth which structure our sense of orientation. The incline and the form of the slope must determine the way in which our roads and buildings are constructed. I shall suggest another very simple law: 'It is forbidden to build on ridges which are potential territorial boundaries'. It is true that very beautiful buildings and even towns have been built on ridges, but the large built-up areas of today have become so difficult to contain that ridges and lakes are the only sufficiently powerful and continuous boundaries; Zurich, Athens and several other European cities have seized in time the opportunity offered by topography. The horizon is a limit even if, as Bollnow draws to our attention, this limit is in reality intangible, because the more we advance, the more the horizon is replaced by new horizons.[124]

Then I shall write about the duality between *centre and periphery* of the region, the town, the neighbourhood, the house. This duality is revealed only when the two are put in relationship to each other. I shall imagine ways of achieving this. I know several; Manhattan and Adolf Loos's Villa Karma in Clarens are two; London will not satisfy me; neither will Athens or Lausanne. I shall let Kevin Lynch[125] talk about the role of *path, edge, node, district and landmark* as territorial references. I shall also quote Louis Kahn. I shall show examples of clear and open structures, like the centre of Turin, as well as confused structures like its suburbs. Numerous elements in this book must reappear there however, especially 'Order and Disorder', and 'Fabric and Object'.

I shall also go into the matter of *interior and exterior*, as two opposing notions which provide perhaps the most fundamental differentiation between places. The means for achieving this is the spatial limit. In the interior there is always room for even more internal places; the last subjective limit is our own body. We have organized the world in increasingly secure interiors which contain each other in succession from the celestial vault, through the nation down to the cradle in which the newborn child is sleeping. I shall return here to the notion of limits and thresholds.

The themes set out here are archetypes; practically all cultures refer to them to orientate themselves in space and time. However, they are not our only guides, nor always the most important. For the second part of the book, I shall collaborate with an anthropologist to talk about orientation in our Western culture in particular, about the way in which certain routes, certain places, objects and layouts, certain movements and repeated rituals provide the necessary familiarity and stability for us to know *where* and *when* we are.

So here are my notes set out on this imaginary book on the problems of cosmic, territorial and temporal orientation. The 'game' has been entertaining for the author and, let us hope, also for some readers. If one admits that *disorientation* is one of the hardest states to take upon oneself in the context of the rapid and gigantic transformations and urbanizations of the twentieth century, the desire to remedy it can no longer be absent from dissertation on architecture. In the past these problems were solved, so to speak, 'naturally' due to the slowness of change. Today it might be useful to evoke some fundamental principles of orientation in order to stimulate our efforts to confront this 'new' problem in our design task. *The Image of the City* and *What Time is This Place?*[126] already written some time ago by Kevin Lynch, as well as some recent research, have begun to prepare the ground.

Dynamics of the path

Our daily comings and goings single or repeated, contribute to forging our image of the environment. They reveal the world which surrounds us by its geometric, spatial and formal characteristics and highlight observed events and meanings evoked along the way. The path enables us not only to move from place to place, to go near to or to cross places, but also helps to remind us of things seen and experienced and to situate us in a wider community. The experience of the path is dynamic and the terms associated with it are verbs of action: to walk, to seek and find, to pass, to penetrate, to discover, to enter and leave, to stop and continue to arrive and depart.... Sometimes this path crosses boundaries, gradually or, on the contrary, suddenly. The idea of the route is therefore identified with that of change. In all change human beings experience the need to situate themselves in relation to their points of departure, their past, and their objectives, their future. For that they refer to their experience which enables them to anticipate the unknown without too many risks of making mistakes.

We are able to travel in unknown territory, cautiously perhaps, but without necessarily making errors. We proceed by analogy with more familiar situations. We still know little about the signs we use; specific research is yet to be undertaken. Kevin Lynch's remarkable work remains relatively isolated; it continues to be a reference for the architect and planner who are concerned with problems of orientation. Recent research has introduced the notion of 'mental maps' which each one of us is said to establish with regard to large-scale environments. They have

improved our knowledge, but are far from being able to penetrate current planning practice. It seems that the experience accumulated during our trips through towns enables us to interiorize *archetypes* or models of spatial organization in order to confront and evaluate new situations. Thanks to these archetypes we can orientate ourselves in unknown space. We formulate generic expectations which are of a topological rather than Euclidean order. Without seeing where the street leads, we know its characteristics of continuity, direction and of an element in a network, which enable us, should the occasion arise, to correct our route.

On a smaller scale it is the same for moving about a house which one enters for the first time: one does not yet know its precise organization, but it is part of the family of all the houses which we have already lived in or visited. Strange as its layout may be, we generally find in it some indications of dimensions connections and degrees of privacy which inform, reassure and guide us.

It seems that for their security in little known or unknown territory, human beings seek to maintain their orientation to their *starting point*: that is their 'escape route', the only one they know! When they move around in open country or in town, they take with them, as it were, their starting point, dividing the journey into stages from one landmark to another. Some of these landmarks are weak and ephemeral, such as some unspecified intersection; others are more lasting, like the beginning of a route or a sudden change in the nature of the route, or even an unusual object. For the interior of a building the reference for the beginning of the route is generally the *entrance* and the stair. Their position plays an important role in orienting us through the entire building.

Streets and internal layouts are some of those archetypes which can cause disorientation and anxiety, should the architect and planner needlessly depart from a familiar typology. That is of little consequence for small-scale interiors, because the disorientation is of short duration. It can even be stimulating, helping to cause surprise and provide the pleasure of discovery. It is different with large-scale public places, towns, neighbourhoods, and, worse still, interiors of large institutions. There, architecture can and must help to guide and orientate. Finding one's way means, in spite of possible changes of direction, intersections and bifurcations, being able to decide the best route to take. A region, a town, a building which one visits for the first time and without a guide, is a space empty of meaning apart from that given by the associations of images. Gradually we fill this emptiness, especially if we have a preferred point of reference from which we can organize this new world.

In towns, two or three archetypes of streets are more familiar to us than others: the corridor-street with adjoining buildings, and the street along which stand isolated buildings. A third type has developed during this century, in the form of a network of paths and roads freely located in park landscapes scattered with freestanding buildings. In this third case the paths are difficult to lay out. It is said that Aalto recommended that one should wait one or two years to see the places where the grass is trampled and then lay the paving stones for the paths there.

Twentieth-century building programmes have introduced complex-es of public buildings of a size comparable to that of a village or a small town. Contrary to the latter, their interiors are most often felt to be labyrinths by a visitor who is not familiar with the place. It is therefore useful to examine here the causes of this problem, with the help of a specific example.

The network of corridors of the new Ecole Polytechnique Fédérale de Lausanne (EPFL), although built on an orthogonal north-south/east-west grid, with a plausible hierarchy from the bird's eye view, is a source of continual, irritating disorientation for visitors. These difficulties arise from the coincidence of several factors which we shall examine by comparing the EPFL to the town centre of Morges, which is about the same size and which accommodates a network of functions more complex than that of the EPFL without, however, posing any problems of orientation (Figures 266 and 267).

In the wide corridor-streets of Morges, the passerby grasps simultaneously important urban fragments and individual buildings, or at least their street façades, constituting subgroupings. He can even form a vague idea of what he does not see. The plan of the town and system of addresses are particularly simple. You only need the street name, number of the building and the name of the business or the resident - the floor being indicated at the entrance. A stranger arriving from another continent will be able to orientate himself with the aid of a small street plan. If he makes a mistake, his route will be relatively easy to correct; it would be even more so if there were more narrow streets perpendicular to the main streets; cardinal orientation is ensured, the network is continuous and there is a directional hierarchy. The individuality of certain buildings, spaces, signs, etc., helps in recognition of places where one has already passed. The reference to other towns is obvious (Figures 267 and 268).

EPFL, on the other hand, reserves the ground level for an efficient service area for deliveries (Figure 271). In order to link all parts of the complex under cover, the pedestrian level is situated on the first and second floors, with the main entrances in a superstructure on the second floor of the central part (Figures 269, 270 and 272).

Internal circulation on the ground floor is treated in the same way as would be the deliveries to a basement (Figure 273). There is no visual communication between these superimposed systems. For reasons of security, in case of fire, control of draughts and for selective accessibility according to timetable, the stairwells act as airlocks and divide the different areas. The network is thus punctuated by breaks without, however, these breaks constituting thresholds.

Beyond the problem of airlocks and floors which produce a series of breaks, the tree-like organization, with a trunk distributing branches ending in very long cul-de-sacs whose ends are not even visible, means that it is advisable not to make a mistake. An aerial view makes it much easier to comprehend this tree-like place than is possible from any of three levels.

In corridors there are frequent changes in direction and when they occur in the absence of a reference to cardinal points, of a directional hierarchy of routes, or of a reference to a familiar exterior, it only take three changes of direction for a normally constituted person to make a 90-degree mistake in his position. The

Figure 266 Morges, small town with complex content, 7 km from EPFL; general plan.

Figures 267 and 268 Main street at ground level with numerous individual signs, without destruction of the overall coherence.

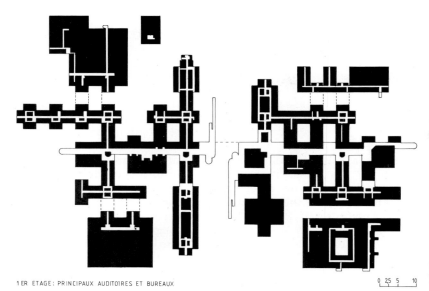

1 ER ETAGE: PRINCIPAUX AUDITOIRES ET BUREAUX   0 25 5   10

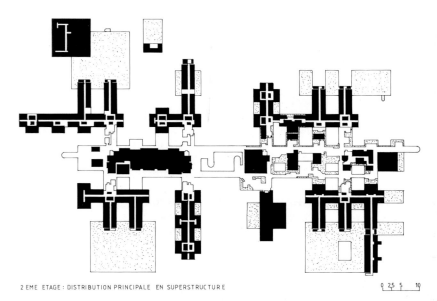

2 EME ETAGE: DISTRIBUTION PRINCIPALE EN SUPERSTRUCTURE   0 25 5   10

Figures 269 and 270 EPFL, general plan
of the university complex, first stage
1973–84 (on the same scale as the city of
Morges, Figure 266).

Figure 271 The ground level reserved for
an efficient delivery system.

Figure 272 Main street at the nth level
with no reference to the ground and no
indications of the overall structure of the
system.

Figure 273 Ground floor . . .

blind bilateral corridors, forming a rectangle around a courtyard or nodal point, are particularly prone to this. There is hardly any similar example in town layouts (Figures 269 and 270).

At EPFL another difficulty for orientating oneself arises from the small scale of the spaces, with the exception of the 'spine' on the second level. A visualization of groupings and even of coherent subgroupings is impossible. The scale of the 'street façade' is reduced to the punctuation of doors, each of which leads to a unit of the complex.

We have mentioned that the individual characteristics of an intersection are of considerable help in orientation. The architects of EPFL have taken notice of this, but, on their own, these signs are insufficient. They are only of secondary importance. On this level the comparison between a town, which has evolved through history, and a large project erected at one moment in time is necessarily unfair. But it must not prevent us drawing several conclusions. The demands of economy and time have not left much scope for giving character to intersections, bifurcations, types of forms, structures and materials. This homogeneity is not a fault in itself – it can even be a good quality – but it does pose problems, because it compounds other factors of disorientation, or rather because it cannot offset them by local variation.

The visitor's insecurity is increased even more by the fact that he or she very quickly loses contact with the entrance, the origin of the journey; the 'escape route', is thus lost. The great 'lump' of the multi-purpose hall prevents the establishment of links with the outside world. When one takes one of the lateral branches, not only does one's

memory of the entrance become confused, but contact with the spine itself is broken. Finally, one must admit that, from the exterior, the absence of a simple limit and of an entrance on the scale of the complex do nothing to ease one's anticipation of the nature of the system of internal routes.

Moreover, as the car parks are practically all situated at the ends of the lateral branches, it is these 'back-stage doors', or emergency exits, which become the real entrances to the complex.[127]

If we have dwelt for some time on this concrete example of a complex which, incidentally, also has some good functional qualities, it is because it reflects a problem of contemporary architecture and town planning ... still awaiting a solution. Similar problems occur in almost all recent large buildings on this scale. It is a new concern; the Greeks took three centuries to perfect their temples. In the same way we must gradually learn to handle problems of orientation which spring from our large building programme of the twentieth century: hospitals, universities, administrative buildings, airports, etc. A sophisticated and costly system of signposting can mitigate design deficiencies, but a real architectural solution lies in a spatial and orientated layout which has little or no need of signs.

These orientation requirements rarely figure in initial briefs. It is apparent from the concerns of the client, and from some entries in the competition for the second phase of EPFL, that the problem of orientation is now felt to be important by all those who at some time have had to suffer the effects of a lack of attention in this respect. One of the entries to the competition for the

second phase of EPFL attempted precisely to solve the problems of orientation and identity of the 'university' as a place by referring to models of internal streets such as the Galeria Vittorio-Emmanuele in Milan.

Observations on these two concrete examples show the need to take account of a whole set of factors much more diversified than the simple relationship to the ground or the creation of a central square. The most basic difference between the corridors of EPFL and the streets of Morges lies in *abandoning the archetype of adjoining buildings and of the street's relationship to the ground and the sky*.

It is probably difficult to build a hospital, a head office of a large company or even a university rationally according to the morphological model of the town of Morges. We have new problems to solve. Some simple suggestions could help us to make a better job of planning orientation in large projects which are mainly horizontal:

- Cardinal, topographic and geographic orientation should be maintained throughout the layout.
- Circulation should be organized in networks rather than in tree form. Long cul-de-sacs and loops should be avoided. A dead end is not a street.
- Networks should be continuous with repeated links; they should be geometrically simple, regular and hierarchic. A systematic differentiation in the character of the circulation system, according to directions, will clarify the image of the whole. If, moreover, this differentiation finds its counterpart in the relationship between the path system and the visible load-bearing structure, the visitor should be

better assisted in his changes of direction and the image of the whole will be reinforced.

- Intersections could be potential places to stop and useful points of reference, provided they are emphasized as an architectural event.
- A spatial and not only functional link should be maintained between superimposed horizontal networks. Breaks caused by doors and stairwells should be avoided as they prevent anticipation of their destination. Staircases belong to all levels.
- 'Blind' circulation routes should be restricted to the absolute minimum; they should be of the greatest geometric simplicity; they should depart from and lead to reassuring points of reference, in principle in straight lines, avoiding dark corners.
- From the main routes one should be able to see coherent groupings of more importance than a repetition of individual units. Indication of the purpose or specific character of these groupings would, moreover, make it possible to introduce variation along the route.
- Reference to points of departure and destination should be facilitated. Reference to a centre which is itself related to the entrance could also be envisaged.
- A large public institution must have a main entrance, a threshold which is representative and which is clearly visible in the façade. As far as possible the entrances, even those from the car parks, must easily lead to it *before* one enters the building. When the building has several entrances, the secondary entrances are not to be treated as 'emergency exits'; they, too, have a welcoming role to play. The system of the circulation network must appear as obvious from the secondary entrance as from the main entrance.

Finally, so that a public institution of the size of a small town can become a memorable place, its architecture has to have a strong and global image.

There are examples of recent buildings in which the problem of orientation within a large complex has been solved quite successfully, as in the administrative building of Hermann Hertzberger's Centraal Beheer at Apeldoorn, or Vittorio Gregotti's University of Cosenza.

In buildings on a small scale we can take more liberties. The play of orientation and subtle disorientation, of the familiar and the surprise, of the hidden and visible, becomes a possible strategy. The purpose of the building influences this strategy; whether it is a museum or an exhibition, we try to *guide without channelling*. In the case of the passengers' mad rush to the plane it is more necessary to channel. The airport is a place which functions as long as one is in a hurry and which becomes distressing as soon as one spends some time there. If we spend some time there, the character of our visit is no longer simply utilitarian, like liquid flowing through pipes. It is a journey and an excursion, part of an existential experience which can be poetic. Poetry needs calm and universality.

7.4 A place for identity

To be at peace with the universe, with society and with themselves people need to be able to situate themselves by affirming their identity:

- identity as a human being, *Homo sapiens*, who is distinct from the physical, mineral, vegetable and animal world;

- identity as a member of a group with which one shares and discusses values; the family, political party, club, etc.

- identity as an individual who maintains a margin of liberty and personal responsibility, distinct from the group and from all others; each person is unique.

The built environment is far from being the only one to influence our sense of identity. Gestures and rituals, clothes and objects, language and many more factors are just as important. Architecture is nevertheless playing an important role in reducing or strengthening our sense of identity.

Rapoport[128] rightly reminds us that we must distinguish two types of manifestations of identity:
(a) Private identity, *the affirmation of identity to oneself and to one's intimate group*: the signs can be relatively 'private' or subtle. They only need to be recognizable by the initiated. Thus the position of objects and icons in an orthodox church guide the behaviour only of those who know its ritual, and that is sufficient.
(b) Public identity, *the affirmation of identity to others* by establishing a distinction between 'them' and 'us': the indications must be clear, redundant and popularized. The architec-

ture of colonial towns imposing itself on a foreign country is a striking example on a large scale. The erection of a monument often has the same aim of communicating or recalling without ambiguity an event or the memory of a personality to those who have not known them or who might have forgotten them.

So that these two concepts of identity may be profitably inserted into the process of architectural design, we must question the practice and codified images of those for whom we act as trustee when we build. In both cases the aid to identity is only effective provided it is known and recognized by others. It implies a tacit or explicit agreement, a convention, a tradition. The terms of this agreement, the distinctive signs of identity, become clearer as we accumulate experience of social life in a given culture. The architect must discover the principal means which ensure this communication of identity.

In order to produce a building reflecting the identity of a group of initiates - for example a family home or a church interior - the architect has the choice between three strategies.

The first is interpretative; it presupposes attentive observation and deep understanding of the values and behaviour of the people and groups concerned, as well as the places and the architectural elements crucial to their identity. When he makes a strict rule for himself that he must observe with sufficient humility, he no longer needs to be part of the observed group in order to succeed in his diagnosis and then in his scheme. Le Corbusier was not a practising Catholic, but he clearly understood the essential characteristics of the sacred Catholic space in order to build Ronchamp and La Tourette.

The second strategy consists in making the future users participate in the design of places. This process presents interesting possibilities in the residential field for allowing those involved to affirm their identity[129], but experience shows that the architect who engages himself merely as a technician at the service of the user produces buildings which are characterized by a non-critical summation of personal tastes at the expense of the collective interest, thus detracting from the lasting quality of the work. Moreover, it is not certain that a place which has been thus created can remain a good aid to identity after the departure of the original inhabitants.

The third strategy proposes the search for an architecture which suitably lends itself to the places and symbols of identity which will be created by the occupants themselves after completion of a strong ordering structure. Herman Hertzberger talks about an 'architecture of hospitality' and has pursued this new strategy which seeks to reconcile mass production and our need for individual identity.

To resolve a building project which involves, to a greater extent, the creation of a place displaying an identity to the public - for example a church exterior or the gateway to a private garden - we must resort to symbols that are comprehensible by everyone. These signs of a place and its underlying identity are effective because they are unique and widely known (like the Eiffel Tower) or because they belong to a typology rather than to a conventional code, deep-rooted in the collective memory of which we are part, such as doorways, fountains or staircases. The place and the form of a door or a specific building have their name

and their history of memorable events. They have been recounted to us and retold sometimes from our childhood. Gradually what was at first only a building or an element like any other takes on a collective value perpetuating itself through time. These 'stories' and connotations are transmitted and modified from one memory to another; they root us in time and place. The architect who intends to refer to this memory which has become collective is bound to respect certain conventional layouts in order that the building can effectively play its role as an aid to public identity. The extent to which the architect can move away from conventions in order to explore new horizons in our culture is in fact a delicate question of judgement; however, it is culturally necessary to do so. But remember: a belfry is not a water-tower!

Reality is often more complex: most briefs and schemes imply both a contribution to public identity and a space for private identity. Sometimes a conflict arises from the contradictions between the demands of a public face and individual requirements. Our architectural task appears once more as an art of compromise: to define places which serve the urban identity whilst retaining a margin capable of accommodating places where private identities can be expressed. The development of some forty dwellings near Berne by Franz Oswald can be quoted as an example of a design process which seeks precisely to manage this double aspect of identity.[130] After fixing certain general rules, such as three widths of plots, the arrangement of dwellings in terraces and alignments, Oswald acts as personal architect to each of his forty individual clients. Having fixed neither the position of the

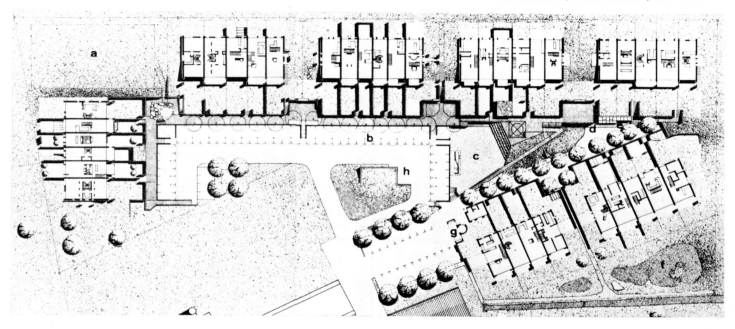

staircase, nor that of the plumbing, he had kept plenty of room for manoeuvre in the design of each terrace house, taking the particular aspirations of the future inhabitants into full consideration (Figure 274). But consultation with the user did not stop there; the summation of these individual expressions would not amount to a coherent neighbourhood: Oswald then asked these 'suburban settlers' for their opinions and involvement in his proposals for the public space and objects, in short, the elements aiding the identity of the neighbourhood. Here the architect knew how to treat the contradictions between the desire for a house on a plot and the desire for town-building in the spirit of con-

temporary culture by engaging, patiently, in a process of participation. In the long term these dwellings are, like the schemes of Hertzberger, a support which offers both an identifiable collective place – the neighbourhood and the street which recall other streets whilst still being unique – and a host of potential private places which will be defined in the course of time by the more modest interventions of the inhabitants themselves. Only architecture with a highly structural morphological character can withstand these alterations 'without losing face'.

Whereas place as an aid to public identity – neighbourhood, court or market square – has been recognized and treated by architects more or

less successfully for centuries, place as a welcome to private identity is a new problem and needs to be treated urgently because of the rapid production of anonymous housing for large numbers of people. This is particularly apparent in *mass housing*. It is therefore worthwhile giving it some consideration.

The real estate market attempts to mitigate the absence of places as aids to identity by producing ready-made advertising images. The numerous homes which are currently being built in suburbs to escape the connotation of living in a block of flats and to indicate having reached higher social status are an example of this. The false traditional Swiss home or the 'English or Spanish col-

163

onial style' home in the USA seek to exploit a convention which announces unambiguously the purchaser's attachment to middle-class values and behaviour to be distinguished from the 'ordinary' member of the public. Unfortunately this purchased identity lacks any depth of meaning.

In order to clarify this concept of private identity which should characterize the dwelling, it is useful to associate it with that of the appropriation of space.[131]

The functioning of the dwelling is an obvious requirement which, on its own, is not sufficient to satisfy the inhabitants. For a dwelling to be transformed into a house, the user must be able to develop links with it and adapt it to himself, his needs and images. In a purely functional dwelling there is little room for this adaptation. In most contemporary cases, however, the user is not in a situation in which he can influence the design of his dwelling. It is therefore essential that, besides its usefulness, this house should have 'personality', even character, which will encourage its inhabitants to take it over. This house should not be neutral; its architecture should be strong and ordered, giving it a stable and distinctive underlying structure. Moreover, its personality can be reinforced by a random and irrational side which is a challenge to the user, making him act and react. Research on appropriation of space shows the usefulness of architectural clues in encouraging this takeover.[132] The dimensions, form and relative position of rooms, as well as the existence of ordering or focal elements, such as doors, windows, fireplaces, recesses, floor pattern, etc., have a considerable influence on the way in which the space is occupied. These physical indicators become anchor points for inventing and modifying the way in which the space is occupied with furniture and activities. A purely functional layout and commercialized sets of furniture (cumbersome because they cannot be broken down) reinforce the tendency not to think about *one's own* way of living and to arrange one's interior according to ready-made schemes.

The effectiveness of these architectural clues is increased when they do not immediately suggest a precise use. Some conflicting situations can even provoke ingenious solutions of which the inhabitants are proud. Thus an excess, and sometimes even a lack, of space encourage an interactive relationship between the occupant and the place in which he lives. The ease with which a door can be blocked up, an implicit subdivision of the space can be reinforced, a large corridor can be given over to other uses, the freedom to cover the walls, the possibility of organizing one's interior by views onto 'set-pieces', etc., in turn stimulate this appropriation. That partially explains the present success of turn-of-the-century and pre-war flats. Their formal characteristics, such as ceilings that are 'too' high, that useless empty space, the waste of space of a landing that is 'too' wide, spacious entrance halls, very uneven natural lighting, the bulkiness of radiators, a veranda that is too narrow, a blind space, apparently only a storage space, etc., are in fact disadvantages which the occupant has time to transform into advantages and where he can imprint his identity.

In a contemporary design, anxious to provide clues for approximation, the difficulty lies in the fact that one must create something not quite complete which stimulates and reassures at the same time: an architecture in between order and disorder, points of reference which ask to be completed. In fact most of the tasks the architect is asked to resolve have this double aspect: to interpret a collective identity and offer the space to active appropriation by an individual or a small group.

These cultural considerations set the limits of 'autonomy of form' or architecture as a three-dimensional art. They are not the only ones, because functionality and economy of construction are other, more obvious ones. The architect who accepts these three conditions – utility, constructions and identity of place – nevertheless retains considerable room for manoeuvre and artistic creativity.

8

FORM AND THE NATURE OF MATERIALS

Overleaf
Window and material.
Hossios Loukas.

8.1 Truth or untruth?

'*To believe that one can attain beauty by untruth is heresy in the practice of art . . .*'[133] As attractive as this aphorism of Viollet-le-Duc appears at first sight, its universality is put in doubt by the fact that art often uses illusion successfully. In architecture, the question of truth and untruth refers to the relationships between form and construction or between form and content. This chapter deals with the first pair: how does form express technique, or how does technique inspire form?

Architecture is an art of compromise: it can be untruth for some while in the same case others see truth in the skill and elegance of a solution appropriate to a problem. Discussions about '*honesty*' have always played an important part in architectural theory. They are articulated around the three terms: *form, expression and construction*.

Auguste Perret, who can be placed at the transition between academic rationalism and the engineer's rationality, said this: '*It is by the splendour of truth that the building attains beauty*'[134]. And by 'truth' he really meant definition of form based on materials and their appropriate use in construction.

That is only *one* of the attitudes amongst those current today. No earlier period witnessed such an ethical plurality on this subject, although the dilemma is as ancient as architecture itself. Today 'all' attitudes are practised simultaneously, giving the impression that it is only a question of the artist's taste. Technique is sometimes *glorified*, becoming the exclusive source of form; sometimes it is simply *used as an image*, as at the Centre Pompidou;

some people try to *falsify* it by giving an illusion of a technique other than that which has really been used; and others even *subject* it to formal ends inspired by the art of abstract painting and sculpture, and then there are those who *tame it* by exploiting the logic of construction, without giving it a privileged and independent status. What is worrying is that the architect who adheres to one of these approaches must all the same recognize from the evidence that each of the others may produce buildings which demand admiration. At best we have become more sceptical about dogmas; at worst we are in an ethical mess which leaves us without criteria for judgement.

The architect is faced with contradictory choices between right and wrong, or the good and the bad path to follow. Lack of certainty is one of the facets of the 'crisis' in contemporary architectural theory. Students are intellectually solicited, not only because there has been an increase in knowledge, but above all because, in the absence of a predominant doctrine, they must make ideological choices by *themselves*. Of course, a teacher will not agree with all the above-mentioned options; he will have a critical attitude and his own soundly argued preferences. But in the next-door garden other philosophies are cultivated and they are exposed to the light of day by our rapid means of communication: magazines, books and travel.

However, there are two fundamental principles which unite the five approaches we shall deal with and which distinguish them from painting, sculpture and to some extent arts and crafts: architecture always has to deal with gravity; its forms by necessity have to express this fact. '*Gravity and rigidity are the aesthe-*

tic substance of beautiful architecture.'[135]

Secondly, architecture always consist of hollow forms in order to accommodate the internal space which is its *raison d'être*.

These permanent truths do not as such determine an approach. The impulses in architectural form are numerous and complex: the discipline of architecture covers territory extending from the laws of vision to socio-psychological and cultural considerations; from the geometric and dimensional properties of the objects and spaces to be built, to the design for light and view to the design of place and path, etc., and now we superimpose on it the dilemma of constructional rationale.

A work of architecture attains its true greatness from the synthesis of these multiple constituents into a unique final design. The relative emphasis of these ingredients cannot be subjected to a rule of general validity. It must find its own balance according to the brief and the site in the wider sense of these terms. Their role and their relative importance will vary depending on whether it is a question of building a public institution, a factory or a dwelling, whether or not it is in the country or in the town, north of the Alps or on the Mediterranean . . .

Construction – especially the load-bearing structure in its interaction with space, the spatial envelope, the openings and light – is the first means of putting into concrete form an idea which belongs to the domain of art. That does not mean that the construction will deny its own laws. On the contrary, these laws are themselves valuable sources for explaining the work, but the degree to which an expressive role may be given to the construction will depend even more on the brief and the site than on the demands of statics and materials. The most mature and the richest architectural works have always subordinated, without betraying it, constructional rationality to that of a more universal architectural idea: structural design, the form and the texture of materials are superimposed and measure and order the design of space, light and place. That is how our best temples, and cathedrals and palaces are built, and likewise our humblest housing and urban fabric, when they stand out from the mediocre commercial development which scarcely merits the name of 'architecture'.

We can divide the attitudes concerning the relationship between form and technique into five categories: the glorification of technique, technique as an image, falsification of technique, technique subjected and technique tamed. This division is a useful simplification. It is certainly not able to cover the whole of reality which is undoubtedly more finely differentiated, but it does provide us with the elements for a better understanding of this fundamental choice in the architectural process.

The glorification of technique

Technique is sometimes itself the justification of an architectural code. In fact, who does not wonder at a fine timber frame, the metallic structure of Tony Garnier's slaughterhouse in Lyons, Paddington Station, the decorative effect of joints and rivets on the Eiffel Tower, the junctions of a suspension bridge cable and the carefully assembled laminated profiles of a building by Mies van der Rohe? Roland Barthes says in his essay on the Eiffel Tower that at the time of its construction it set a new value against the secular image of sculptural beauty, that of functional and technical beauty, which has since conquered the world[136]. In this the nakedness of a logical construction lies the condition for an aesthetic; it reflects an economical response to the laws of nature: gravity and the resistance of materials or, as Konrad Wachsmann puts it

... building is, in the end, a material struggle against the destructive forces of nature. That obliges us to draw on the consequences of the progress of science and from technical discoveries and inventions ... These revolutions in construction methods, which were limited until then by the rules of craftsmanship, have provided stimulation to which the sensitive and creative mind had to react.[137]

The poetic emotion aroused by a Robert Maillart bridge, a Pier Luigi Nervi exhibition hall, a covered market by Eduardo Torroja, a three-dimensional structure by Konrad Wachsmann, or that canopy by Santiago Calatrava (Figure 278), is created by expressive and elegant use of a technique in which the play of static forces and the method of assembly give a certain distinction to the work. The approach of these pioneers is experimental: intuition and artistic sensitivity are the driv-

Figure 275 Technical expressionism is established here as a principle of art: Joseph Paxton, Crystal Palace, 1851 Exhibition, London.

168

ing force. They are not content with the purely structural shape which depends too much on knowledge and not enough on feeling.[138]

In the twentieth century technical means attain the rank of a generating principle in art. The technical aesthetic gives the impression of a mathematical and therefore 'natural' logic of construction, but this remains equivocal; there are manifold possibilities. Calculation is only one means of control, after intuition and invention, of a constructional system. 'Form obeys the demands of expression, not calculation. One cannot separate structure from spatial reality.'[139]

The glorification of technique presupposes a task of construction *dominated* by questions of statics and technical means. It is most successful when there is an unequivocal brief, as in civil engineering: a bridge or a large covered market to span. In these briefs the fundamental problem is that of the stability and assembly, of the fixings and junctions between elements without interference by multiple or contradictory requirements. In the case of

Figure 276 'Revolutions in construction methods have provided stimulation to which the sensitive and really creative mind had to react' (K. Wachsmann) Pier Luigi Nervi, exhibition hall Giovanni Agnelli, Turin, 1947/49.

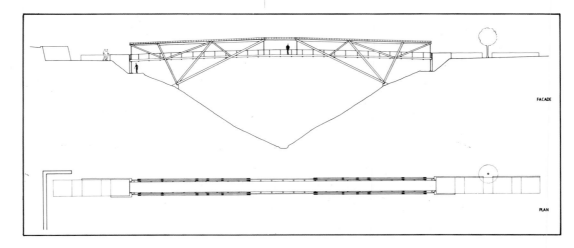

Figure 277 Glorified technique is helped by an unequivocal brief, such as this timber footbridge; student project, EPFL, 1984.

169

a dwelling, the expression of technique as an aesthetic aim does not follow very easily the complex spatial and cultural nuances required by this use.

These works in which technique is the very basis of architectural expression, present another characteristic worthy of attention and likely to arouse our critical thought: it is difficult for them to abandon their object-status in order to become a stitch in the urban fabric. That is precisely where their limitation lies: this building type cannot be generalized. When, on the other hand, their status as object is justified by the location and purpose of the building, the architecture of the town is enriched by it.

Another limitation to this approach is imposed by the risk of 'styling'. By this we mean the partial abandonment of structural truth for the sake of image. It is a delicate matter to define this limit, because even the works mentioned above are obviously not the expression of only material necessities. Considered from the restricted point of view of resistance of materials, articulation between the two segments of Calatrava's canopy could have been reduced. It is the need for the understanding of a structural phenomenon by the eye which required this accentuation. In this case, the choice is perfectly justified.

Some late works by Nervi and some civil engineering and 'industrial design' works undertaken with excessive aesthetic pretensions go beyond these limits. We are already touching on the approach to *technique as an image*.

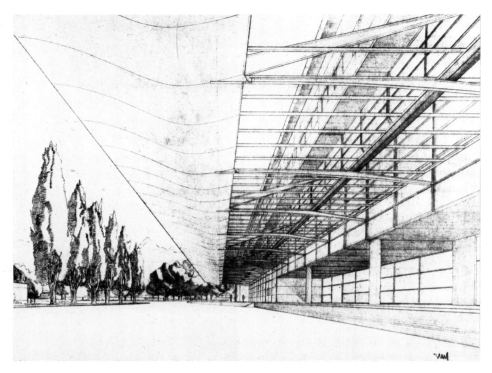

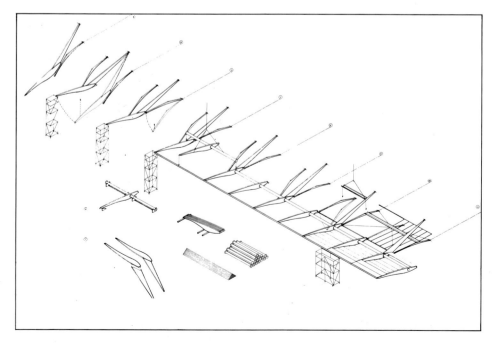

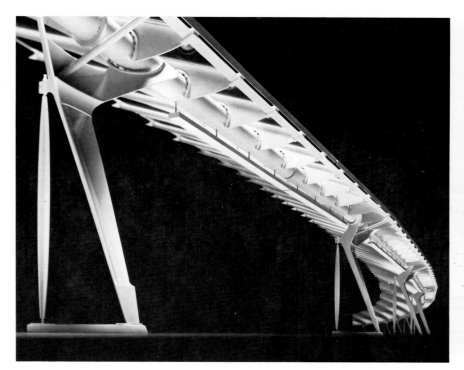

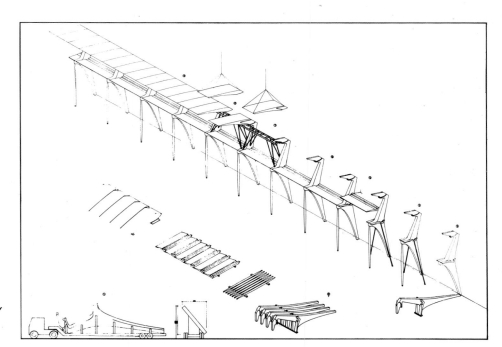

Figure 278 Bold canopies or railway station awnings: Santiago Calatrava counts among the few contemporary civil engineers who knows how to glorify technique to the benefit of enjoyment and beauty.

Technique as an image

This principle is undoubtedly best illustrated by the utopian projects of the British group Archigram (1960s-1970s) and by its largest 'child': the Centre Pompidou by Piano and Rogers in Paris.

Contrary to the 'glorification of technique' in which form is guided by the expressive articulation of the potential inherent in a technology, here it is a question of an opposite process: one designs the technical image and *then* looks for a technology which enables it to be built, even by craft methods if need be. Frampton observes quite fairly that '... Archigram was more interested in the seductive appeal of space-age imagery and, after Fuller, by the overtones of survival technology, than in the process of production or the relevance of such a sophisticated technique to the tasks of the moment.'[140]

Sputnik and Apollo broke the imaginable limits of technology. One no longer needed to be Jules Verne or to be led by the engineers. Everything became possible once one had imagined it: creations such as 'Plug-in City', 'Space Capsule', 'Instant City', illustrating technology serving pleasure.

Technological imagery has been a catalyst in the debate on the inertia of conventional forms. It finds scope for experiment and a show-case in national and world exhibitions, world fairs, sets for various shows, and temporary buildings, but it hardly has a place in urban architecture or in that which has to transcend generations.

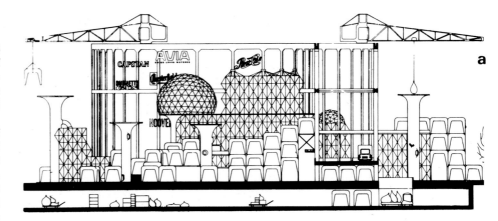

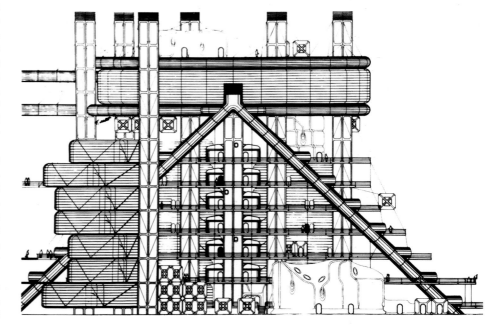

Figure 279 If the nineteenth and twentieth centuries not only introduced technology as an artistic message, they also assume the right to substitute the technical image for technical reality. 'Archigram was more interested in the attraction of space-age imagery ... than by the production or perfection of a really sophisticated technology for present day purposes' (K. Frampton)[140].
Archigram, Peter Cook and David Green, Nottingham Shopping Viaduct, 1962, and Peter Cook, Plug-in City 1962/64.

Figure 280 Technical illusion produced by the resemblance to mass-produced industrial products such as cars; symbols for clients eager to prove the virtue of progress. Piano and Rogers, Centre Pompidou, Paris, 1975.

Falsification

When the appearance of a technique is 'disturbing' one is inclined to make it disappear behind decoration which expresses what one would have wished to see. In the last years of Archigram (and the Beatles) a significant change came about. They saw themselves as precursors of a popular movement. Who wants to live in a 'capsule'? Archigram, back-pedalling, produced its last projects, amongst which were 'Hedgerow City' and 'Crater City'. All the sophisticated technology is buried, hidden behind the curtain of nature, in the same way as, today, some conceal it behind a neo-classical or pseudo-vernacular decor.

Other architects use economical techniques which they transform and reclothe in such a way as to *simulate* another technique from an earlier period and of greater 'prestige'. For Andrea Palladio brick columns, a timber architrave covered with stucco and false stones of stucco were legal currency.

In this respect it is important to make the distinction between the architecture of Greek antiquity and that of the Renaissance. It is true that the Greek temple in marble would not have its mutules or its modillions if its language were not derived from timber construction.

Figure 281 With the aim of creating an image, Palladio had no fears about restoring to a decor which simulates technique other than that actually used. Detail of the Villa Badoer di Fratta Polesine, Andrea Palladio, 1557. Frank Lloyd Wright retorted; 'Instinctively all forms of pretension fear and hate reality. The hypocrite must always hate the radical' (Frank Lloyd Wright, The Natural House, p. 60.)

Figure 282 'The Romans, judicious people, provided with our large pieces of iron, would have left the forms borrowed from the Greeks on the side in order to adopt new ones' (Viollet-le-Duc) R. Bofill, aedicule at St Quentin-en-Yvelines, 1982.

However, *at no moment is it a question of imitation of wood*, whereas Palladio mixes the stone base, the brick column, the wooden architrave, the brick tympanum, etc., and covers it all with stucco which undisguisedly *imitates* stone in order to create an *illusion* (Figure 281).

At the other extreme Viollet-le-Duc asserts '... that to clad iron columns with brick cylinders or stucco rendering, or to cover iron supports with masonry, is neither the product of calculation nor of imagination ...'[141]. Thus, towards the end of the nineteenth century, Viollet-le-Duc recognized in constructional falsification a resistance to innovation. The forms that have emerged from new building methods have not yet acquired the status of aesthetic

value; we cover them up in order to satisfy tastes from the past. Lack of familiarity always acts as a brake to the diffusion of an invention. Viollet-le-Duc launched into a fight for renewal which would bear fruit in the twentieth century.

Towards the end of the twentieth century this phenomenon of substitution does not have the same significance. It is no longer a question of resistance to innovation in the case of the Krier brothers in the 1970s and 1980s. They do not refuse invention as far as it serves an image which 're-fossilizes' the town by recalling the principles of construction in stone and brick. Their propositions are merely a criticism of the material heterogeneity of the modern city.

Their strength lies more, however, in the proposition of a spatial order for the town by giving back to the public space a clear and recognizable form, than in the promotion of obsolete material methods. The substitution of an economic and constructional reality by recourse to the imagery of old techniques cannot be the basis of a contemporary aesthetic. The cry of alarm by the adherents of a fossilized town in the image of the past will never have the power of those who confidently use modern methods.

Technique subdued

With the technical means of the twentieth century, architecture has been able to assume the great formal freedom which we know. From the 1920s onward, modern architecture has sought its renewal by moving closer to the conceptual world of abstract painting and sculpture, especially Cubist and Purist. Thus, contrary to widely held opinion today, its inspiration is not only derived from the expression of function or technique. The latter was often the servant of artistic expression for the great majority of avant-garde architects. Architecture has itself become plastic art manifest in such examples as Rietveld's Schroeder house, Lissitzky's Constructivist designs, Terragni's Frigerio house, Le Corbusier's church at Ronchamp and so many other outstanding works.

Peter Collins, a critic and historian of modern architecture has admirably grasped these contemporary phenomena in his book *Changing Ideals in Modern Architecture*. Let us quote a key passage from it:

The new theory of abstract art led to the complete interchangeability of artistic disciplines; it also inevitably suggested that the Vitruvian qualities of usefulness and stability were artistically of little importance as compared with the abstract aesthetic value which every building potentially possessed. ... The ideal of a complete fusion of abstract sculpture, abstract painting and building technology was expressed by J. J. P. Oud in his manifesto *On the Architecture of the Future,* published in 1921, in which he announced that 'a self-created architecture is possible at last, to which the other

arts are no longer subordinated. ... The Bauhaus students were initiated into the study of architecture by manipulating abstract shapes without any reference to building functions or the ultimate strength of materials, but solely with a view to achieving ornamental appeal in terms of 'significant form'

This relatively dematerialized approach to design, to criticism and teaching has opened undreamt-of routes to the flourishing of architecture as an authentic art of the twentieth century. Today it is architects like Richard Meier and Peter Eisenman[143], critics like Colin Rowe and Robert Slutzky [144] and teachers like John Hejduk and Daniel Libeskind[145], who have best grasped, manipulated and developed these

Figure 283 Between frame and vault: as for the Baroque, Jörn Utzon's plastic and spatial intentions take precedence over constructional reality. Baqsvaerd church, Copenhagen, 1973–76.

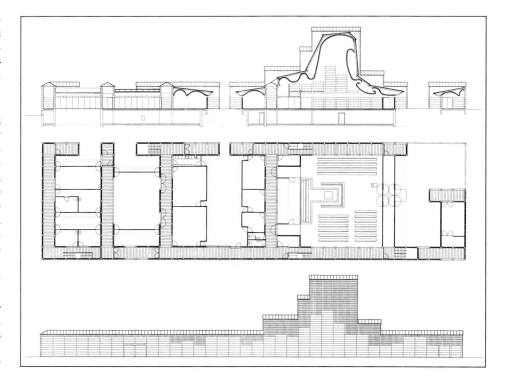

newly acquired constructional freedoms with the objective of applying contemporary plastic art to architecture.

They exploit the technical possibilities by subordinating them to a formal end. A column represents a vertical line, a balustrade becomes a strip, walls and floors are planes – the whole able to be covered with a white or coloured rendering in order to complete its dematerialization.

In practice, this approach sometimes leads us down dangerous paths because, by playing down constructional constraints, it can produce weaknesses in weather resistance or premature ageing of the building. It also deprives the building of a certain common sense which emanates from the logical indications of its being built. Let us emphasize, on the other hand, the enormous didactic advantages when such an approach is considered as *one of the steps* in the architect's training. Without functional or constructional alibis, the student must temporarily turn his attention to the inherent potential within the means of geometry and form in order to develop a concept.

Architectural form is certainly linked to use and technique, but it also enjoys a certain independence. On one hand, the same techniques and the same content do not in any way determine a precise form. On the other hand, built form proves to be a less ephemeral reality than use. There are very few examples of buildings whose life span does not extend beyond that of their initial use and meaning.

Figure 284 'The new architecture is elementary. It develops from elements of construction in the widest sense: function, mass, surface, time, space, light, colour, material, etc..., these elements generate form' (Theo van Doesburg, extract from the De Stijl Manifesto, 1924).

Plastic art in architecture by the de-composition of the plane of the façade in closely spaced layers: Giuseppe Terragni, Casa Frigerio, Como, 1939.

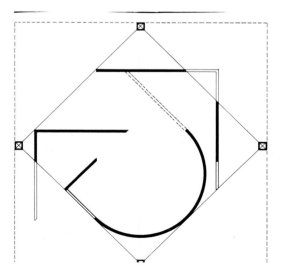

Figure 285 The student, working without functional and constructional alibis, temporarily centres his attention on the potential inherent in the methods of geometry and form: this is an irrefutable didactic advantage. Student exercise, EPFL, 1975–83.

Technique tamed

Technology has become part of the everyday order of things. It preserves us from famine, it offers us comfort and health, an extraordinary freedom of movement and also gives us the luxury of time for thought, study or play. Its failures provoke disruption according to the degree of our dependence on it. Technology can also be threatening by its harmful effects and the waste it creates. The earth already shows the scars of its inconsiderate exploitation inflicted by the frantic cycle of production and consumption.

The last quarter of the twentieth century is thus seeking rather to conceal technology without abandoning it as such. It simply refuses to elevate it to a monument. It is obviously not sufficient to hide it; it must be reinvented, and its impact on the planet on which we live must be regulated. In this intermediate phase in which we are living, technology will continue to influence form and appearance but it might no longer express itself loudly. That is what gives the works of Kahn, Scarpa, Botta and others a special

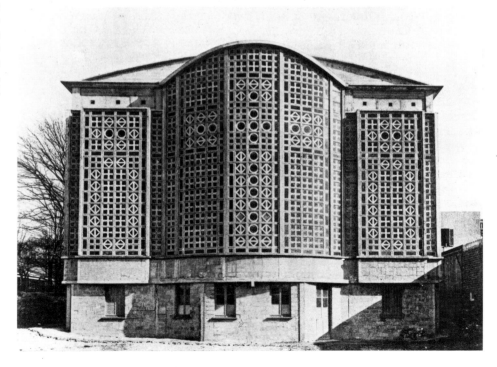

Figure 286 'Was Gothic architecture because of stone or regardless of it?' (F. L. Wright). Rouen Cathedral.

Figure 287 'Decoration does not only mean a surface modified by man's imagination, but imagination giving a natural design to the structure ... articulating and making visible the material structure of the building, just as the structures of trees or lilies are articulated ... it is these qualities which distinguish the essence of architecture from the simple act of building' (F. L. Wright). Perret, Notre Dame du Raincy, 1923.

relevance. Technique is tamed when it concerns itself with habitability and enjoyment with neither pride nor shame in its own rationality and laws.

Not being ashamed does not mean emphasizing all traces of construction. Let this anecdote recounted by Tessenow puts us on our guard against extremes:

An old, experienced and influential craftsman once said: if, for example, one nails two planks of wood together to make a door, one must show quite openly how it is made, and if possible one should show where the nails have gone through the plank and reappeared at the back, etc. If during this operation a splinter is pushed out, one should simply tear it off and do nothing more about it.

One can say that this story is nothing more than an image, but it shows where honesty can lead. A sort of 'bang-bang honesty' exists. It is these extremes of which we are afraid ... We want craftsmanship to be truthful as a general rule, but we do not want, indiscriminately, to see each nail and every glued joint[146].

Once tamed, technique that is made visible is allowed and even called for, but the objective must remain an overall one. An elegant trace of the building process becomes an integrated ornament, as F. L. Wright would say, but this decoration must have a meaning in the architectural and artistic concept of the building. It cannot be the simple result of a building process. The project exploits technique as a resource for motifs for structuring the form without, however, allowing itself to be dominated. 'Beauty is the true and chosen expression of the material elements available and of the physi-cal or moral needs that must be satisfied ...'.[147]

At their best, form and technique have a balanced relationship, each emphasizing its qualities and its claims. It is when neither technique nor form try to dazzle us on their own that we come closer to architecture. 'Technical honesty' must not take precedence over general honesty.

Gothic cathedrals remain perhaps the most sublime example of technique tamed. Frank Lloyd Wright suggests that it is not the stone which inspired the cathedrals. It is a limiting factor; it makes one wonder whether Gothic architecture is of stone or whether it is what it is in spite of the stone.[148] Stone is no doubt used in it with a greater knowledge of its characteristics than was the case in Greek antiquity. The material is carried to extreme limits of performance owing to a structure whose logic is not intrinsic, but the product of an alliance between technique and the objective of religious glorification of the period.

Figure 288 A symbiosis which seeks its perfection in the balance between man's artistic urge and the physical 'urge' inherent in the materials; Mario Botta, house at Ligornetto, 1978.

How to choose?

The critical review of the five attitudes towards materials and their utilization could lead us to espouse or oppose one rather than another according to our tastes. However, it would not be too difficult for most of us to agree with Viollet-le-Duc when he said: 'The Romans, judicious people, provided with our large pieces of iron, would have left the forms borrowed from the Greeks on one side in order to adopt new ones'.[149] Frank Lloyd Wright and many other moderns could just as well have said it. Truth must lie in the nature of materials. By adopting this position we would at least have reassuring directives for attaining 'an architecture of truth'.

It is no longer necessarily an adequate theory for our culture, as we near the end of the twentieth century, because our sophisticated technology allows us, on one hand, to make a 'perfect' and cheap imitation of a technique by substituting it with another, and on the other hand more than ever opens the way to cladding because of the requirements of thermal insulation.

Frank Lloyd Wright rejects these realities, saying that imitation is the natural tendency of man, not of mankind[150]. Perhaps we should make a clear distinction between *imitation* (or substitution) and apparent *dematerialization*. The latter is no longer 'a sin' these days. We have seen that, by de-materialization, we mean a design process whereby the sculptural play of the geometry of spaces, forms and surfaces dominates to the extent that the different materials with which they are created must be made homogeneous under a unified facing (Gerrit Rietveld, Theo van Doesburg, J. J. P. Oud, Jörn Utzon, Peter Eisenmann, Richard Meier, John Hejduk, etc.). With an architecture of facing to which our thermal demands are leading, such a tendency acquires a justification. Moreover, some buildings would gain by being covered with a unifying layer rather than 'honestly' displaying their heterogeneous range of materials. De-materialization has therefore become today one of the legitimate approaches and a potential for contemporary expression.

Little used, condemned by the majority of great contemporary architects, this approach conflicts with another which refuses to deprive architecture of the language of materials and their utilization. Without going as far as the nails which show through the assembled planks of the door, material as surface and texture as well as elements whose joints are a decorative feature originating in construction will always remain a valuable ingredient of architecture, as we can clearly see in the works of Louis Kahn and Carlo Scarpa.

The approaches of technique as an image, and the technique of substitution, are without any doubt the most debated and the most debatable. Architecture can never be merely an image. It would be deprived of its foundation, of its role in organizing territorial space into private places for accommodating human life. One can therefore hardly impose the same criteria of truth and untruth on architecture as on art in general. If illusion is the medium of picturesque expression, it cannot be the basis of architecture, whose role remains more concrete and thematic.

Stage sets are a kind of architecture, but architecture is not a stage set.

8.2 Materials have their own propensities

It is enough to know the physical and economic capacity of materials in order to build as a contractor. For an architect this type of performance is not very satisfactory. The form and space of architecture *are qualified* by the character of the materials and the way they are prepared and put in place. Light is a contributory factor. The result is '*an ambience*'; it is exactly this word 'ambience' which is suitable here, a valuable word which does not really have an equivalent in the English language. We are obliged to use this foreign word to talk about the character of a place. In the definition of place, forms play their role by means of the material. When we run our hands or our eyes over it, it shows itself to be fragile or resistant, soft or hard, cold or temperate. According to its surface treatment the same material will be smooth or rough, matt, satiny or shiny. Polishing is what shows up its internal structure by laying it bare. Materials also have symbolic significance: they can evoke opulence or austerity, the ephermeral or the eternal, vegetable, mineral or artificial mixture, the private or the public, industrial or craft. Building materials thus potentially carry connotations.

Examination of the subjective impressions conveyed by stone, concrete, wood, metal or fabric indicates that connotations evolve with technology and culture. They sometimes go beyond their immediate constructional role, as the three following examples might show.

Hewn stone, extracted skilfully from its bed, then carefully worked and jointed, gives us an assurance of its long life in exchange for man's sweat. When polished, it can become a cladding, showing off its veins and its colours. Each time that man has sought to secure its most important values by anchoring them in time, it is to stone that he has turned (Figure 289). Its meaning has hardly changed; its connotation of durability is the result of thousands of years of experience and resistance to fire. More resistant than the sandstone of Swiss cathedrals, less than the marble of Athens, *concrete* has become the 'rock' of twentieth century's builders. The mould is easy enough to construct; it is even reusable!

Reinforced, well gauged, vibrated and protected, concrete knows hardly any limits.

Wood, softer, easier to work as a structural and cladding material, even accepts tension; it has not always been as well regarded as today. Sensitive to weathering, it requires protection on the exterior (Figure 290). Deeming it to be too dark and less noble than stone, its true character has sometimes been stifled by a covering. The woodwork in rooms of eighteenth-century houses was filled and painted. At other periods wood was not only considered as a poor material, but it

constituted a risk. Fires in the Middle Ages led to a hostility towards wood, whereas today interior walls and ceilings in wood are appreciated because they evoke shelter and warmth compared with the 'coldness' of industrial products.

Pressed metal, thin and supple metal sheets that are pressed on moulds in order to give them great rigidity has transformed the face of our environment. Transport vehicles, packaging, some pieces of furniture, etc., can release an extraordinary sensuality of form. And yet pressed or folded metal used in building has already fallen some-

Figure 289 Hewn stone – assurance of longevity; Segestum, Sicily.

Figure 290 Wood, easier to work, perhaps more ephemeral, but it remains a valuable component of man's shelter; v. Meiss, Collomb, Natterer, Le Châtelard school, Lausanne, 1979.

what into disgrace. Assimilated to our consumer products, it removes something from the idea of the longevity of the town and it symbolizes a progress which is no longer unanimously welcomed (Figure 291).

We could just as well have spoken about plastics. The distinction between 'natural' and 'synthetic' materials does not, however, make much sense, because paper, stainless steel and resins are not in conflict with nature, rather adding, by man's intelligence, to it, and he is already part of this nature.

The three examples - hewn stone, wood and pressed metal - present materials as bearers of messages from history and culture with a potential for poetics. That is only one aspect of their character.

It would be a mistake to consider materials as more or less neutral or inert bodies awaiting our imagination and our application. Materials also have their own urge, their 'soul'. In order to make judicious choices, the architect must consider them in a dialogue with his sensitivity.

He must first of all question the materials about what they want to be. That means not asking too much of them, nor too little. For this one must learn to know their inherent characteristics. Each material has its own 'structural potential' because it suggests certain volumetric and spatial forms. It also has its own 'application potential', of assembly, and formation of joints. Then it has its own 'cladding potential'. These resources are sufficiently rich for it not to be necessary to force one material to resemble another. The painted imitation of precious marbles in the Baroque churches of Bavaria, where there were none of these marbles, is certainly a demonstration of skilled craftsmanship, but it hardly shows a way to the future. Imitation by industrial methods has become *too easy* to be credible and respectable. The apparent perfection of false rustic expanded polystyrene beams stuck onto a reinforced concrete ceiling, and the photographic wood finish under plastic laminate surfaces have devalued imitation. To find its right to art again, imitation must be diverted from its original function and be displayed as such. Trix and Robert Haussmann work with talent and humour in this surprising and almost surrealist mode (Figure 292).

Questioning a material on what it can and wants to be in terms of formative structure of architectural spaces, is to give it authority and restrict our choices. Hewn stone will express other spaces and lights and textures than brick, wood, reinforced concrete or steel ... Frank Lloyd Wright is certainly correct when he says that 'a stone building will no

Figure 291 Pressed or folded metal – connotation of consumer products and industrial precision; corner detail of an industrial shed; Jean-Daniel Baechler, Fribourg, 1981.

more *be* nor will it *look* like a steel building. A pottery, or terracotta building, will not be nor should it look like a stone building. A wood building will look like none other, for it will glorify the stick. A steel and glass building could not possibly look like anything but itself. It will glorify steel and glass....'[151] Alas, this general principle does not serve as much of a guide; within each technique there exists a multitude of possible forms.

What then, together with the choice of material, are the variables manipulated by the architect, the craftsman and the labourer? The 'tactility' of a building always has a triple aesthetic aspect: *the form, 'massiveness' and the texture/ colour combination*, whether it is a question of an element of construction prepared before being put to use, such as brick, the panel of a façade, one step of a flight of steps, or whether it is an element of composite architecture such as a wall, façade or staircase.

Figure 292 'Function follows form'; five functional metamorphoses of a conventional element by Trix and Robert Haussmann, 1977–78. A game with history or history as a game? Artistic quality permits ethical transgression. Furniture design may be more permissive than buildings.

Form and material

By material 'form' we mean *the geometry of the volumetric envelope* of an element with a view to making it capable of production, resistant, manipulable and capable of assembly in order to serve and delight man.

To illustrate our point, we shall use the example of *brick*, this material used for thousands of years which has never lost its contemporary usefulness, in fact quite the opposite, since new sorts of brick are continually being invented. Terracotta or concrete block replace laboriously hewn stone. Working only in compression, it borrows structural and spatial forms from stone: wall, arch, vault and dome. But its manufacture makes it quite different: clay or malleable concrete at the outset, baked or hardened respectively, it can be given a form and relief which respond with less effort to our intentions in terms of surface texture. Its oblong geometry, size and weight have nothing arbitrary about them; they fit the mason's hand, the other hand remaining free for the trowel. The first use of brick is *the wall* - whether it be load-bearing or not. To be rigid it requires perfect verticality and bracing angles or curvatures; their frequency determines the ratios between thickness, height and length. To be as homogeneous as possible it requires the mortar beds to be perfectly horizontal and the vertical joints to be alternated. To be economical, the brick wall requires the dimensions of length, width and height to be a multiple of its elements and joints. To remain sound, this material demands secure foundations and, when it is porous, to be protected from humidity in the ground, from rain and from frost on its surface. Such are the requirements of the wall and brick combined.

But brick can do more than the wall. Louis Kahn said: 'If you ask a brick what it wants to be, it would say, 'an arch'. Sometimes you ask concrete to help the brick and brick is very happy.'

Would certain materials therefore harmonize with certain forms and vice versa? Kahn's attractive aphorism conveys with great relevance the form by which man attains the greatest virtuosity using brick intelligently. With the dome, brick is at its best (Figure 293). Kahn does not say that brick demands the vault, but he identifies the sublime use of brick in architecture when it outwits gravity.

In the economy of contemporary building, the vault and dome have given way to the reinforced concrete slab. The idea that brick may 'be helped' by concrete is considered by purist adherents of glorified technology as a perversion. But should we reject metal fixings in a timber frame in order to return to the onerous technique of pegging? Why should we prevent an ancient mate-

Figure 293 With the dome, brick is at its best: church of the Virgin Theotokos, Hosios Convent, Greece, about AD950.

184

rial being helped by new techniques thanks to composite structures?

Let us take the example of the interlocking brick of synthetic material, measuring 100 × 100 × 200 mm, developed and used at the Laboratoire d'Expérimentation Architecturale (LEA) at the Ecole Polytechnique Fédérale in Lausanne. It is used as a teaching aid for design through full-scale simulation of architectural spaces. Consequently the constructions must be easily modifiable, demountable and remountable, hence the use of a light brick with accurate, dry joints, requiring precise interlocking to ensure the stability of the wall. This means it is not possible to alter the thickness and treatment of the joint, nor the facing. The walls are built on the ground without foundation. Not being loaded, their stability is precarious; corners and braces are necessary.

In an exercise on the bonding and modulation of walls carried out with students at the EPFL, we have done experiments in which the constraints of this particular material were to become design stimuli. The walls tended to transform themselves into arcades and, from one transgression to another, a pyramidal dome of about 3 m in diameter has appeared, an archetype which, until then, was reputed to be unfeasible with LEA's interlocking bricks (Figures 294–296).

This example shows how form and the system of construction sustain relationships stimulating composition to the point of fascination. Design and experiment can explore the farthest limits of stability with respect to one material, *or* explore its decorative capacities, in the correct meaning of the word.

Brick becomes clever in the hands of the Roman mason. It assists the

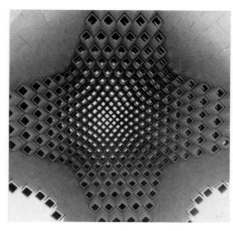

Figures 294–296 The constraints of an interlocking brick become a stimulation for the design of walls, archways and domes. Laboratoire d'Expérimentation Architecturale, EPFL, 1980.

pozzolana concrete, and not the opposite, in order to build the gigantic vaults of the thermal baths. It accepts the role of formwork.

It is fascinating to use a material by pushing its performance to the limits. The bricks forming the inclined columns at Antonio Gaudi's Colonia Güell in Barcelona excite the imagination by their audacity in having touched the bounds of credibility. He had to be an architect-builder of very great experience to manipulate materials with such ease. When brick is used with such virtuosity, without even being assisted by concrete, it is no longer a simple question of design, nor calculation, but much more the product of reason and practice, trial and error (Figure 297).

Materials do not tolerate excess; within the limits of their resistance, manufacture and installation, they grant a considerable margin to form. The great formal diversity of brick buildings is proof of this. The kind of thought that we have just given to the material aspects of brick and form, must be given, and in even greater depth, to the nature of all building materials.

Figure 297 Brick pushed to the limits of credibility thanks to the great expertise of Antonio Gaudi. Colonia Güell, Santa Coloma de Cervello, 1898.

Thickness

If the volumetric envelope is a fundamental characteristic of form, its 'massiveness' is a particularly significant complementary attribute. The same form can appear thin or thick, solid or hollow. Mass influences our perception of things. The thin sheet metal of a car body and the massive mould on which it is pressed are judged in a totally different way. However, they have the same exterior form (Figure 298). The two images show very clearly the opposition in nature between the hollow and the solid form. The sheet metal is pressed so that its shell form becomes sufficiently rigid to resist normal stress, whilst at the same time providing, with the greatest economy of material, space for other parts. Its mould is built to resist the extraordinary force of the press; it does not have an interior.

We have said that architecture is an art of the hollow. The perception that one has of the spatial envelope of a building depends largely on the way in which we modulate and perforate the thickness of this envelope. A façade with deeply recessed windows will evoke 'fortress' and security whereas the urban Baroque Viennese window carefully placed on the exterior surface of a wall of the same thickness is agreeably deceptive, giving the whole building an appearance of lightness and elegance (Figures 299 and 300).

From the interior the thickness of a spatial envelope qualifies the space around the opening. A window placed in an 80 cm wall represents this envelope in a completely different manner from a window set in a 20 cm or less wall (Figure 301). Each opening creates a 'space of wall thickness' and causes reflections of light on the reveals. In a thin wall or a curtain wall, space and reflected light are negligible. The space of wall thickness can become a place between the inside and the outside; accessible or not, it is one of the attractions of many traditional stone buildings.

Mass influences not only the manner in which we see architecture, but also its connotation of resistance and longevity. Rightly or wrongly, thin seems less permanent than thick, even if this thickness is sometimes only fake. In the Baroque a wall which appears very solid is often only the combination of two relatively thin shells concealing its hollow character. What interests us, in short, is the *apparent* rather than the actual massiveness.

Thinness also has a poetic potential. The circular stairs of Nervi's

Figure 298 The thin sheet metal of a car body is experienced in a totally different way from the solid mould on which it has been pressed. However, they have the same exterior form. Volkswagen factories, 1985.

Figures 299 and 300 Massiveness or lightness as a result of the position of windows in the thickness of the façade. Baroque Rome, where each window aspires to be a deep aedicule, and Baroque Vienna, where the subdued profiles of the windows constitute an elegant surface texture.

Figure 301 Openings in the wall reveal its thickness. There exists a 'space of the wall thickness'.

stadium in Florence, whose thickness is reduced to as little as 4 cm. Candella's large-span thin membranes, the elegant curtain wall of Mies van der Rohe's Seagram Building, or Frei Otto's daring tents, need not envy the massiveness of the pyramids.

The creation of architectural form, therefore, also requires a '*design for the thickness of spatial envelopes*' in harmony with other more general aspects of the plan such as the site, brief, theme, space, light, and building methods.

Texture and surface modulation

The arrangement of coursing and bonding in masonry construction and mouldings and trimstone regulate the surfaces which surround us by the control of profiles, joints between elements and changes in materials (Figure 302).

Le Corbusier stresses this potential:

Surface modulation is the architect's touchstone. He reveals himself either as an artist or simply as an engineer.

Surface modulation is free from all constraint. It is no longer a question of habits, traditions, building processes, nor of adaptation to utilitarian requirements.

Surface modulation is a pure creation of the mind; it calls for the sculptor.[152]

These observations are of considerable relevance. They reflect a determination to defend the autonomy of architectural form with formal or

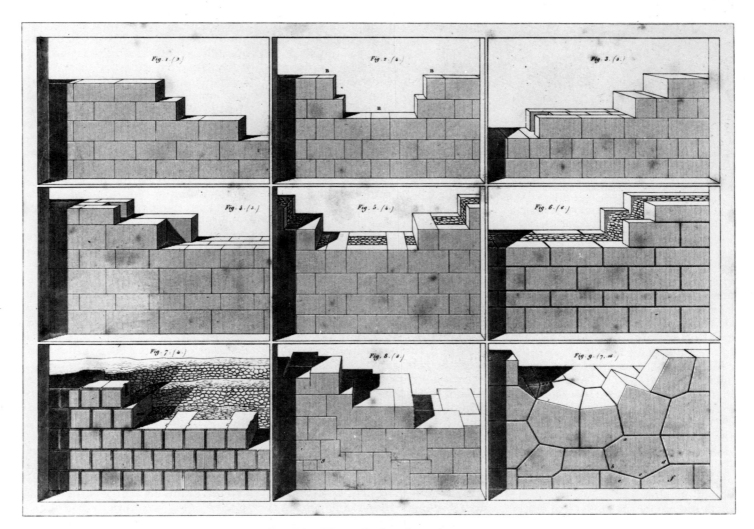

Figure 302 Wall bonding according to Jean Rondelet. Theoretical and Practical Treatise on the Art of Building, 1810–17.

Figure 303 Pure volumes and underlying texture without surface modulation, Cyclades.

symbolic objectives and not as the mere result of realities of production. Nevertheless, surface modulation is only exceptionally a pure creation of mind (stage set design for example); in fact it is *also* the reflection of a compromise by a designer who has to arrange the material and to join the elements together.

The surface texture and colour of the materials used, their combination and their jointing give the space its ultimate character, its 'status' and its 'temperature'. Traces of the chisel, bush-hammer or polishing machine model the surface of stone; joints between bricks, marks of formwork or the grain of wood on moulded concrete, the metal plate

taking the oblique forces of a timber frame, the lack of precision of a cut with an axe or the precision of the plane, the enamelling of a surface, the bend of sheet metal are all traces of fashioning which, together with colour, model the surfaces. They inform us about certain attributes of the building, for example its thickness, which we discussed earlier.

Frank Lloyd Wright enables us to rediscover the value of 'integral ornament - the nature-pattern of actual construction' as a confrontation with material, as opposed to symbolic decoration. Integrated decoration is not, however, just the result of physical necessity.[153] Man's power of imagination modifies the surface by structuring it in harmony with his intentions and the material used. This also distinguishes architecture from ordinary building activity.

The precision of fashioning materials has always been an aim and a measure of human mastery of nature. *Polishing*, which reveals the internal structure of the material, is the ultimate stage of it. It erases the idea that the object has been made with tools; all that remains is the object itself. As architecture most often produces fairly coarse objects, it is nevertheless useful to know and to exploit the decorative effects of traces of fashioning and especially their capacity to differentiate reflections of light. The Greeks knew how to make the most of their tools to exploit the potential of reflected light which results from differences in texture of the same material.

Since an architectural element is composed of several parts, acknowledgement of the traces of assembly often becomes inevitable, unless a cladding is applied (Figure 303). A stone or brick wall is not, primarily, a geometric plane or panel. The

many standardized elements and their joints form a texture, a lasting trace of the act of construction (Figure 304). The recessed or projecting articulation between these elements shows the bonding at a detailed level. Instead of amounting to a uniform texture, these individual elements can constitute groups in such a way as to produce a design on a larger scale: *surface modulation*.

To discuss bonding and surface modulation we shall take the example of brick again, in a precise context. The art of Palaeo-Christian and Byzantine building is based on Roman inherited skills: the spatial enclosure of the vault and the dome and the composite wall construction of roughly cut stones alternating with beds of precise bricks. Byzantium developed the Roman techniques by increasing both the spatial possibilities (Saint Sophia in Constantinople) and the decorative effects of the bonding in order to save the expense of an exterior facing. In building a wall it is the corners and the openings which require the most care in construction. The corners are then carried out in precisely cut stone and the face of the wall in rubble, or roughly cut stone, sometimes surrounded with brick, thus creating surface modulation (Figure 305). Builders of Byzantine churches and palaces, incidentally, often economized on the cutting of stone by framing two or three arched windows in brick, thus emphasizing the form and importance of the openings. Sometimes the simple turning of the bricks by 45 degrees, without special bricks or the addition of more expensive materials, accentuates the outline of the windows in the roughness of the wall. The infill brick chips of the tympanum, in their matrix of mortar, form, in turn, a surface decoration. Long experience of working with materials, and not the design itself, opened the way towards this method of economical treatment. The heavy elements in hewn stone can be restricted to capitals and centre columns of the windows whose slenderness prohibits the use of brick.

Each material is used within its own working logic, but with an overall objective. Brick has served the window well. The rational and refined combination of stone and brick guarantees the coherence of the whole. The exact places where there are changes in the form of assembly or in the material coincide with key locations in terms of the building as a whole: plinth, corners, openings, cornice, principal façade, lateral façade (Figure 305). The result is a design which makes it possible to accentuate edges and to introduce order on a larger scale than the simple additive texture of stones.

This example shows that the economy of cladding does not in any way exclude a decorative effect of the structure of the surfaces and architectural elements, when the materials are chosen, dimensioned and assembled with sensitivity, imagination and intelligence. Among contemporary examples one can cite the work of Mario Botta or, less well known, the repair of the breach in the Munich Pinakothek by Hans Döllgast after bomb damage (Figure 306).

Figure 304 Bonding and surface modulation without facing: detail of the side façade of Leon Battista Alberti's Sant' Andrea in Mantua.

Figure 305 Bonding becoming surface modulation; Saint Sophia, Monemvassia, Greece.

Figure 306 A great lesson in architecture: the Munich Pinakothek, damaged by bombs in the Second World War, emerges from its rubble with the greatest economy of means in the post-war period. The architect has known how to honour the sumptuous past by the modest means of salvaged brick and steel which were available immediately after the war.

Support structure and cladding

The appearance of the surface of walls, floors and ceilings is important enough for a more resistant or higher quality cladding to be often applied to the mass of a structure which has been built with cheaper materials.

Italy, from the time of the Romans to the Renaissance and Baroque, hardly bestowed the stamp of respectability upon fair-faced brickwork, quite the opposite to Byzantium and, later, the Nordic countries. Brick is considered to be an economical means for building *a structure to be subsequently clad* by a superior material: marble slabs, stucco frescoes, mosaics, etc. Rome's wealth had limits which would have made a massive construction in hewn stone without cladding too costly to cover the thermal baths, the Pantheon, or to build a prestigious villa. With the exception of columns Rome therefore used cheaper structural material with cladding to lend the desired glamour to its buildings. The Renaissance, upholding the idea and the image of the building more than its constructional reality, differentiated the scenic role of the main façades of a religious building and often treated the sides and the back as 'common sheds' (Figure 307). Conversely, Greek antiquity, Byzantine and Gothic architecture considered buildings as precious objects of which neither the sides nor the rear deserve to be neglected. One can see a conceptual difference here between these civilizations.

There has been a period in modern architecture when the principle itself of cladding has been rejected in favour of the rough appearance of 'real' materials (the 1960s). The Greek temple with its columns and walls in solid marble was then recognized as a model of honesty. Viollet-le-Duc did not hide his preference for the Greek, who did not distinguish construction from deco-

Figure 307 'Scenographic' cladding of the principal facade during the Renaissance period. The side and back are relegated to the rank of 'ordinary sheds'; Leon Battista Alberti's Sant' Andrea in Mantua.

ration, whereas he accused the Roman of being an 'upstart dresser' who only called on the artist once the material requirements (structure and space) were met.[154] More than Rome, one could have denounced Palladio (Figure 281) but this contempt for cladding would be excessive. Rome and Byzantium could not have financed their dreams in solid marble; it was brick and cladding which provided them with an economical method compatible with their ambitions. Gottfried Semper said: 'Form which is the expression of an idea must not contradict the material of which it is made, but it is nonetheless not indispensable for the material as such to be added to the work of art.'[155] – an opinion which is diametrically opposed to that of Viollet-le-Duc or Wright, which we discussed earlier.

Semper's proposition corresponds fairly well to certain demands of contemporary building. Thermal economy is directing us by necessity towards 'composite envelopes'. The development of an architectured cladding is therefore a real task for our times. The fact that thermal insulation, which is by necessity light and fragile, would be more effectively placed on the exterior than on the interior of the structure will perhaps alter the appearance of our buildings. It is only resistance to change which means that, for the moment, this 'overcoat' continues most of the time to assume conventional forms.

Cladding allows the surface, and even space, great formal freedom. Its laws are not necessarily guided by structural requirements. Its thinness means it is possible to use high quality, more resistant and more expensive surface materials than those used for the structure. Their unit size and modulation can follow a logic which more easily complies with the formal intentions of architecture.

Besides purely technical considerations, we can pick out roughly two uses of cladding: one which does not fundamentally alter the space produced by the structure, following it closely or even exaggerating it; the other contradicts structural reality by producing different spaces and objects, as we have shown in the abbey church of Einsiedeln (Figures 190 and 191). This path has become a precarious one to follow. There is no longer that unifying theme which governed the space of illusion as there was in the Baroque period. Consequently there is a risk of illusion causing alienation.

On an apparently more technical level, cladding which closely follows structure can, in turn, be divided into two categories.

Some very thin claddings *adhere* to the whole surface of the structure, for example paint, rendering, wallpaper, mosaics and tiles. If the texture of the structure is sufficiently pronounced and if the cladding consists of mosaics or a thin film which is flexible at the moment of application, the texture of the support shows through, but its irregularity is less apparent.

Other claddings come in the form of slabs or panels which are *fixed* individually to the structure, for example marble, glass, metal or wood. Their geometry and joints introduce a new modulation which does not necessarily correspond to that of the hidden structure. The fixing can be hidden or visible. In the latter case it introduces a new texture which accompanies the rhythm of the panels, as in Otto Wagner's Postsparkasse in Vienna.

The wise and sensitive combination of these two methods of cladding, by adhesion or fixing, has made it possible to create some extremely refined buildings, as we shall see by examining the Byzantine example of the church of the convent of Hosios Loukas built in the eleventh century not far from Delphi (Figure 308). I shall describe its interior:

The walls up to the springing of the arches, vaults and dome are clad in solemn dress as for a celebration: an arrangement of slabs of polished marble, in grey, emerald, reddish brown, pink and ochre, large, simple rectangles which mutually encircle, juxtapose and superimpose themselves on each other in harmony with the spatial structure, making the transition between heaven and earth. A very thin ribbon of white marble, in slight relief, surrounds the slabs and gives them a relative autonomy. A geometric abstraction, the wall is thus clothed with classical simplicity which inspires respect for the place (Figure 309).

This dress is not a 'wall', it does not disappear in the ground in search of support. The marble cladding swells out slightly at its base and merely brushes the ground. The dress has its hem: the plinth with the slight relief of its white marble mouldings (Figure 310). Faithful companion to the wall, not straying at all from its master's path, the plinth traces, or rather retraces with its clear line, the ground plan of the church – and it does so superbly.

Above this plinth the rhythm of the rectangles does not start immediately. First of all there is horizontal band of monochrome marble, calm and smooth, contrasting with the verticality of the space or, rather, counterbalancing it. Two fine threads of white marble moulding accompany it, one at eye level and

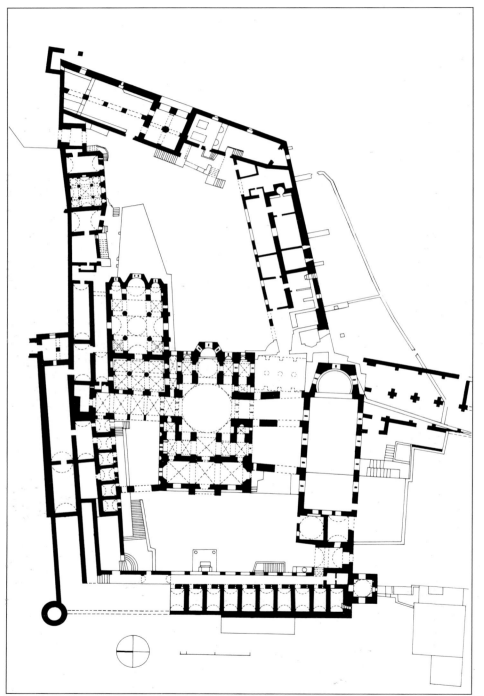

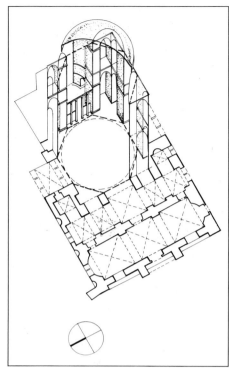

Figure 308 Hosios Loukas, Byzantine convent in Attica with two churches, and one of the tenth and one of the eleventh centuries; plan and axonometric.

Figure 309 '...the wall is thus clothed, without paintings, or statuary, with classical simplicity which inspires respect'.

Figure 311 'Two threads of marble accompany the 'ribbon' of the base, one at eye level and one at raised arm level'.

Figure 310 '... the dress has its hem, it does not disappear into the ground'.

Figure 312 'From behind this sober and dignified clothing appears, for a moment and for the first time, the skin of the building, with the evangelists'.

Figure 313 'Above the rigorous and articulated geometry of the cladding rises in great splendour the naked body of the building with its skin of mosaics'.

the other at raised arm level (Figure 311).

Between the lower level of recesses and vaults and those at the top, there is the *string course*, in white marble like the plinth, but with a delicate, repetitive, carved ornament. It gives scale to the height. In contrast to the plinth, which escapes discreetly towards the edge, the string course continues around the central square and the apse. But, before we get to the string course, something extra ordinary happens. We discover that underneath the dress there is a body! The dress has four openings which reveal the nakedness of the wall with its skin clad in gold and 'tattooed' with portraits of the four evangelists - openings which are forerunners of the vaults and the dome (Figure 312).

Above the string course, still in marble, are large, polychrome rectangles and white threads, which end with the 'collar', a simple white frieze like the string course. Here *suddenly and magically emerges the 'real' body, the load-bearing structure which escapes from the rigour of its dress and transforms itself immediately into arches, vaults, pendentives and dome.* A *skin* of mosaics covers the flesh. The contrast is controlled in a masterly fashion; from the rigorous and articulated geometry of the man-made dress emerges the continuity of the sensuous forms and textures of the body (Figure 313).

What a superb lesson in architecture and building, which manages to create, with confidence and economy of means, this contrast between the spirituality of the ceiling - because the dome seeks to be untouchable, a sky well beyond the measure of man - and the serene and rational beauty of the marble on the walls! The height of refinement is perhaps in

Figure 314 The line conveys the spatial idea.

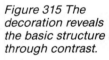

Figure 315 The decoration reveals the basic structure through contrast.

the announcement by the four semi-domes of the evangelists - these lanterns on the walls, four tear-drops fallen from heaven, forming the ceiling of the recesses.

This subtle duality comes to us from Constantinople, but we come across it again elsewhere, especially in the Baroque period, whereas the Gothic, Renaissance and the Neo-classical tended more to extend rationality to relate it to the whole of the work. We are far from the 'inte-grated decoration' of Frank Lloyd Wright; without denying its aesthetic

potency, it should not be elevated to a dogma. Wright broke this rule him-self: the decoration of the internal space of Unity Temple in Oak Park is articulated less from material than from a spatial idea (Figure 314).

Some contemporary architects have been able to exploit the potential of articulation between body and clo-thing without necessarily referring to the divine. At the Castelvecchio Museum in Verona, Carlo Scarpa uses the contrast between structure and cladding to articulate and make visible both history and the present.

His building reveals the precision of geometric control of our contempor-ary tools (especially the design on paper) whilst at the same time show-ing the geometric approximations from the past. History becomes explicit without being too voluble (Figure 315).

The final choice of surface treat-ment for the interior and exterior of the building is not easy to make. It requires knowledge of underlying associations. A cube covered in fur does not make one think of the same thing as the identical cube in polished steel. It was not by chance that Renaissance theorists insisted on *conformity* of surface treatment according to the type of building. Precious materials were, in the first place, intended for places of worship (Alberti and Palladio); rustication was particularly suited to fortified buildings (Serlio).[156]

Nowadays there are many different cladding materials available; the distinctions between 'precious' and 'poor' have become blurred. We find something of the place of worship in a villa, office, school ... everywhere. The old labour-intensive methods are being replaced by new materials and processes. Glass and metal have, with their cheap, shiny surfaces, replaced polished marble. Mass-produced veneers and wood-photo laminates are making the former luxury of solid wood into something commonplace. The ease with which we produce and reproduce these elements in large numbers has ended up by devaluing the rich associations of shininess. The precision of the craftsman's movements in shaping material, which since the beginning of time has been a sign of human skill, has been caught up with and overtaken by the machine. With the machine, unprecedented precision has been made possible, even compulsory, for industrially produced articles. Values have thus been reversed. Imperfect objects gain the symbolic value of personal investment; perfect objects no longer enjoy the same admiration. Many people scrutinize an object in search of imperfections, proof that it is 'hand-made'. Industrial production has gone as far as the simulation of hand-crafted finishes. This art of 'faking' will perhaps lead to temporarily satisfactory solutions, but certainly not to a real architecture for our time.

In the contemporary scene of the profusion of 'easy cladding', it is necessary to remind ourselves of the principles which govern the architectural potential of the covering and its basic relationship with the structure as a body. Hosios Loukas, where nothing is left to chance, could teach us a lesson: to cover is not simply to hide a body in order to falsify appearances; on the contrary, the cladding attains perfection when it acknowledges what it is covering (Figure 316).

Figure 316 Acknowledging what is being covered and in what place: Christo wrapped the Kunsthalle in Berne fairly roughly in 1968. For the Pont Neuf in 1985 he respected the cultural demands of Parisian 'haute couture'.

9

EPILOGUE: DESIGN

Overleaf
Design for a window which will become the modern show-case of an ancient window.
Carlo Scarpa, pencil drawing on photograph, Castelvecchio Museum, Verona.
Photo made available by Prof. Licisco Magagnato, Verona.

The method of carrying out an ordinary architectural design has not always been the same. A few centuries ago clients and craftsmen could agree on a simple building to erect, without resorting to a plan. A few discussions and site visits were sufficient, given that the *models* of spatial layouts and building methods hardly ever changed. If the window dimensions varied slightly from one building to another, their verticality, proportions, manufacture, position or even their setting in the thickness of the wall did not need to be specified. They built 'according to the rules of the art', an expression which conveys very well the *tacit agreement* which at that time linked the craftsman and designers in any one region.

This stability of techniques and forms contributed to a certain homogeneity of appearance, which imposed itself quite naturally both on the public and on the producer. Whatever kind of craftsmen were responsible for the 'design' and its execution, the buildings were similar. The fact of knowing implicitly what sort of object one could expect from a new building obviated the need for various stages of what we nowadays call the 'design process'. The fact that change in technical and formal conventions was slow also engendered familiarity, and consequently popular acceptance of an architectural language. When there is tacit agreement it is easier to adhere to it or, if necessary, *to surprise* by rule-breaking or invention. Such deviation from the norm was generally reserved for authority, which sought in this way to leave a lasting record of its own genius. These special buildings, innovatory and more complex, required study, a plan and sometimes even prototypes. Their construction took much

longer. The building of cathedrals was so slow that a prior drawing-up of plans by specialists was necessary in order to ensure continuity and co-ordination of the work, which would only be completed in the distant future.[157]

In the wake of Vitruvius, the Renaissance established a distinction between the architectural concept and the methods of its execution, thus creating the beginnings of the specific activity of design. Let us remember that, at this period, the recognized architect was, at the same time, a man of letters and science, knowledgeable about the laws of music, a painter, sculptor and, especially, an engineer and site foreman. Architectural design was not necessarily his principal occupation (for example, Leonardo da Vinci, Michelangelo, Raphael, Bernini, etc.). One of the last famous people whose name can be added to this humanist lineage was probably the third president of the United States, Thomas Jefferson (1743-1826), who planned, and built, some remarkable buildings such as the University of Virginia and his own mansion at Monticello.

Nowadays, even buildings of lesser importance are of such technological complexity that they require division of labour, as much in the design stage as in the factory and on site. The scheme, a concrete proposal to be negotiated, developed and built, has become an inescapable necessity and even a legal requirement. Our profession has thus become an institution.

Paradoxically, and in spite of this growth in logical (rather than scientific) planning, it appears that the range of 'possible solutions' has increased enormously in all directions rather than converging towards a new, authentic and coherent

architectural language. There are several reasons for this which have already been discussed in earlier chapters. These are notably the hitherto unimaginable and greatly diversified resources and technical possibilities enabling production of 'any shape at all' at virtually the same price, which threaten to turn architectural form into a simple consumable product subject to rapid changes in fashion. And so construction breaks off its partnership with experience, making illusory any possible contribution of a tacit agreement to the establishment of a conventional code.

The state intervenes: complex legislation fills the gap left by the lack of a tacit agreement, trying to co-ordinate public interest, health, security and the different planning, practical, aesthetic and economic constraints. All these contingencies are added to private interests of people involved in the particular project. Acting basically in reaction to publicly denounced excesses – which are more a reflection of symptoms than of causes – contemporary legislation seeks to introduce, with a certain degree of authority, a stabilizing element to built form. For example, it requires window openings to correspond to a certain proportion of the floor area of the room, it specifies the height of the window sill and the size of the opening lights to ventilate the room; it stipulates its degree of thermal insulation and, in old villages and towns, it requires traditional style windows or, in the case of demolition, it imposes conservation or identical reconstruction of the street façade regardless of the new use of the building. The façade is then nothing more than a mask which hides the true space.

The architect's field of skill has been considerably reduced since the

Renaissance. Architecture has been undergoing the consequences of the general tendency towards specialization, from the discipline of structural engineering in the nineteenth century, to the congestion of legislation of the twentieth. Lucky are those few contemporary buildings which have *one designer* who has known how to subordinate and contain technical and functional complexity by linking the design to a dominant architectural intention. Every true scheme must have an underlying ethic, the desire for a better environment, for a fairer, more beautiful and most welcoming building and town. Every true scheme demands a clear, sophisticated synthesis and especially one that is made simpler than the numerous problems it seeks to solve.

In our discussion on design, let us borrow a few words which Paul Valéry gives to Thèdre in the fable *Eupalinos et l'architecte*: When I compose '*... I seek this form passionately, endeavouring to create an object which will delight the eye, which will converse with the mind, which will be in harmony with reason and with good manners ...*'[158].

'*Which will delight the eye ...*' is this not an appeal to sensitive mastery of the world of forms? What of a window that is well proportioned, carefully executed, in harmonious materials and colours, pleasant to look at and to touch, inserted with so much love that its absence or removal from the composition of the façade would disturb the over all order and balance - a window which also reveals and enhances the interior space by lighting surfaces and objects. '*Nur das Schöne ist der höchsten Liebe fähig*' said Friedrich Schinkel[159].

'*Which will converse with the mind ...*' is not this an appeal to the pleasure of intellectual stimulation? Architecture has no need to borrow the unequivocal language of advertising, an unambiguous message understood in seconds. The hidden meanings of architecture, which are sometimes riddles and provocations, are revealed through allusions to the laws of the universe as well as to the experience of man. If we say experience we imply memory. The element of creativity in memory has been relevantly recalled by Italo Calvino (section 7.3).

'*Which will harmonize with reason and with good manners ...*' is to say that there are dialectic relationships between love, the mind and reason. *Love* is the safeguard of *reason* and vice versa. Maillart could never have built his bridges without love, neither could Gaudí have built the Colonia Güell without engineering spirit, and nor could Botta have built his houses without an empathy with the stonemason.

Good manners are also safeguards and abettors of reason and love at the same time. They become a disaster when they bar the way to one or the other, when convention becomes totalitarian, when an architectural language is erected out of obligation, devoid of meaning for the future. But good manners become valuable sources of the scheme when they exploit the lessons of architecture in a critical and creative way and when they help to *perfect a type* which has good reason to exist.

These three interwoven concepts - the pleasure of beauty, stimulation of the mind and reasoned adaptation to existing conditions - are the basic themes of this book. Design is consequently no longer seen as a mere satisfaction of need and its technical and economic resolution. It involves an intellectual, artistic and public dimension which goes beyond the explicit professional mandate.

All attempts to make design into an essentially deductive process have failed. Even the computer has been unable, until now, to change this. This is not only due to the cultural dimension of architecture, but also to the impossibility of defining in advance all the important nuances of an architectural and planning problem. *In reality design is itself an instrument of research into the problem posed and not simply the search for a solution!*

People outside this process, the public, political authorities, clients and engineers sometimes experience some difficulty in understanding and admitting this uncertainty, this inductive aspect of architectural design, this method of '*producing certainties through design*'.

The philosopher Karl Popper has given a pertinent explanation of the nature of design in *Objective Knowledge*:

We start, I say, with a problem, a difficulty. It may be practical or theoretical. Whatever it may be when we first encounter the problem we cannot, obviously, know much about it. At best, we have only a vague idea what our problem really consists of. How, then, can we produce an adequate solution? Obviously, we cannot. We must first get better acquainted with the problem. But how?

My answer is very simple: by producing an inadequate solution, and by *criticizing* it. Only in this way can we come to understand the problem. For to understand a problem means to understand its difficulties; and to understand its difficulties means to understand why it is not easily soluble - why the more obvious solutions do not work. We must therefore produce these more obvious solutions; and we must criticize them, in order to find out *why* they do not work. In this way, we become acquainted with the problem, and may proceed from bad solutions to better ones - provided always that we have the creative ability to produce new guesses, and more new guesses.

This, I think, is what is meant by 'working on a problem'. And if we have worked on a problem long enough, and intensively enough, we begin to know it, to understand it, in the sense that we know what kind of guess or conjecture or hypothesis will not do at all, because it simply misses the point of the problem, and what kind of requirements would have to be met by any serious attempt to solve it. In other words, we begin to see ramifications of the problem, its sub-problems, and its connection with other problems.[160]

This argument remains totally relevant if we replace the word 'problem' by 'design'. The latter is, in fact, the production of knowledge by means of an interactive process of conjecture and refutation.

Cultural sensitivity, field of knowledge and the experience of the designer will decide the level at which this process of conjectures and refutations can take place. Listening to the forces and aspirations of our times, critical respect for human achievements of the past, and the patient search for a method all lead towards discovery of the design. Innocence does not make genius; it makes uncertainty. Knowledge and experience give the architect a deeper understanding of the world in which he functions and provide him with architectural me-

thods on which he can draw; that is the message of this book.

Certainly, speech is a limitation on architecture; even if it is used to reason and learn, an *a posteriori* debate *on* architecture is never as rich as architecture itself, which has less need to 'speak' than to 'exist with man'. The built works of great architects are therefore always finer than their writings. Architecture is silence, light and material; so let us be silent and build!

REFERENCES

Chapter 1

1 Collins, Peter (1965) *Changing Ideals in Modern Architecture*, Faber and Faber, London.
2 van Eyck, Aldo: aphorism appearing in several of van Eyck's writings (see the Dutch Forum 1959-63).
3 Boullée, Etienne Louis (1968) *Architecture: Essai sur l'art*, Hermann, Paris, p. 67. (Original version written at the end of the eighteenth century, pub. for the first time in 1953).
4 Perez-Gomez, Alberto (1983) *Architecture and the Crisis of Modern Science*, MIT Press, Cambridge, Mass.
5 Perez-Gomez, Alberto, *Architecture and the Crisis ...*, op. cit., p. 253.
6 Germann, Georg (1980) *Einführung in die Geschichte der Architekturtheorie*, Wissenschaftliche Buchgesellschaft, Darmstadt.
7 Tzonis, Alexander and Lefaivre, Liane (1986) *Classical Architecture; the poetics of order*, MIT Press, London.
8 Zevi, Bruno (1972) in *Encyclopedia universale dell arte*, Architettura, Sansoni, Firenze, pp. 615-652.
9 Vitruvius, Pollio (1960) *The Ten Books on Architecture*, Dover Publications, New York.
10 Palladio, Andrea (1965) *The Four Books on Architecture*, Dover Publications, New York.
11 Blondel Francois, 1675-1683 *Cours d'architecture dans l'Académie Royale d'architecture*, P. Auboin and F. Clouzier, Paris, 1675-1683, chap. XX, p. 786.
12 Germann, G., *Einführung ...*, op. cit. p. 188.
13 Durand, Jacques Nicolas Louis (1819) *Précis des leçons d'architecture*, 2 vol., Paris.
14 Guadet, Julien (1909) *Elements et théorie de l'architecture, Librarie de la constr. moderne*, Paris, vol. 1. p. 98.
15 Semper, Gottfried (1981) *Die vier Elemente der Baukunst*, Vieweg, Braunschweig, (orig. edn 1851).
16 Rykwert, Joseph (1972) *On Adams House in Paradise*, The idea of the primitive hut in architectural history, The Museum of Modern Art, New York, p. 38.
17 Le Corbusier, (1923) *Vers une architecture*, Les éditions G. Crès & Cie, Paris.
18 Perez-Gomez, A., *Architecture and the Crisis ...*, op. cit. pp. 5-6.
19 Alexander, Christopher (1971) *Notes on the Synthesis of Form*, Harvard University Press, Cambridge, Mass.
20 Alexander, Christopher (1977) *Pattern Language*, Oxford University Press, Oxford.
21 Serres, Michel, broadcast by France-Musique 18.12.83.
22 Rowe, Colin (1980) Architectural Education in the USA, in *Lotus international* No 27, pp. 42-46.
23 Laugier, Abbe Marc-Antoine (1972) *Essai sur l'architecture*, Minkoff Reprint, Genève, (orig. edn 1755).

Chapter 2

24 Grandjean, Etienne (1983) *Précis d'ergonomie*, éd. d'organisation, Paris (orig. edn Germany, 1979).
25 Saraus, Henry (1978) *Abrégé d'ophtalmologie*, Masson, Paris-New York, 4th edn.
26 Ludi, Jean-Claude (1986) *La perspective "pas à pas"*, Manuel de construction graphique de l'espace, Dunod, Paris
27 Koffka, Kurt (1935) *Principles of Gestalt Psychology*, New York.
28 Wertheimer, Max (1923) Untersuchungen zur Lehre von der Gestalt, II in Psychologische, Forschung, no. 4, pp. 301-350.
29 Katz, David (1961) *Gestaltungspsychologie*, Benno-Schwab Verlag, Basel/Stuttgart.
30 Guillaume, Paul (1937) *La psychologie de la forme*, Flammarion, Paris.
31 Metzger, Wolfgang (1975) *Gesetze des Sehens*, Waldemar Krämer, Frankfurt 3rd edn. (1st edn 1936).
32 Gregory, Richard Langton (1966) *The Eye and the Brain: the psychology of seeing*, Weidenfeld and Nicolson, London.
33 Gibson, James J. (1950) *The Perception of the Visual World*, Houghton Mifflin, Boston.
34 Arnheim, Rudolf (1974) *Art and Visual Perception*, a psychology of the creative eye, Univ. of California Press, Berkeley (1st edn 1954).
35 Arnheim, Rudolf (1977) *The Dynamics of Architectural Form*, Univ. of California Press, Berkeley.
36 Gombrich, Ernst H. (1979) *The Sense of Order, A study in the psychology of decorative art*, Phaidon Press, New York.

37 Zevi, Bruno (1975) *Architecture as space: how to look at architecture*, Ed. Horizont, New York.

38 Norberg-Schulz, Christian (1963) *Intentions in Architecture*, Universitätsforlaget, Oslo.

39 Arnheim, R., *Art and Visual Perception*, op. cit.

40 Metzger, W. *Gesetze des Sehens*, op. cit.

41 Le Corbusier, *Quand les cathédrales étaient blanches*, Denoël/Gonthier, Paris, (orig. edn 1937).

42 Droz, Remy (1983) Erreurs, mensonges, approximations et autres vérites, in *Le genre humain*, 7-8.

43 Boullée, E. L., *Architecture: Essai sur l'art*, op. cit., pp. 62-63.

44 Gombrich, E. H., *The Sense of Order*, op. cit.

45 Droz, Rémy, La psychologie, in *Encyclopédie de la Pleiade*.

Chapter 3

46 Gombrich, E. H., *The Sense of Order*, op. cit.

47 Tessenow, Henrich (1955) *Hausbau und dergleichen*, Waldemar Klein, Baden-Baden, p. 20.

48 Gombrich, E. H., *The Sense of Order*, op. cit.

49 Slutzky, Robert, 'Aqueous humor', in *Oppositions*, Winter/Spring 1980, 19/20, MIT Press, Cambridge, Mass, pp. 29-51.

50 Rowe, Colin and Slutzky, Robert (1964) 'Transparency, literal and phenomenal', *Perspecta* 8, Yale.

51 Hoesli, Bernhard (1968) Kommentar zu *Transparenz* Rowe, C., Slutzky, R. Birkhäuser, Basel.

52 Palladio, A., *The Four Books ...* op. cit.

53 Venturi, Robert (1966) *Complexity and Contradiction in Architecture*, The Museum of Modern Art, New York, (French edn 1971).

54 Arnheim, R., *The dynamics ...*, op. cit. p. 163.

55 Arnheim, R., *The dynamics ...*, op. cit. p. 171.

56 Schinkel, Friedrich (1840) *Gedanken und Bemerkungen über Kunst*.

57 Conrads, Ulrich, '*Building - On this side of imperial victories*', in Diadalos 7/1983 'On order and disorder'.

58 Gombrich, E. H., *The Sense of Order*, op. cit. p. 31.

59 Tessenow, H., *Hausbau und dergleichen*, op. cit.

Chapter 4

60 Rodin, Auguste (1921) *Les cathédrales de France*, Armand Colin, Paris p. 1.

61 Vitruvius, *The Ten Books ...*, op. cit.

62 Vitruvius, *The Ten Books ...*, op. cit.

63 Slutzky, R., *Aqueous Humor*, op. cit.

64 Wittkower, Rudolf (1967) *Architectural Principles in the age of humanism*, Alec Tiranti, London, (1st edn 1949).

65 Jerusalem Bible, The Book of Wisdom, chap. 11/20 cited by von Naredi-Rainer (1982).

66 von Naredi-Rainer, Paul (1982) *Architektur und Harmonie*, Du Mont Buchverlag, Köln, pp. 150-183.

67 von Naredi-Rainer, P., op. cit. pp. 177-179.

68 von Naredi-Rainer, P., op. cit. p. 193.

69 Woodworth, R. S. (1938) *Experimental Psychology*, New York, p. 387.

70 Boullée, E. L., *Architecture: Essai sur l'art*, op. cit. pp. 64-65.

71 Tessenow, H., *Hausbau und dergleichen*, op. cit.

72 Gombrich, E. H., *The Sense of Order*, op. cit.

73 Klee, Paul (1965) *Pädagogisches Skizzenbuch*, Kupferberg, Mainz, (orig. edn 1925), p. 33.

Chapter 5

74 Eisenman, Peter (1974), Real and English; The destruction of the box I, in *Oppositions*, no. 4, Oct. pp. 5-34.

75 Eisenman, Peter (1971) From Object to Relationship II: Giuseppe Terragni, Casa Giuliani Frigerio, in *Perspecta* 13/14, Yale.

76 Rowe, C. and Slutzky, R. '*Transparency ...*' op. cit.

77 Norberg-Schulz, Chr. *Intentions in Architecture*, op. cit.

First interlude

78 Arnheim, R., *The dynamics ...*, op. cit. pp. 22-23.

Chapter 6

79 Bollnow, Otto Friedrich, *Mensch und Raum*, Kohlhammer, Stuttgart (3rd edn 1976). (orig. edn 1963), pp. 30, 37.

80 Germann, Georg (1985) Höhle und Hütte in *Jagen und Sammeln*, Vlg Stämpfli, Bern.

81 Schmarsow, August (1897) *Barock und Rokoko*, Eine kritische Auseinandersetzung über das Malerische in der Architektur, Leipzig, Verlag S. Hirzel, pp. 6-7.

82 Fueg, Franz (1986) *Les bienfaits du temps*, Presses polytechniques romandes, Lausanne, (orig. edn Germany, 1982).

83 Moholy-Nagy, Laszlo (1968) *Von Material zu Architektur*, Neue Bauhausbücher, Kupferberg, Mainz, (orig. edn 1929).

84 Arnheim, R., *Art and visual perception*, op. cit.

85 Alberti, Leone-Battista (1955) *Ten Books on Architecture*, reprint of the 1755 ed. Joseph Rykwert, London.

86 Ching, Francis D. K. (1979), *Architecture: Form Space and Order*, Van Nostrand Reinhold Co., New York, pp. 115–174.

87 Gibson, J. J., *The Perception of the Visual World*, op. cit.

88 Gibson, J. J., *The Perception of the Visual World*, op. cit.

89 Rowe, C. and Slutzky, R. '*Transparency...*' op. cit.

90 Giedion, Siegfried, (1922) *Spätbarocker und romantischer klassizismus*, F. Bruckmann, München.

91 Rowe, C. and Slutzky, R., '*Transparency...*' op. cit.

92 Arnheim, R., *Art and Visual Perception*, op. cit. pp. 304–305.

93 Alberti, L. B., *Ten Books...* op. cit.

94 Le Corbusier, *Vers une architecture*, op. cit. p. 16.

95 Arnheim, R., *Art and Visual Perception*, op. cit. p. 317.

96 Heidegger, Martin (1971) 'Building, dwelling, thinking' in: *Poetry, Language, Thought*, Harper & Row, New York.

Second interlude

97 Elytis, Odysseus (1982) *Marie des Brumes*, Maspero, Paris, p. 72.

98 Bachelard, Gaston (1983) *la poétique de l'espace*, Presses universitaires de France, Paris, (orig. edn 1957), p. 17.

99 van Eyck, Aldo, *in Forum* 4/1960, Amsterdam.

100 Heidegger, M., 'Building, dwelling, thinking', op. cit.

101 Alberti, L. B., *Ten Books...*, op. cit.

102 Ronner Heinz, Sharad J. and Vadella A. (1977) *Kahn, Louis Complete Work 1935–1974*, Birkhäuser, Basel/Stuttgart, p. 390.

103 Rossi, Aldo (1982), *The architecture of the city*, MIT Press, Cambridge, Mass.

104 Devillers, Christian and Huet, Bernard (1981) *Le Creusot, Naissance et développement d'une ville industrielle 1782–1914*, Champ-Vallon, Seyssel.

105 Frampton, Kenneth, On reading Heidegger, in *Oppositions* no. 4, MIT Press, Cambridge, Mass, Oct. 1974.

Chapter 7

106 Note: i.e. Chr. Norberg-Schulz, *Genius Loci*; G. Bachelard, *La poétique de l'espace*; W. Hellpach, *Geopsyche*; ...

107 Note: i.e. U. Eco, *Le nom de la rose*; E. Canetti, *Auto-da-fé; visibles*; M. Proust, *A la recherche du temps perdu*; ...

108 Lynch, Kevin (1960) *The Image of the City*, Harvard University Press, Cambridge, Mass.

109 Lynch, Kevin (1962) *On Site Planning*, MIT Press, Cambridge, Mass.

110 Gregotti, Vittorio (1982) *Le territoire de l'architecture*, L'Equerre, Paris, (orig. edn Italy, 1972) (to be published in English by Rizzoli International, New York).

111 Gregotti, Vittorio *Le territoire...*, op. cit. p. 85.

112 Bourdieu, Pierre (1970), *Esquisse d'une théorie de la pratique*, Droz, Paris.

113 Van Eyck, A., op. cit.

114 Eliade, Mircea (1961) *The Sacred and the Profane*, Harper and Row, New York.

115 Lawrence, Roderick, *Espace privé, espace collectif, espace public*, l'exémple du logement populaire en suisse romande 1860–1960, 483, EPF, Lausanne, 1983.

116 Lawrence, Roderick (1980) 'The simulation of domestic space: users and architects participating in the architectural design process; in *Simulation and Games*, 11, 3, pp. 279–300.

117 Smithson, Alison and Peter (1968) *Team Ten Primer*, MIT Press, Cambridge.

118 Luchinger, Arnulf (1981) *Structuralism in architecture and urbanplanning*, Eyrolles/Kraemer, Paris/Stuttgart.

119 Perec, Georges (1974) *Espèces d'espaces*, Gallilée, Paris, pp. 51–53.

120 Arnheim, R., *The Dynamics...*, op. cit. p. 21.

121 Kaschnitz, Marie-Louise (1979) *Beschreibung eines Dorfes*, Suhrkamp, Frankfurt.

122 Cassirer, Ernst, *Philosophie der symbolischen Formen*, Band II, Berlin, 1923–1929, p. 108.

123 Calvino, Italo (1979) *Invisible Cities*, translated from the Italian by William Weaver, Picador, Pan Books, London.

124 Bollnow, O. F., *Mensch und Raum*, op. cit. pp. 74–76.

125 Lynch, K., *The Image of the City*, op. cit.

126 Lynch, K. (1972). *What Time Is this Place?* MIT Press, Cambridge, Mass.

127 Bassand, Michel, Corajoud G., Perrinjaquet R., Pedrazini Y. (1985) *L'adequation d'un édifice public*, Le cas de l'Ecole Polytechnique Fédérale à Ecublens; Institut de Recherche sur l'Environment Construit, Dépt. d'Architecture EPFL, Lausanne.

128 Rapoport, Amos (1981) Identity and Environment: a cross-cultural perspective in J. S. Duncan, *Housing and Identity: Cross-Cultural Perspectives*, Croom-Helm, London.

129 Noschis, Kaj and Lawrence, Roderick (1984) Inscrire sa vie dans son logement: le cas des couples;

in *Bulletin de Psychologie*, vol. 37, no. 366.

130 Oswald, Franz (1982) Vielfältig und veränderbar, Wohnquartier Bleiche, Worb (Bern), in *Werk, Bauen und Wohmen* 4.

131 von Meiss, Pierre (1979) Avec et sans architecte, in *Werk-Archithèse*, 27–28.

132 Lawrence, Roderick (1982) Un laboratoire vivant pour la conception des maisons, in *Bâtiment international*, 10 (3), pp. 52–60.

133 Viollet-Le-Duc, Eugène (1977) *Entretiens sur l'architecture*, Mardaga, Bruxelles, (orig. edn 1863–1872), Vol. 2, p. 120.

Chapter 8

134 Perret, Auguste (1949) Contribution à une théorie de l'architecture, in *Techniques et Architecture* I, 2.

135 Schoppenhauer, Arthur (1818) Die Baukunst, in *Die Welt als Wille und Vorstellung*.

136 Barthes, Roland et Martin Andre (1972) *La tour Eiffel*.

137 Wachsmann, Konrad (1959) *Wendepunkt im Bauen*, Krauskoff, Wiesbaden.

138 Tessenow, H., *Hausbau und dergleichen*, op. cit.

139 Zevi, B., *Encyclopedia . . .*, op. cit.

140 Frampton, Kenneth (1980) *Modern Architecture, a critical history*, Thames & Hudson, London, p. 281.

141 Viollet-le-Duc, E., *Entretiens . . .*, op. cit. vol. 2, p. 67.

142 Collins, P., *Changing ideals in modern architecture*, op. cit. p. 271–284.

143 Five Architects, exhibition catalogue, Oxford University Press, New York, 1975.

144 Rowe, C. and Slutzky R., *Transparency*, op. cit.

145 *Education of an Architect*, Cooper Union School of Art and Architecture, exhibition catalogue, New York, 1971, and
Libeskind, Daniel, (1980) *Symbol and Interpretation/Micro Megas*, Cranbrook Academy of Art, Archantic Publications, Helsinki, and ETH Zürich, 1981.

146 Tessenow, H., *Hausbau und dergleichen*, op. cit., pp. 18–20.

147 Viollet-le-Duc, E., *Entretiens . . .*, op. cit., vol. 2, p. 120.

148 Wright, Frank Lloyd (1975) *In the Cause of Architecture*, Wright's historic essay for Architectural Record, 1908–1952, Architectural Record, McGraw Hill, New York.

149 Viollet-le-Duc, E. *Entretiens . . .*, op. cit., vol. 2, p. 76.

150 Wright, F. L., *In the Cause of Architecture*, op. cit., p. 190.

151 Wright, Frank Lloyd (1954) *The Natural House*, Horizon Press, New York, p. 60.

152 Le Corbusier, *Vers une architecture*, op. cit.

153 Wright, F. L., *In the Cause of Architecture*, op. cit.

154 Viollet-le-Duc, E. *Entretiens . . .*, op. cit. vol. I, p. 90.

155 Semper, Gottfried (1878) *drei Hauptrichtungen der Baukunst*, in Der Stil in den technischen und tektonischen Künsten, Fr. Bruckman, München.

156 Germann, G., *Einführung . . .*, op. cit., pp. 55, 114, 136.

Chapter 9

157 Germann, G., *Einführung . . .*, op. cit., p. 31.

158 Valery, Paul (1944) *Eupalinos*, L'âme et la danse, dialogue de l'arbre, Gallimard, Paris.

159 Schinkel, Karl Friedrich (1840) *Gedanken und Bemerkungen über Kunst*, Berlin.

160 Popper, Karl (1972) *Objective Knowledge*, Oxford University Press, London, p. 260.

Quotations in the captions

161 Calvino, I., op. cit. pp. 15, 54, 73, 106.

162 Serres, Michel (1985) *Les cinq sens*, Grasset, Paris, pp. 23, 35, 51, 93, 180, 184, 185, 335, 336, 348.

BIBLIOGRAPHY
A Selection

Alberti, Leone-Battista *Ten Books on Architecture*, reprint of the 1755 edn, ed. Joseph Rykwert (1955) London

Alexander, Christopher (1971) *Notes on the Synthesis of Form*, Harvard University Press, Cambridge, Mass

Alexander, Christopher (1977) *Pattern Language*, Oxford University Press, Oxford

Arnheim, Rudolf (1974) *Art and Visual Perception*, a psychology of the creative eye, University of California Press, Berkeley (1st edn 1954)

Arnheim, Rudolf (1977) *The Dynamics of Architectural Form*, University of California Press, Berkeley

Bachelard, Gaston (1983) *La poétique de l'espace*, Presses universitaires de France, Paris (orig. edn 1957)

Barthes, Roland and Martin, André (1972) *La tour Eiffel*

Blondel, François, (1675-83) *Cours d'architecture dans l'Academie Royale d'architecture*, P. Auboin and F. Clouzier, Paris

Bollnow, Otto Friedrich, *Mensch und Raum*, Kohlhammer, Stuttgart, (3rd edn 1976), (orig. edn 1963)

Boullée, Etienne Louis (1968) *Architecture: Essai sur l'art*, Hermann, Paris, p. 67 (orig. version written at the end of the eighteenth century, pub. for the first time 1953.)

Bourdieu, Pierre (1970) *Esquisse d'une théorie de la pratique*, Droz, Paris

Calvino, Italo (1979) *Invisible Cities*, trans. from the Italian by William Weaver, Picador, Pan Books, London

Cassirer, Ernst (1923-29) *Philosophie der symbolischen Formen*, Vol. II, Berlin

Ching, Francis D. K. (1979) *Architecture: Form, Space and Order*, Van Nostrand Reinhold, New York

Collins, Peter (1965) *Changing Ideals in Modern Architecture*, Faber and Faber, London

Devillers Christian and Huet Bernard (1981) *Le Creusot, Naissance et développement d'une ville industrielle 1782-1914*, Champ-Vallon, Seyssel

Durand, Jacques Nicolas Louis, *Précis des Leçons d'architecture*, 2 vols, Paris

Eisenman, Peter (1971) 'From Object to Relationship II: Giuseppe Terragni, Casa Giuliani Frigerio', in *Perspecta* 13/14, Yale

Eisenman, Peter (1974) 'Real and English; The destruction of the box I', in *Oppositions*, no. 4 Oct. MIT Press, Cambridge, Mass, pp. 5-34

Eliade, Mircea (1961) *The sacred and the profane*, Harper and Row, New York

Frampton, Kenneth (1974) 'On reading Heidegger', in *Oppositions*, no. 4, Oct. MIT Press, Cambridge, Mass

Frampton, Kenneth (1980) *Modern Architecture, a critical history*. Thames & Hudson, London

Fueg, Franz (1986) *Les bienfaits du temps*, Presses Polytechniques romandes, Lausanne, (orig. edn Germany, 1982).

Germann, Georg (1980) *Einführung in die Geschichte der Architekturtheorie*, Wissenschaftliche Buchgesellschaft, Darmstadt

Gibson, James J. (1950) *The Perception of the Visual World*, Houghton Mifflin, Boston

Giedion, Siegfried, *Spätbarocker und romantischer Klassizismus*, F. Bruckmann, München, 1922

Gombrich, Ernst H. (1979) *The Sense of Order, a study in the psychology of decorative art*, Phaidon Press, New York

Gregory Richard Langton (1966) *The Eye and the Brain: the psychology of seeing*, Weidenfeld and Nicolson, London

Gregotti, Vitterio (1982) *Le territoire de l'architecture*, L'Equerre, Paris, (orig. edn Italy, 1972)

Guadet, Julien (1909) *Eléments et théorie de l'architecture*, Librarie de la constr. moderne, Paris

Heidegger, Martin (1971) 'Building, Dwelling, Thinking' *Poetry, Language, Thought* Harper and Row, New York (orig. edn Germany, 1954)

Hoesli, Bernhard (1968) Commentary on Rowe, C., Slutzky, R., *Transparenz*, Birkhäuser, Basel

Katz, David (1961) *Gestaltungspsychologie* Benno-Schwab Verlag, Basel/Stuttgart

Klee, Paul (1965) *Pädagogisches Skizzenbuch*, Kupferberg, Mainz (orig. edn 1925)

Koffka, Kurt (1935) *Principles of Gestalt Psychology*, New York

Le Corbusier (1923) *Vers une architecture*, Les éditions G. Crès & Cie, Paris

Le Corbusier (1977) *Quand les cathédrales étaient blanches*, Denoël/Gonthier, Paris, (orig. edn 1937, Plon, Paris)

Laugier, Abbé Marc-Antoine (1972) *Essai sur l'architecture*, Minkoff, reprint, Geneva (orig. edn 1755)

Liebeskind, Daniel (1980) *Symbol and Interpretation/Micro Megas*, exhibition catalogue, Cranbook

Academy of Art, Archantic Publications Helsinki/ETH Zürich

Luchinger, Arnulf (1981) *Structuralism in architecture and urban planning*, Eyrolles/Kraemer, Paris/Stuttgart

Lynch, Kevin (1960) *The image of the city*, Harvard University Press, Cambridge, Mass

Lynch, Kevin (1962) *On Site Planning*, MIT Press, Cambridge, Mass

Lynch, Kevin (1972) *What Time Is this Place?* MIT Press, Cambridge, Mass

Metzger, Wolfgang (1975) *Gesetze des Sehens*, Waldemar Krämer, Frankfurt 3rd edn (1st edn 1936)

Moholy-Nagy, Laszlo (1968) *Von Material zu Architektur*, Neue Bauhausbücher, Kupferberg, Mainz (1st edn 1929)

Norberg-Schulz, Christian (1963) *Intentions in architecture*, Universitetsforlaget, Oslo

Oswald, Franz (1982) 'Vielfätig und veränderbar, Wohnquartier Bleiche, Worb (Bern)', in *Werk, Bauen und Wohmen* 4

Palladio, Andrea, (1965) *The Four Books on Architecture*, Dover Publications, New York

Perec, Georges (1974) *Espèces d'espaces*, Gallilée, Paris

Perret, Auguste (1949) 'Contribution à une théorie de l'architecture', in *Techniques et Architecture* I, II

Perrez-Gomez, Alberto (1983) *Architecture and the Crisis of Modern Science*, MIT Press, Cambridge, Mass

Popper, Karl (1972) *Objective Knowledge*, Oxford University Press, London

Rapoport, Amos (1981) 'Identity and Environment: a cross-cultural perspective in J. S. Duncan, *Housing and Identity: Cross-Cultural Perspectives*, Croom-Helm, London

Rodin, Auguste (1921) *Les cathédrales de France*, Armand Colin, Paris

Ronner Heinz, Sharad, J. and Vadella, A. (1977) *Kahn, Louis I, Complete Work 1935-74*, Birkäuser, Basel/Stuttgart

Rossi, Aldo (1982) *The architecture of the city*, MIT Press, Cambridge, Mass

Rowe, Colin (1980) 'Architectural education in the USA', in *Lotus international* no. 27

Rowe, Colin and Slutzky, Robert (1964) 'Transparency, literal and phenomenal', *Perspecta* 8, Yale

Rykwert, Joseph (1972) *On Adams House in Paradise, The idea of the primitive hut in architectural history*, The Museum of Modern Art, New York

Schinkel, Karl Friedrich (1840) *Gedanken und Bemerkungen über Kunst*, Berlin

Schmarsow, August (1897) *Barock und Rokoko, Eine kritische Auseinandersetzung über das Malerische in der Architektur*, Verlag S. Hirzel, Leipzig

Schoppenhauer, Arthur (1818) 'Die Baukunst' in *Die Welt als Wille und Vorstellung*

Semper, Gottfried (1878) 'Drei Hauptrichtungen der Bakunst', in *Der Stil in den technischen und tektonischen Künsten*, Fr. Bruckmann, München

Semper, Gottfried (1981) *Die vier Elemente der Baukunst*, Vieweg, Braunschweig (orig. edn 1851)

Serres, Michel (1985) *Les cinq sens*, Grasset, Paris

Slutzky, Robert (1980) 'Aqueous humour', in *Oppositions*, Winter/Spring, 19/20, MIT Press, Cambridge, Mass, pp. 29-51

Smithson, Alison and Peter (1968) *Team Ten Primer*, MIT Press, Cambridge, Mass

Tessenow, Heinrich (1955) *Hausbau und dergleichen*, Waldemar Klein, Baden-Baden

Tzonis, Alexander and Lefaivre, Liane (1986) *Classical architecture; the poetic of order*, MIT Press, London

Valery, Paul (1944) *Eupalinos, L'âme et la danse, dialogue de l'arbre*, Gallimard, Paris

Venturi, Robert (1966) *Complexity and contradiction in architecture*, The Musem of Modern Art, New York

Viollet-le-Duc, Eugène (1977) *Entretiens sur l'architecture*, Mardaga, Bruxelles (orig. edn 1863-72)

Vitruvius, Pollio (1960) *The Ten Books on Architecture*, Dover Publications, New York

von Naredi-Rainer, Paul (1982) *Architektur und Harmonie*, Du Mont Buchverlag, Köln

von Meiss, Pierre (1979) 'Avec et sans architecte', in *Werk-Archithèse*, 27-28, April

Wachsmann, Konrad (1959) *Wendepunkt in Bauen*, Krauskoff, Wiesbaden

Wertheimer, Max (1923) Untersuchungen zur Lehre von der Gestalt, *II* in *Psychologische Forschung*, no. 4, pp. 301-350

Wittkower, Rudolf (1967) *Architectural Principles in the Age of Humanism*, Alec Tiranti, London (1st edn 1949)

Wright, Frank Lloyd (1954) *The Natural House*, Horizon Press, New York

Wright, Frank Lloyd (1975) '*In the cause of architecture*', Wright's historic essay for Architectural Record, 1908-1952, *Architectural Record*, McGraw Hill, New York

Zevi, Bruno (1975) *Architecture as Space: how to look at architecture* Ed. Horizont, New York

ICONOGRAPHIC REFERENCES

In order of appearance in the book.

Technikum Winterthur, Seminarwoche 1980: 2
Ino Ioannidou and Lenio Bartzioti, photographers, Athènes: 7, 9, 43, 69, 71, 118, 129, 162, 243, 256, 303

Engravings by Bernard Piccart, in *Cérémonies religieuses*, Amsterdam, 1723-28: 8, 95

Drawings by Florence Kontoyanni; scholarship IKEA foundation, Lausanne/Athens, 1983: 14, 27, 36, 39, 45, 46, 207, 308

Antoniades, E.M. Ekphrasis of Saint Sophia, Athens, 1907-09; greogoriades, Athens, 1983: 16

MacDonald, W. *Early Christian and Byzantine Architecture*: 17

Choisy, A., *Histoire de l'achitecture*, E. Rouveyre, Paris, vol. II p. 49; I: 18, 54

Arnheim, Art and Visual Perception, p. 13: 20

Leonardo da Vinci, fragment of the Joconde: 23

Weinbrenner, F., *Architektonisches Lehrbuch*, 1811, Part, I, Plate X, Fig. XVIII: 24

Werk-Bauen und Wohmen No. 4, 1984: 63

Keller, R., *Bauen als Umweltzerstörung*, Zürich: 6a, 115

Reynaud, L., *Traite d'architecture*: 78

Heusler, J. M., *Travail d'analyse*, EPFL: 96

Rayon, J. -P., Lausanne: 100b, 137, 171, 280, 300

Encyclopédie Diderot: 105

Atelier Cube, Lausanne: 109, 110

Graphische Sammlung, ETH Zurich: 111, 112, 157

Herman, P., in *Baroque, Architecture universelle*, Office du Livre, Fribourg: 130

Flammer, A., Locarno: 176

Gerster, G., Zurich: 190

Cyril, M., *Architecture Byzantine*, 1981: 197, 213

Guisan, J., Lausanne: 236

Aalto, A., Editions Girsberger-Artemis, Zurich: 240

Aerocamera, Bart Hofmeester: 248

Spence Air Photos: 249

Saint-Exupéry, *Le Petit Prince*: 263

Le Corbusier: 264, 265

Helfenstein, H., Zurich: 278c, d

Centro Internazionale di studi di architettura Andrea Palladio, Vicence: 281

Margot, P., Cully: 286

Les albums d'art Druet No 1, A. et G. Perret, Paris, 1928: 287

Ed. Poligrafia S. A., Barcelone: 297

Volkswagen, Wolfsburg: 298

Lamey, U., Munich: 306

When the source is mentioned in the caption or when the pictures come from the author or one of his close collaborators, no reference is given.